Author'

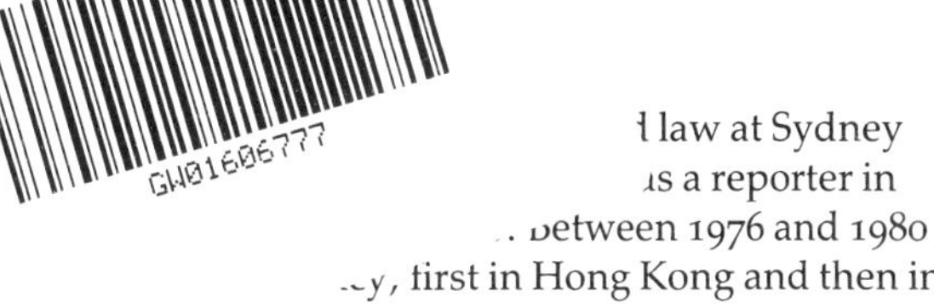

Born in E   l law at Sydney
Universit   is a reporter in
Hong Kon   . between 1976 and 1980
he worked   y, first in Hong Kong and then in
Peking.

Graham Earnshaw became the Peking correspondent for the *Daily Telegraph* in August 1980. He is married to a Hong Kong Chinese and has one daughter.

ON YOUR OWN IN CHINA

The Independent Traveller's Guide

GRAHAM EARNSHAW

CENTURY PUBLISHING
LONDON

To Fung-Yee and
Jennifer – and my Mum

First published in Great Britain in 1983
by Century Publishing Co. Ltd,
76 Old Compton Street, London W1V 5PA
ISBN 0 7126 0248 8
Photoset in Palatino by
Rowland Phototypesetting Ltd
Bury St Edmunds Suffolk
Printed in Great Britain by
Richard Clay (The Chaucer Press) Ltd,
Bungay, Suffolk

CONTENTS

INTRODUCTION

> Some foreign guests feel they are isolated in capsules and are given little or no chance to meet or to acquaint themselves with the Chinese people. These sealed capsules, which are identical with barriers, should be removed, and the sooner the better.
>
> Letter in the *China Daily*

Most foreigners visiting China still travel in 'capsules'. Until the early 1980s, there was no other choice: if you wanted to travel to China, you had to join a group tour, and often one masquerading as a delegation of medical workers or sociologists. An elaborate framework was constructed in the 1960s and early 1970s in which foreigners could travel through China rarely, if ever, meeting or talking to ordinary people, or seeing Chinese society as it really is. Foreign tourists were, and largely still are, carefully shepherded from one place to another in groups, staying in segregated hotels, eating in segregated restaurants, and rarely given the chance to stray off the beaten track.

This book is aimed at those who want to break out of the 'capsule' and see China on their own. Tourists are allowed to visit a growing list of cities and towns around the country, and budget travellers who have gone round without any help from officialdom say it can be done with little trouble, even if you don't speak a word of Chinese.

The first crack in the group-tour-or-nothing façade appeared in Hong Kong in 1981 when advertisements appeared on the notice-boards of a number of hostels frequented by young budget travellers, offering individual visas for China for about UK £20 each. Apparently, the owners of the hostels were arranging their own 'group' tours, with members of the 'group' travelling independently. Whether it was all above-board or not was uncertain, but no one was asking too many questions for fear of the visas disappearing. The intrepid tourists who obtained the visas took the train up to Canton and then struck out on their own, blazing trails as they went.

The individual visas offered in Hong Kong at that time now appear to have been a test by China's tourist authorities to see what problems would crop up. Their caution was understandable. When Chairman Mao Tse-tung died in 1976, China effectively had no tourist industry at all, unless the 'study groups' of trendy Western Maoists are counted. Even in 1978, China received less than 50000 foreign visitors. The figure in 1982 was probably ten times that.

China is a lot more open than it used to be, and the authorities are losing their fear of foreigners wandering about unaccompanied. More and more individual tourist visas are being issued, and the various organisations around China that deal with tourists are gradually gaining experience in how to handle people who suddenly turn up out of nowhere. China's tourism authorities estimate that individual tourists will account for 20 to 30 per cent of foreign visitors by 1990, and up to 40 per cent by the end of the century.

Barring another political upheaval, tourist travel around China is likely to get easier and easier. At present, well over 90 per cent of the country's total area is still closed to foreigners, but the list of places that are open is growing all the time. Restrictions on travel are also being gradually eased. The pragmatic government of Deng Xiaoping, China's leader, has realised that the less restrictions there are, the more tourists will come, and the more foreign exchange the country can amass.

This book will show you how to travel through China without any help from the China International Travel Service (CITS), the organisation charged with handling foreign visitors. In fact, the Travel Service can be very useful indeed for the individual who wants to save time and effort, or who feels like travelling in comfort. At any stage in your travels, you can ignore the various pieces of travel information in this book and just have the Travel Service arrange everything for you. *Or* you can do it by yourself. The choice is yours.

This book also gives you information and tells you stories about China that you are unlikely to find anywhere else. The emphasis is on events in the past few decades, an era of great change in China that most guidebooks almost ignore.

I have used the Pinyin romanisation system for Chinese words throughout the guide, except for a few names which have well-known, or relatively well-known, equivalents in English or in the old Wade-Giles romanisation system, such as Peking, Canton, Tibet, Chiang Kaishek and the Yangtse River. The Pinyin system, with its unpronounceable Zs, Xs and Cs, is far from perfect, but it has already been virtually accepted as the standard. Most of the names of roads are rendered completely in Pinyin to make it easier for travellers to ask for directions. For a short introduction to Pinyin, and to the Chinese street and road-naming system, please consult the Language section, page 25.

The China tourism scene is changing so fast these days that some of the information in this book may prove to be outdated. Any criticisms or additional information will be gratefully received.

I would like to thank the people who helped me put this book together, particularly my wife Lam Fung-yee, Richard Pascoe, Tony Walker, Beverly Lum-des Jardins, Fred Bourke and Tim Grindell.

Graham Earnshaw
Peking, March 1983

GETTING THERE

Visas and permits

To get a tourist visa for China, first apply to the nearest Chinese embassy. If, for some bureaucratic reason they do not issue you with one, you can get one in Hong Kong.

There are a number of places in Hong Kong which offer individual visas for China. Firstly, China now has an official visa office in the British colony (387 Queen's Road East), although at the time of writing it rarely issues tourist visas to casual travellers; this may change soon.

A number of private companies and hostels have also offered individual tourist visas in the past, and probably still do so. They include:

Travellers' Hostel, 16th floor, Chunking Mansions, Block 'A', Nathan Road, Kowloon (opposite Hyatt Regency Hotel), tel: 3-687710.
Hong Kong Student Travel Bureau Ltd, Room 1020, Star House, Kowloon (near the Star Ferry Terminal), tel: 3-694847.
China Tour Centre, Room L1-55, New World Centre, Tsimshatsui, Kowloon, tel: 3-683207.

The official China Travel Service (77 Queen's Road, Central) has also been known to issue individual tourist visas masquerading as group visas. Some people have been designated as a group of one (themselves). If you are with a friend or friends, ask if you could be designated a 'group'. Another possibility is to join one of the regular China Travel Service-operated tours to Canton and get your visa extended when you get there.

Some tourist visas are valid for a month, some for a week; it varies wildly. But once you are in China, you can get the visa extended by the Public Security Bureau (the police) at least once and probably twice. Some PSB offices are more generous than others; the large offices, particularly those in Peking and Shanghai, have the reputation of being less helpful in this regard.

In the past for travel within China, every foreigner had to have an Aliens' Travel Permit, issued by the Public Security Bureau, listing all the places which the traveller was allowed to visit. However, since November 1982, tourists have been allowed to visit 28 selected cities and towns without a permit.

If you want to travel beyond these places, you will still need the Aliens' Travel Permit. Go to the Public Security Bureau foreign affairs office in any large city, and write out a list of cities you want to visit on the application form. Some of the places may be crossed off, but don't worry; apply again at the next city. For some particularly out-of-the-way places, you can only get permission at the nearest provincial capitals.

The following is a list of the main places that are now open to foreign tourists.** Those marked with an asterisk (*) are the 'open' cities which travellers can visit without a permit; the rest require Aliens' Travel Permits. There is no harm in applying to visit places not on this list – all they can do is turn you down.

Peking (Beijing)*
Shanghai*
Tianjin (Tientsin)*
Anhui Province: Hefei, Huang Shan.
Fujian Province: Fuzhou (Foochow), Quanzhou, Xiamen (Amoy).
Gansu Province: Dunhuang, Jiayuguan, Lanzhou.
Guangdong (Kwangtung) Province: Canton (Guangzhou)*, Conghua, Foshan*, Hainan Island, Shenzhen (special economic zone next to Hong Kong), Zhaoqing*, Zhuhai (special economic zone next to Macao).
Guangxi Province: Guilin (Kweilin)*, Liuzhou (Liuchow), Nanning*.
Hebei Province: Beidaihe (Peitaiho), Chengdu*, Qinhuangdao*, Shijiazhuang*.
Heilongjiang Province: Daqing oilfield, Harbin*.
Henan Province: Kaifeng*, Linxian County, Luoyang*, Shaolin Monastery, Zhengzhou*.

** Several places listed as 'open' have not been included in the text – either because there is little to say or insufficient information to warrant an entry. Qinhuangdao is a seaport east of Peking important as a coal trans-shipment point. Linxian County is known for its man-made irrigation canal called the Red Flag Canal. Changzhou, Xuzhou and Zhenjiang are three little towns on or near the Grand Canal. Jilin is the name of a province and not a place name as such. Anshan is the site of a large iron and steel works. The Shengli oilfield is – no prizes for guessing – an oilfield! Zhaoqing is a tourist spot in Guangdong Province.

Hubei Province: Wuhan*, Yichang*.
Hunan Province: Changsha*, Shaoshan.
Inner Mongolia: Baotou, Huhehot (Hohhot), Xilinhot.
Jiangsu Province: Changzhou*, Nanking (Nanjing)*, Suzhou*, Wuxi*, Xuzhou, Yangzhou (Yangchow)*, Zhenjiang.
Jiangxi Province: Jingdezhen*, Jinggangshan, Lushan, Nanchang.
Jilin Province: Changchun*, Jilin.
Liaoning Province: Anshan, Dalian (Luda, Dairen), Shenyang (Mukden)*.
Shaanxi Province: Xi'an (Sian)*, Yan'an (Yenan).
Shandong Province: Jinan*, Qingdao (Chingtao)*, Qufu (Chufu), Shengli oilfield, Tai'an, Taishan, Yantai.
Shanxi Province: Datong, Dazhai (Tachai; sometimes), Taiyuan*.
Sichuan Province: Chengdu*, Chongqing (Chungking)*, Dazu*, Emei Shan, Leshan*.
Xinjiang (Sinkiang) Autonomous Region: Shihezi, Tianchi*, Turfan (Turpan), Urumqi.
Yunnan Province: Kunming*, Xishuang Banna.
Zhejiang Province: Hangzhou (Hangchow)*, Ningbo, Shaoxing, Wenzhou.

The Yangtse River from Chongqing down to Wuhan – which takes in the famous Yangtse Gorges – is 'open', but the towns along the river are almost all 'closed'.

Tibet is a special case. Its capital, Lhasa, is sometimes 'open', and regular tourist groups have visited the city, but it is still officially classified as 'closed'.

Apart from those places already mentioned, virtually all of the rest of China is off-limits to foreigners. However, in the hope that more areas will be put within the reach of tourists, other, officially 'closed' areas have also been included in this guide.

Customs

Chinese customs officers are primarily interested in Hong Kong Chinese, who are the ones most likely to be smuggling things in and out of the country. Other foreigners are usually given a fairly cursory inspection. The important thing is to declare all your electrical goods, watches, tape recorders, etc. when you enter the country, otherwise you could have trouble when the time comes to leave. If you lose any declared item during your travels, go and see the Public Security Bureau.

At Peking airport, one of the most common points of entry, the customs people X-ray all baggage but rarely open suitcases, another sign of their primary interest in electrical goods. You can bring as much foreign currency as you like into the country. Non-resident foreigners are allowed to bring in four bottles of alcohol and 600 cigarettes duty-free.

Unlike most East European Communist countries, there are virtually no controls on what books foreigners can bring into China. English and other European languages are double Dutch to the average Chinese customs official, and he has no way of telling a racy pornographic novel from a damning critique of Chinese Communism. One exception has arisen recently however: copies of *New York Times* correspondent Fox Butterfield's book on China, *China, Alive in the Bitter Sea*, have been seized at customs checkpoints, so if you are reading that, it might be an idea to put it at the bottom of your bag.

Things to bring

Clothes

Don't bring too many. As a tourist, you won't need anything more formal than casual wear, even for banquets. Jeans are ideal. Most of the foreigners' hotels can return laundry within 24 hours, so don't bring too many changes of clothes. In summer, most of China is very hot, so T-shirts will be useful, but bring along a sweater or light anorak for use on cool evenings or when you climb mountains. In the winter time, China is cold: temperatures in Peking, for instance, can drop to 10°F or even 20°F below freezing (−7°–12°C). Down south in winter, the temperatures aren't so low, but the added humidity can chill you to the bone. Make sure that you have thick shoes, heavy-duty socks, long-johns, and a thick jacket. You might like to buy one of the huge padded greatcoats, coloured green or blue, which everyone in China wears. They may not be much use back home, but they are among the best buys in the country.

Shoes

Bring a sturdy, comfortable pair of walking shoes. Tourists in China do a lot of walking, up and down the Great Wall, traipsing through temples and factories, investigating the back streets of cities, etc.

Books

Bring your own. Most major cities have 'foreign language book stores', but they stock few books of interest to foreigners. A handful of bookstalls, mostly in top hotels, also have some foreign paperbacks on sale, but if you're a reader, it would be best to have your own supply. If you plan to travel by train a lot, you will be thankful of a thick novel or two.

Film

Kodak colour film (slides and prints) is available in most major cities in the foreigners' shops or hotels, but at higher prices than outside China. Elsewhere only locally made black-and-white film is available. Colour prints can now be developed in Peking in one day; there are film-processing counters at the Peking Hotel and the International Club.

Cigarettes and alcohol

A wide selection of foreign-brand cigarettes and some alcohol is available in the Friendship Stores. The local cigarette brands are pretty strong, and the rice wine is formidable, but the beer is generally good.

Electrics

China's electricity is 220 volts, 50 cycles.

Coffee

A couple of places (Peking and Canton) now sell foreign instant coffee at exorbitant prices. The local coffee is mostly terrible, so if you're a connoisseur, bring your own.

Radio

A shortwave radio is an excellent idea if you want to stay in touch with what's happening in the world. The Voice of America (VOA) can be picked up loud and clear in most of China, but the BBC is quite weak, especially in the north. Without a radio, up-to-date world news is hard to come by except in Peking, Shanghai and Canton where the *Herald Tribune* and the Asian edition of the *Wall Street Journal* are available, a couple of days late. There is also the official English-language daily newspaper, the *China Daily*, which provides relatively objective coverage of international events.

Other ideas

A couple of phrase books. If one book doesn't have it, the other one will. Some people write down lists of useful questions and have someone write the Chinese underneath. A better method is to put each question on a separate card.

Multi-vitamin tablets are a good idea, particularly if you intend to eat mostly where the ordinary Chinese do.

A water bottle is useful in summer. In many places there is nothing available but sweet iced lollies and sweet fizzy drinks, neither of which really quenches the thirst.

Many Chinese hotels have only baths and no showers, and the baths in some places can be pretty dirty. So, if you like soaking in a bath and intend to travel beyond Peking, Shanghai and Canton, some bath-cleanser would be useful. If you prefer showers, a handy item is a plastic shower nozzle which can be attached to bathtaps.

If you have any favourite soap, toothpaste, make-up, etc., you should bring adequate supplies with you.

Money

One yuan = 100 fen, 10 fen = one mao

China's currency is the *renminbi* (people's money), but most foreign visitors in China don't see too much of it. In an effort to put a stop to black-marketeering and financial funny business between local Chinese and outsiders (mostly Hong Kong Chinese), in 1980 the authorities introduced a new form of currency known as 'foreign exchange certificates'. Unauthorised local people are not supposed to possess the new notes, which can be used to buy things in the foreigners' shops, where quality is higher and stocks greater than in ordinary shops.

As a result, the obvious happened: a black market in the certificates developed, and foreign tourists are sometimes badgered by local people (especially in the south) to exchange ordinary money for the prized certificates. Occasionally the government appears to spread rumours that the certificates are about to be abolished in order to scare local people into unloading their holdings. But despite the problems, and criticism from many people who object to the existence of two kinds of Chinese currency – one high-class type for foreigners, and a lower-class one for ordinary Chinese – the Chinese government has apparently decided to stick with the foreign exchange certificates.

As a foreign tourist, it is perfectly legal to possess either type of currency. The main difference is that the certificates can be changed back into foreign currency (on presentation of the original currency exchange receipts), while ordinary *renminbi* cannot be changed and cannot be taken out of the country. Some places (foreigners' hotels, airline ticket offices, etc.) only accept the foreign exchange certificates, but the ordinary *renminbi* is useful out on the streets. Many shops will eagerly accept the certificates as well, but in off-the-beaten-track areas, you may find people who have never seen the certificates who will insist on *renminbi*.

One thing to watch: when you pay in foreign exchange certificates, make sure you get your change in the certificates, or you will end up with a pile of ordinary money that you can't exchange when you want to leave the country. Also remember to save all your currency exchange receipts for when you want to convert back to foreign currency.

As a rough guide, here are some exchange rates, valid at the time of writing:

US$1 = 2 yuan
UK£1 = 3 yuan
1 yuan = HK$3

Hotels

The major cities of China have three or four different kinds of accommodation including hotels for foreigners, overseas Chinese and government officials and lowly inns for the 'masses'. The rooms in the foreigners' hotels generally range from 30 to 60 yuan a day, and foreign tourists will be constantly pushed to take rooms at the top end of the range. If you are travelling on a budget, don't give in until you're convinced that there are no alternatives: there are almost certain to be some (*see* Budget accommodation below). Booking ahead is virtually impossible; hotels in China only like to deal with people actually standing at the reception desk, although CITS can usually help. The only hotel in China with a formal reservations system is the Jianguo Hotel in Peking, co-managed by the Peninsula Hotel Group in Hong Kong.

Hotel rooms for foreigners in China are generally spartan but acceptable. There will be two single beds, two chairs with a small table in between them on which is placed a flask of hot water and some cups. In some places, there will be a television set. Most tourist rooms have private bathrooms, but the plumbing is not always very reliable and some rudimentary knowledge of toilet cisterns is useful. Even if you don't have such knowledge before your trip, you may well have by the end.

In just about every hotel in China, on each floor, near the elevators there is a counter behind which sit the roomboys. They are there to clean the rooms, deliver laundry and also to keep an eye on the guests. It's all part of the Communist Party's belief that it has a right to concern itself with just about every facet of the lives of everyone in China.

Some hotels have heating and air conditioning, some don't, and the same applies to the showers and baths. In some hotels, the hot water is not turned on in the mornings, so it is best to shower or bathe in the evening. If you want an early morning wake-up call, ask the service desk on your floor of the hotel. Laundry usually takes a day, but don't hand in any particularly delicate fabrics for washing.

Budget accommodation

Many of the people who have travelled China as individual tourists in the past couple of years have been budget travellers, on their way through Asia on-the-cheap, who managed to get visas in Hong Kong. Those who have done it this way say it is possible to get by on an absolute minimum of about US$50 a week, depending on how much travelling you do. A more reasonable estimate would be US$80–100 a week.

Most cities in China have at least one hotel with dormitories which foreigners can stay in for between five and ten yuan per bed-space per night. That is more expensive than similar accommodation in most places in Southeast Asia and India, but the standard is generally higher, too. There are usually clean sheets, and sometimes a bathroom attached to the room (if not, then down the hall).

The attendants in some hotels may deny the existence of a dormitory or swear that all the bed-spaces are full. When this happens, as it will many times during your travels, remain calm and polite, and say you will sit down and wait until a bed becomes vacant. You may have to wait an hour or more, but eventually your patience will almost certainly be rewarded. Whatever you do, don't get angry.

Transport

Airlines

The Chinese airline, CAAC, has a comprehensive domestic network, but planes fill up quickly so it is wise to book several days in advance. Airline ticket prices for foreigners are not extortionate (about UK£50 Peking–Shanghai, £80 Peking–Canton), and are only slightly more expensive than first-class train tickets for the same route. Some airports in China are a long way out of the city, so it is useful to know that there is always an airport bus leaving from the CAAC office in the centre of town, which is free for ticket-holders.

The airline is rather strict on its baggage limit of two suitcases and 20 kilos (44 lb) maximum weight, but as more groups check and weigh in for flights collectively, this is not usually a problem, unless your baggage is drastically overweight.

Trains

The most convenient form of surface travel is the railways, and there is a good service linking all but one of the major cities of the People's Republic: the exception is Lhasa in Tibet. The trains are clean, and usually punctual. Long-distance trains are divided into three classes: soft-sleeper, hard-sleeper and ordinary hard seats. The soft-sleepers, which consist of cabins for four people, with frilly curtains and potted plants, are the preserve of foreigners and high-ranking Communist Party officials. The other Chinese and the more adventurous foreigners rough it in the hard carriages. The hard-sleepers are, in fact, not hard at all, and are perfectly adequate for most travellers. Ticket prices for the three classes vary widely, with the added complication that foreigners pay almost double the amount that the local Chinese do for the same tickets.

Train tickets are sold at the stations, but there can be long queues in front of the ticket offices. It is usually possible to buy tickets through CITS or some foreigners' hotels. Trains are sometimes fully booked, so buy your tickets a couple of days in advance. Keep your ticket with you when you get off the train: you will need it to get out of the station.

Food is sold on the trains. Attendants move through the hard-class carriages before mealtimes and sell ticket vouchers exchangeable for cheap containers of rice with some vegetables and meat. Better food is available in the restaurant cars, but beware you don't get over-

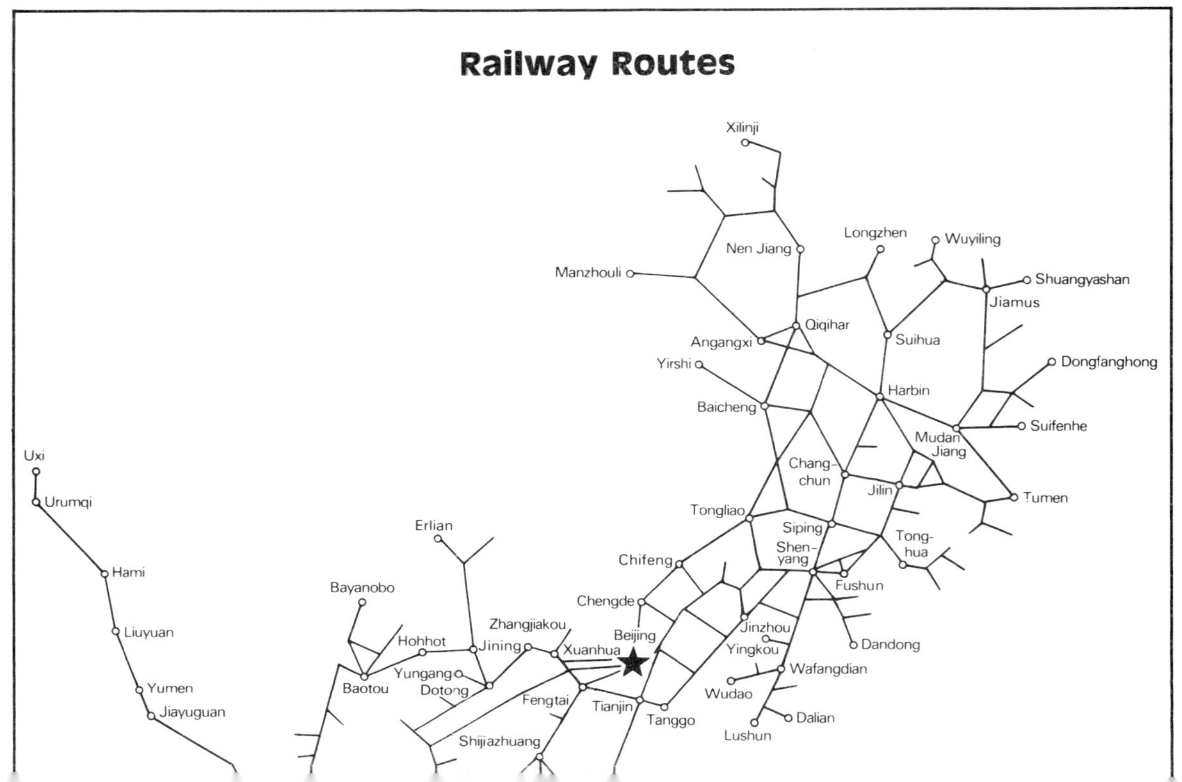
Railway Routes
Xilinji
Longzhen
Wuyiling
Nen Jiang
Manzhouli
Shuangyashan
Jiamus
Qiqihar
Angangxi
Suihua
Dongfanghong
Yirshi
Harbin
Baicheng
Suifenhe
Mudan Jiang
Chang-chun
Uxi
Jilin
Tumen
Urumqi
Tongliao
Siping
Erlian
Tong-hua
Shen-yang
Chifeng
Hami
Fushun
Bayanobo
Chengde
Zhangjiakou
Jinzhou
Liuyuan
Hohhot
Beijing
Dandong
Jining
Xuanhua
Yingkou
Yungang
Wafangdian
Baotou
Yumen
Dotong
Wudao
Fengtai
Tianjin
Jiayuguan
Dalian
Tanggo
Lushun
Shijiazhuang

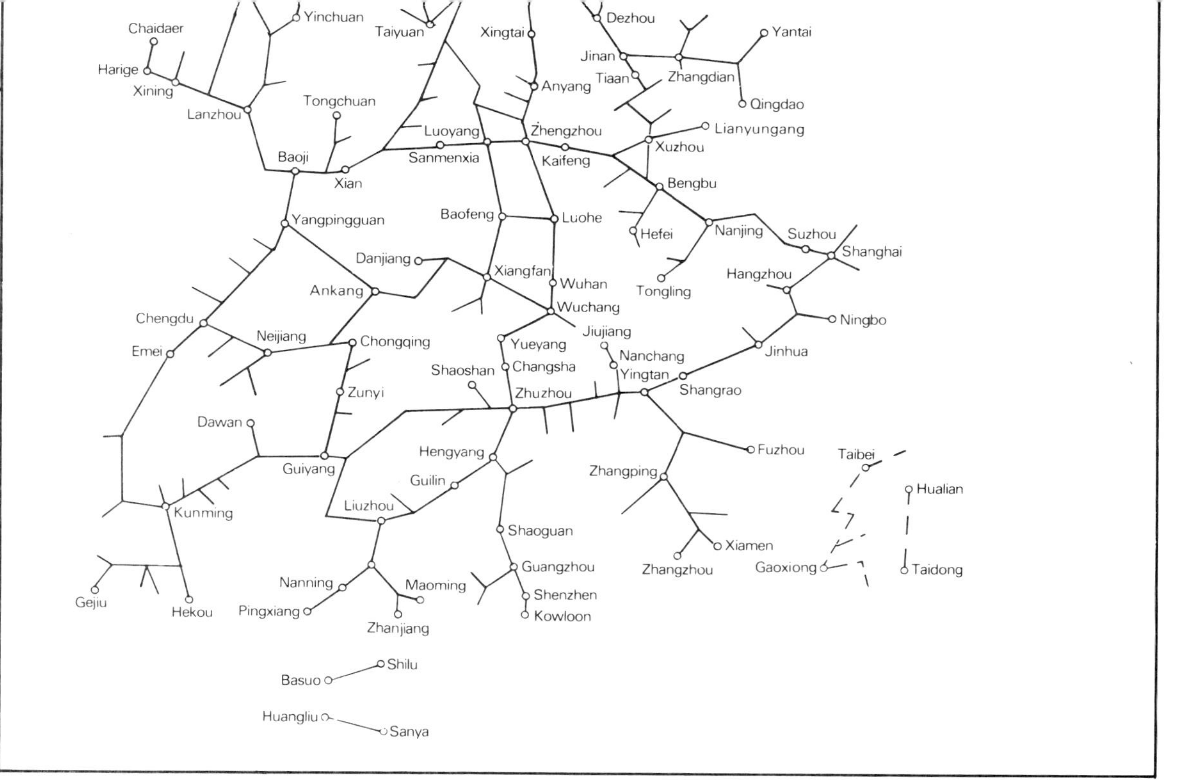

Yinchuan
Taiyuan
Xingtai
Dezhou
Chaidaer
Yantai
Harige
Jinan
Xining
Tiaan
Zhangdian
Anyang
Tongchuan
Lanzhou
Qingdao
Luoyang
Zhengzhou
Lianyungang
Xuzhou
Baoji
Sanmenxia
Kaifeng
Xian
Bengbu
Baofeng
Luohe
Yangpingguan
Hefei
Nanjing
Suzhou
Shanghai
Danjiang
Xiangfan
Hangzhou
Wuhan
Tongling
Ankang
Wuchang
Ningbo
Chengdu
Jiujiang
Neijiang
Chongqing
Emei
Yueyang
Nanchang
Jinhua
Shaoshan
Changsha
Yingtan
Shangrao
Zunyi
Zhuzhou
Dawan
Hengyang
Fuzhou
Taibei
Guiyang
Zhangping
Guilin
Hualian
Liuzhou
Kunming
Shaoguan
Xiamen
Guangzhou
Zhangzhou
Gaoxiong
Taidong
Nanning
Maoming
Shenzhen
Gejiu
Hekou
Pingxiang
Kowloon
Zhanjiang
Shilu
Basuo
Huangliu
Sanya

charged. Attendants come round every so often to fill up tea mugs with hot water; if you are travelling hard-class, bring your own mug.

Buses

There are buses operating between virtually all cities in China, but foreigners are not allowed to use most of them, because they travel through, and stop in, 'closed' areas. However, there are some places where buses can be ridden. They are not as comfortable as the trains, but they are cheap, and give you a good view of the countryside. Buses in the cities are usually very crowded, and you will often have to fight your way on with the crowd, but they are a convenient way of getting round. City bus route maps are usually available at major bookshops and at the railway stations. The bus services in most cities stop running at about 9.00 p.m. or 10.00 p.m. at the latest, and often a lot earlier.

Boats

There are regular services along the coast and along the major rivers, but foreigners are often refused permission to go aboard. Regular services operate from Shanghai, Fuzhou and Xiamen to Hong Kong. There are river ferries on the Yangtse River which foreigners can use, and also on the Grand Canal between Hangzhou and Suzhou (however, some people have been refused permission to make this trip).

Taxis

The large cities of China now have taxi fleets for the use of foreign visitors, but only in Canton (so far) can they be hailed in the street. In other centres, you must go to a regular taxi stand to get one, and most are situated at the main tourist hotels. The taxi fares vary depending on the size of the car rented, and are generally about 50 fen per kilometre. Waiting time is cheap, and it is often a good idea to keep a taxi driver hanging around for the return fare if you are going somewhere out-of-the-way. In smaller cities and towns, the only taxis available for foreigners are generally under the control of CITS, and there are often only a handful. So if you want a car to go somewhere, it would be wise to make arrangements the day before.

How to get from the station to the hotel

This is a crucial, and sometimes exhausting, problem for the independent traveller. The easy way is to check in with CITS at your last stop and arrange for a guide to meet you with a car. To get to the hotel on your own, check the individual travel sections of this book which, in most cases, will give you the information you need. Usually, the standard form of local transport is the public bus, and there is a bus terminal near just about every railway station in China. Sometimes there are pedi-cabs, especially in southern China – agree on a price before you get on board – and sometimes the hotels are within walking distance.

Guided tours

Tourist groups in China at present travel on group visas which the tour guides hold. Individual passports are not stamped with visas unless you specifically ask for one.

Most people on group tours of China are very experienced travellers, but they quickly discover that China is something different. Basically, you have to accept things as they come; there is almost nothing that can be done to effect changes, so try to develop a calm, Zen-like acceptance. There may be sudden changes of itinerary. You may be put in hotels outside town, or in accommodation that is of a considerably lower standard than you are used to. Just accept it. Any changes are usually the result of bureaucratic foul-ups by CITS, an organisation which is still feeling its way through the mass tourism business, and it has to deal with huge numbers of people that are, as it were, dumped on it from above (*see* p. 33).

The foreign tour companies have effectively no control over which hotel you stay in: it is all decided by CITS. Sometimes it is necessary to share rooms, especially during the summer and autumn when the hotels are very full. On most tours, it is not impossible for groups or individuals to deviate from the list of cities given beforehand, if they want to, although, in some cases, CITS is forced to alter the itinerary for its own reasons.

On most tours, group meals are provided at the hotels as part of the deal, but you can skip meals and go out and explore some local restaurants whenever you want, at your own expense, of course. If you intend to eat in the foreigners' section of a restaurant, you should make a reservation, and once the reservation is made, you will generally have to pay whether you turn up or not. If you want to go somewhere on your own, you can hire a taxi at the hotel. Except in Canton, it is virtually impossible to hail a taxi in the street, and very few of the taxi drivers speak any English. Take along a card or pamphlet with the name of the place where you want to go and the name of your hotel in Chinese to help you get there and back.

The sight-seeing itinerary for the group in each city will have been arranged long in advance. If you have some special suggestion as to what the group should visit, bring it up as early as possible after arriving in the city concerned. You are likely to visit schools, factories, communes, museums, temples, etc., and the pace can be very wearing, so take it easy and find time to relax. When on visits to factories and other 'units', there will be standard introductory speeches given by some responsible official while you sit around drinking tea. If you have questions, be sure to keep them simple and phrase them clearly.

In all of the cities you visit, you will be completely free to wander around the streets as you wish, and going for a walk is often far more interesting than going to see yet another handicrafts factory. Again, take along a hotel envelope or something similar in case you get lost. There will be many opportunities for shopping. The official Chinese guides will continually herd you in the direction of the local Friendship Store, antiques and handicrafts shop (*see* What to buy, p. 31), but you should also go and look at some local shops.

Most important of all, keep a sense of humour, and be considerate, especially if your tour is a long one. You're going to have to live with your fellow travellers right through to the end.

Contacts with Chinese people

The thing that makes touring China as an individual traveller really pleasurable is the contacts you can have with the ordinary people. Most Chinese will show you great courtesy and kindness, and many will go out of their way to help 'foreign guests'. Even the bureaucrats and police officials are generally pleasant and helpful, and there are none of the problems of petty corruption which make travel in many Third World countries so unpleasant.

Riding in the hard-class sections of trains, you are bound to come across people who can speak some English and who want to practise with you. The most interesting ones to talk to are generally the older people who learned their English before 1949. However, it is important to remember that if you talk to or befriend Chinese people, they could possibly get into serious trouble as a result. How the situation is handled depends largely on how conservative the local branch of the Public Security Bureau is, but there have been many cases of people being detained by the police after simply chatting to a foreigner in the street. So be careful.

Language

China has effectively only been open to tourists for a few years, and many of the people you will come into contact with will not be able to speak English, let alone any other foreign language. However, there are times when it seems as if just about every person in China under the age of 30 is learning to speak English, and at some time during a trip around China, you are certain to be approached on the streets by some earnest young student wanting to practice the latest phrases from *English by Radio*.

If you do come across an impenetrable language barrier, one good tip is to keep an eye open for one of the thousands of young Hong Kong travellers who make their way around China on the cheap. The Hong Kong Chinese, usually very distinctive because of their Western style of casual dress and their hair styles, generally speak some English, and can get by in Mandarin, even though their native language is Cantonese, a very different dialect.

Phrase books are useful, but do not always include all the words or sentences you need, particularly if you are travelling on a budget. A good idea is to put your most commonly used questions on separate cards, and have someone write the Chinese next to them.

The Pinyin spelling system used to romanise Chinese characters is rather confusing. Here are some pronunciation hints:

X sounds like an ordinary 's'
Q sounds like 'ch'
C sounds like a hard 'ts'
Z sounds like a soft 'dz'
Zh sounds like an ordinary 'j'

With words ending in 'ong', the middle vowel sounds like a long 'oo' (as in 'shoe'). 'Dong', for instance, sounds like 'doong'.

Words ending in 'eng' sound like the English 'ung' (as in 'sung'). The surname of China's leader, Deng Xiaoping, is pronounced in a similar way to an English synonym for manure.

Pronunciation is complicated by the existence of four tones in standard Mandarin, the national language. A sound can have many different meanings depending on its tone.

Here are some useful Mandarin phrases:

Hello / how are you? – Ni hao ma?
Goodbye – Zai jian.
Sorry / excuse me – Dui bu qi.
I don't understand – Wo bu dong.

There are a number of ways of saying 'hotel' in Chinese, as you will find in this guide. Here are some of them:

binguan – guesthouse, usually a high-class place for foreigners
fandian – hotel
luguan – (small) hotel

Most of the street names in the guide are written in Pinyin to make it easier for you to ask people directions. Most thoroughfares in China are named either 'lu' (road) or 'jie' (street) as in English. They often have a direction added, too. Here are the Chinese directions:

Bei – North
Nan – South
Dong – East
Xi – West

So, 'Zhongshan Bei Lu' means 'Zhongshan Road North'; 'Jiefang Dong Jie' means 'Jiefang Street East'.

Food and drink

Food

Chinese food is rightly considered to be one of the greatest of the world's cuisines. There are a number of different styles around the country, the most notable of which are Cantonese, Peking, Shanghai and Sichuan, but the food in each region has its own special qualities. It's purely a matter of personal taste as to which is best. The quality of the food varies widely, depending mostly on the size of the city or town you are in. Shanghai, being the largest city in China, probably has the best food of all, both for local people and the foreigners. In some places, especially in northern China in winter, the food can be just awful.

The foreigners' hotels all have restaurants which are generally reasonable in price, and the food is usually of a better quality than in ordinary restaurants outside. But you should try at least a couple of local restaurants, especially if you are travelling on a budget.

Mealtimes in ordinary restaurants in China are much earlier than most Westerners are used to. Lunch starts at 11.00 a.m. or soon after, while the main evening meal is generally over by 7.30 p.m. and even earlier in rural areas. At set mealtimes, every restaurant in China seems to be bursting at the seams.

Foreigners often get special treatment in the ordinary restaurants, even if they don't want it. Many of the bigger restaurants in Peking and other major cities have a special room for foreigners in which they are served large meals at exorbitant prices, out of sight of the ordinary Chinese. Being pushed off into a corner and ripped off is objectionable, and many travellers would much prefer to rough it with the locals. One problem, however, is that, in restaurants without the discreet backroom, the staff can sometimes be a little too eager to please and roughly press other patrons to hurry up and finish to make room for the 'foreign guests'. It's outrageous, but there's often nothing that can be done about it.

Most ordinary restaurants have no menus: items available that day are chalked up on a noticeboard and rubbed off as the kitchen runs out. If you speak no Chinese, either have some favourite dishes written down in Chinese to show the attendants, or else point to dishes other patrons are eating. Food prices vary widely. A backroom feast in a top restaurant in Peking could cost 20 yuan or more per head. A meal in a grubby backstreet noodle shop may cost only 30 or 40 fen. The choice is yours.

For strict vegetarians, China can be a difficult place to tour. The Chinese eat a lot of pork and much of the fried food is cooked in animal fat, so some vegetarians simply give in and eat meat for the duration of the trip. But it's not impossible. There are vegetarian restaurants in some cities, and usually a vegetable dish or two on the menus of most restaurants. I met one Australian traveller who was so strict a vegetarian that he didn't even drink milk or eat eggs and cheese. He had been travelling around China for nearly three months when I met him and he looked fit, although very thin. His advice for strict vegetarians was: bring some simple cooking pots with you, buy your own vegetables and cook them yourself. He passed on a do-it-yourself cooking method for those willing to take the trouble: buy one of the hot water thermos flasks which everyone in China uses, place the food you want cooked in the bottom, pour boiling water on top and let it stand for between 2 and 12 hours depending on what it is. For vegetables, two hours is about enough; for grain and rice, 12 hours is sufficient.

Drink

All the major tourist centres of China now stock a wide selection of foreign liquors, which are quite expensive but at least they are there. In the old days (before 1979), you either brought your own or you did without.

The local beer throughout China is generally good, although beer-drinkers agree that the best brands are Tsingtao and Beijing (Peking) beer. In Shanghai, the beer, the soft drinks, everything, tastes of mud, but if you're there long enough you cease to notice it.

There is a vast choice of Chinese-made wines, ranging from cheapo rice wines at about one yuan a bottle (which will knock you out if you can force the fiery liquid down your throat), to 'Dynasty' white wines, produced near Tianjin as a joint venture with the French company Remy Martin. A Hong Kong wine expert said of one of these wines: 'Its fruity bouquet and fine taste complements seafood perfectly, and as an accompaniment to shark's fin, it's simply unparalleled.'

The alcoholic drink prized most highly by the Chinese themselves is Mao Tai, made from sorghum (a type of millet), which is the traditional drink for toasts at official banquets. It is an expensive drink, and people wanting to grease the palm of some official often give Mao Tai as a 'present'. As a Chinese joke so wisely puts it, those who buy Mao Tai don't drink it, and those who drink it don't buy it. Some foreigners even claim they enjoy Mao Tai. Like any alcohol, it tastes better after the fifth glass.

For real connoisseurs, and for those who think they've tried everything, may I suggest Hejie Jiu (lizard wine), produced in Guangxi Province in the southwest. Each bottle contains a long-tailed, four-legged (dead) lizard floating perpendicularly in the clear alcohol. The creatures look glassy-eyed, but after soaking in such fierce alcohol for so long, who wouldn't? Even if you don't fancy trying it, a bottle of lizard wine makes a great souvenir to take home to offer your guests.

In the soft drinks line, Coca Cola is now produced in Peking although it is produced mostly for foreigners and not the locals. To many people, it doesn't taste quite like the real thing. Perhaps it's the water.

Virtually each city in China has its own brand of fizzy soft drink, all of them incredibly chemical-tasting. In Peking, it's a sort of orange flavour; in Canton and Shanghai, it's an extremely orange flavour; Fuzhou has something allegedly flavoured banana; and so on. Some people go around China sampling and comparing the beers, others, the soft drinks. You, too, can be an instant connoisseur expounding on the subtle reasons why Wuhan beer is superior to Xi'an beer.

Nightlife and entertainment

Compared to other tourist destinations in Asia, China has little of either, and markedly less now than in the very early 1980s. Peking used to boast one or two theoretically 'foreigners-only' discos, but the Communist Party's fear of Western culture and ideas gaining a hold among the ordinary people of China led to them all being closed. At the time of writing only one hotel in Peking has permission to hold dances – the Jianguo Hotel, which is co-managed by the Peninsula Hotel Group from Hong Kong.

Shanghai went one better and had live bands playing in two or three 'foreigners-only' bars around the city. The musicians were veterans of dance bands which played in the old Shanghai before the Communist take-over in 1949, and some of them weren't bad. But alas, they also fell victim to the campaign against so-called 'bourgeois liberalism', and all the bars were shut down in August 1982. Hopefully, they will be allowed to start playing those old Glenn Miller hits again soon.

Other, more proletarian and ethnic, entertainment basically consists of films or theatrical productions in local theatres. Tickets are often hard to get, so it is best to arrange them through the hotel or through the local CITS office (*see* p. 33). But with Chinese opera, plays or films, you would not be blamed if you could not sit through an entire performance.

Chinese opera is definitely an acquired taste. One English 'China expert' of the nineteenth century, a Mr Arthur H. Smith, had this to say: 'If there is in China any such thing as singing, it may safely be said never to come to the ears of foreigners. The shrill falsetto cackling of the Chinese-style singing is, to those who have never heard it, quite indescribable. Those who have heard it, require no description.' The opinion of Mr Smith, cultural chauvinist, can be safely dismissed, but it is true that Chinese singing can sound raucous to the stranger's ear, and can be wearing after a while. However, a real proletarian opera, especially in the smaller cities, is always worth going to, more to watch the audience than what's going on on stage. It's very much a social event, with kids and grandmothers wandering round chatting to acquaintances, spitting out melon seeds and occasionally acknowledging a solo from one of the players with the appreciative expletive '*Hao!*' (good). On summer evenings in some cities, there are opera performances in the parks. Peking operas tend to be harder on the foreigner's ear than the more melodic operas of the south.

Films are a different matter. The standard of film-making in this, the largest movie market in the world, is appalling. The audiences know the films are bad, but go anyway because there's nothing else to do. The film-makers themselves know their products are bad, but there is little they can do about it because they are supervised at every turn by Party watchdogs who tend to veto anything even slightly adventurous. Plots are usually predictable, characters are generally cardboard stand-ups.

Nevertheless, things are better today for Chinese movie-goers than at any time in the past 15 years or more. During Mao's Cultural Revolution and after, only a handful of films were made each year, all to the same boring formula, featuring revolutionary goody-goodies and reactionary baddies. Today, movie production has increased, and some detective and love stories get shown along with the usual blatant propaganda. A few foreign films have also been imported – *Death on the Nile* was a box-office hit in 1982, for instance. You should go to the cinema at least once in China. It doesn't matter too much if you can't understand Chinese – in 99 films out of 100, the plot will be so transparent that you will have no trouble following it. But the audience can be very vocal in its approval or disapproval, which is fun.

Another form of entertainment is, of course, television, although the mainland Chinese variety is not all that entertaining. Huge numbers of viewers in southern China buy large aerials so that they can pick up Hong Kong or Taiwan television instead. An average evening of television viewing in China begins at 6.30 p.m. with a 'learn English' programme called *Follow Me*, bought from the BBC. Then at seven o'clock, there is the news – snippets of film about a model commune in Hunan or how study of the latest political line has helped raise production in the No. 13 bicycle factory in Taiyuan. At about 7.20 p.m. comes one of the most revolutionary things that has happened to China in the past 30 years – ten minutes of satellite news film from the West which gives the Chinese people their first reasonably objective view of the outside world. The authorities generally go to great lengths to keep their citizens away from information and influences from 'outside', but the news film fits in well with their efforts to emphasise the negative aspects of Western society – the wars and street demonstrations, the riots and crises. At 7.30, there might be a travelogue programme on some part of China, or perhaps on Yugoslavia, followed by a Peking opera or a feature film. Some relatively good television dramas have been produced in recent years, especially ones set in classical China, but the television audience still seems generally dissatisfied. The huge number of families that have invested in television sets in recent years want to get some value for their money. Station close-down comes at about 10.00 or 10.30 p.m.

The best evening's entertainment in China, especially in southern China in the warmer months, is walking around the streets. Compared to many Western cities, there is very little street crime in China, and a foreigner is almost certainly immune from attack.

What to buy

Every foreigner who visits China ends up going to at least one of the ubiquitous Friendship Stores, the government-run foreigners-only shops which could be described as China's only franchised chain of retail outlets. The shops have been set up in just about every major Chinese city, primarily to get visitors to open up their wallets and donate a bit more foreign exchange to the Chinese revolution. They are better stocked than ordinary shops, and often have items which are perennially in short supply outside. The other advantage is that you don't need ration tickets or letters of approval from your work unit to buy things at the Friendship Store. Local people lucky enough to have relatives living outside China eagerly wait for them to visit so that they can have access to the Friendship Store and buy whatever they cannot get in the normal shops – bicycles, sewing machines, cooking oil, clothing material, television sets or tape recorders.

The Shanghai Friendship Store has one of the best addresses in China, that of the former British consulate on the Bund, but the Peking Friendship Store is the largest, and also features a real Western-style supermarket. In other cities, the main department stores often have small backrooms which only open up when they know a foreign tourist group is coming through. You frequently have to bang on the doors for a while to wake the slumbering staff inside. Out in the provinces, where the quality of the food can be pretty terrible, the Friendship Stores are a godsend for the simple reason that they are often the only place in town which sells chocolate, that convenient and tasty source of quick energy.

Some visitors leave China convinced that there's nothing worth buying in the Friendship Stores. Others depart loaded down with goodies. It all depends on what you're looking for. For a start, almost everything for sale in the Friendship Stores is also available in the Communist department stores in Hong Kong, which have a better range to choose from and sometimes cheaper prices. Most Friendship Stores have an antique section – some cities have separate antique shops – but the experts say that there are few bargains to be had. The Chinese authorities are well aware of prices on the international market and mark up prices accordingly. But there are some good-value items on sale, even if they are just knick-knacks to take home as souvenirs of a trip to China.

Top of my list are the paper rubbings of old stone inscriptions and carvings which many foreigners' shops around the country sell. The rubbings, usually black and white, can be very beautiful and often sell for as little as 1.50 yuan. Mounted or framed, they make great wall hangings. Next come the Mao caps, green or blue with a red star on the front just like the old Chairman used to wear. Many visitors buy a Chinese chop (seal) and have their names, or Chinese characters approximating them in sound, carved on the end. Prices for the chops start at about 20 yuan and work up close to infinity. Other good buys include cashmere jumpers and cardigans, silk T-shirts (very slinky) and carpets which, although expensive, are still cheaper than similar-quality carpets overseas.

If you do buy an antique, make sure it has a red seal attached to it. You will be given a receipt, and it is imperative that you don't lose it. In fact, keep all your receipts for expensive items: you never know what the customs official at the airport might pounce on. At some of the larger Friendship Stores, it is possible to get things crated and shipped back to your home country.

Visitors to China in the late 1960s and early 1970s, when Chairman Mao was an almost god-like figure, could buy a bewildering array of Mao junk – Mao badges, Mao lamp-shades, Mao mugs, Mao bed-spreads, and Mao alarm clocks with a Red Guard on top waving a Little Red Book back and forth in time to the tick-tock of the clock – but they're all gone now. These days, the only faint echo of that time to be found in the Friendship Stores is a series of black-and-white woven portraits of Marx, Engels, Lenin and Stalin, which make great table place-mats.

Medical matters

Anyone contemplating a visit to China, either as an individual tourist or on a package tour, should be certain they are reasonably fit: China tourism is not a matter of lying around on a beach soaking up the sun. It is generally hard work, and for some people it proves to be too much. An especially large number of older tourists have made the trip through China since it opened up in earnest to foreign visitors in 1978, and every year some of them die, at least partly through the strain of the heavy schedule. It has become such a regular phenomenon that it even has a name: 'Death by Duck'. A typical ageing victim clambers up and down the Great Wall, a difficult task even if you are young and in reasonably good shape, and then goes back to Peking where he consumes a large, greasy Peking Duck dinner. The result: heart failure. One should not be an alarmist, but Chinese tourism can be very tiring.

The most common ailment among visitors is a heavy cold. There is not much you can do to guard against it, but drink lots of liquid, and bring a good supply of tissues. Getting really sick in China is not much fun either. The Chinese authorities will provide foreigners with the best facilities available, and sometimes seem overly cautious with their treatment. But, especially away from the major cities, the standards of medical treatment are, by Western standards, very low. Certain kinds of treatment can also be expensive, so it is worth taking out travel insurance which covers medical treatment before you go.

China International Travel Service (CITS)

Travel in China has long been the responsibility of two organisations: the China Travel Service (CTS) for overseas Chinese and Hong Kong visitors, and the China International Travel Service (CITS) for other foreigners. CITS was traditionally a lethargic beast, only occasionally bothered by small groups of well-behaved foreigners who were happy to be herded round factories, communes and kindergartens. Things changed drastically in the late 1970s when the Chinese leadership decided to open the country up to foreign tourism to earn some money. CITS has been stretched to the limit by the flood of tourists, but generally has done a good job in the face of very difficult conditions. There are inevitable bureaucratic foul-ups, but the guides themselves are mostly open, friendly and helpful.

The travel service is well equipped to help individual tourists wanting to tour China in comfort. You can book guides, taxis, travel and theatre tickets and hotel rooms. All you have to do is visit the CITS office in one city and have them send a message to the branch in the next city, detailing your needs. Of course, things sometimes go wrong but, overall, CITS is pretty efficient. If you are a budget traveller, you will not find CITS much help. They want you to spend money, as much as possible, and will constantly steer you towards the most expensive hotels, train berths and restaurants. But in an emergency, they are there.

The following is a list of the addresses and phone numbers of the main CITS offices around China:

CITY	TELEPHONE	ADDRESS
Baotou	5687	Baotou Guesthouse
Canton (Guangzhou)	34831	179 Huanshi Lu
Changchun	38495	2 Stalin Da Jie
Changsha	22250	130 Wuyi Lu, Sanxing Jie
Chengdu	8225	Jinjiang Guesthouse
Chongqing (Chungking)	51449	Renmin Guesthouse
Dalian (Luda, Dairen)	25103	56 Fenglin Jie
Datong	2704	Xinjian Lu
Fuzhou (Foochow)	33962	Wusi Lu
Guilin (Kweilin)	2648	14 Ronghu Bei Lu
Hangzhou (Hangchow)	22487	10 Baoshu Lu
Harbin	31495	124 Dazhi Jie
Hefei	2221	Jiang Huai Hotel
Huhehot (Hohhot)	4494	Huhehot Guesthouse
Jinan	35351	372 Jingsan Lu
Jiujiang	2526	77 Nansi Lu
Jiuquan	2943	2 Cangmen Jie
Kaifeng	3737	102 Ziyou Lu, Zhong Duan
Kunming	4992	68 Huashan Xi Lu
Lanzhou	4962	14 Xijin Xi Lu
Luoyang	7006	Friendship Hotel
Lushan	2497	–
Nanchang	62571	Jiangxi Guesthouse

CITY	TELEPHONE	ADDRESS
Nanking (Nanjing)	85153	313 Zhongshan Bei Lu
Nanning	4793	Xinmin Lu
Peking (Beijing)	755374	2 Qianmen Dong Da Jie
Qingdao (Chingtao)	28877	9 Nanhai Lu
Qufu (Chufu)	–	Confucius Mansion
Shanghai	217200	59 Xianggang Lu
Shenyang (Mukden)	34653	3 Zhongshan Lu, Yi Duan
Shijiazhuang	8962	Weiming Lu
Suzhou	4646	115 Youyi Lu
Tai'an	3259	Dai Zong Fang
Taiyuan	29155	Yingze Da Jie
Tianjin (Tientsin)	34831	55 Chongqing Dao
Wuhan	23505	1395 Zhongshan Da Dao
Wuxi	25461	7 Xinsheng Lu
Xiamen (Amoy)	4286	444 Zhongshan Lu
Xi'an (Sian)	21191	272 Jiefang Lu
Yan'an (Yenan)	2363	56 Yan'an Shi Da Jie
Yichang	3103	Tao Hua Ling
Yueyang	2282	Qingnian Lu
Zhengzhou	5578	8 Jinshuihe Da Dao

Embassies and consulates

The following is a list of the telephone numbers of some of the foreign embassies in Peking:

Australia 52-2331
Austria 52-2061
Belgium 52-1736
Canada 52-1475
France 52-1331
Germany, West 52-2161
Greece 52-1391
Ireland 52-2691
Italy 52-2131
Japan 52-2361
Malaysia 52-2531
New Zealand 52-2731
Norway 52-3631
Spain 52-1967

Sweden 52-3331
Switzerland 52-2831
United Kingdom 52-1961
USA 52-2033

Consulates in Shanghai:
France 37-7414
Japan 37-9025
Poland 37-0952
USA 37-9880

Consulates in Canton (located in the Dongfang Hotel):
Japan .... 69-900×2785
USA .... 69-900×1000

Further reading

Here is a short selection of books about China:

Denis Bloodworth, *The Chinese Looking Glass* (Farrar Straus and Giroux, New York, 1980).

David Bonavia, *The Chinese, A Portrait* (Penguin, 1982): a good general introduction to modern-day China.

Fox Butterfield, *China, Alive in the Bitter Sea* (Hodder & Stoughton, 1982): an anecdote-filled guide to the dark side of Chinese life.

Roger Garside, *Coming Alive! China after Mao* (McGraw-Hill, 1981).

Simon Leys, *Chinese Shadows* (Penguin, 1977): one of the first books to explode the Mao myth.

Jean Pascalini, *Prisoner of Mao* (Penguin, 1976): an extraordinary account of the Chinese labour camp system written by a former French–Chinese inmate.

Edgar Snow, *Red Star over China* (Penguin, 1968): the monumental book which first introduced the Chinese Communists to the outside world in 1936, telling the story of the Long March.

Almost no fiction of worth has been written in the Chinese language since 1949. One of the few great books is *The Execution of Mayor Yin* by Chen Jo-hsi, published by Indiana University Press in 1978, a semi-fictional account of the madness of the Cultural Revolution from the inside.

One of the best translations of classical Chinese literature is *Monkey*, translated by Arthur Waley (Penguin, 1961), also known as *Travels to the West*, which is the best Chinese fairy story of all time. The greatest classical Chinese novel is considered to be *The Dream of the Red Chamber*, the best translation of it (called *The Story of the Stone*) being by David Hawkes (Penguin, 1973, 1977, 1980).

Of guidebooks, the most important is Nagel's *China*, a heavy tome filled with very detailed information on historic monuments, although much of it is now out of date. An excellent guide to old Shanghai is Pan Ling's *In Search of Old Shanghai* (Joint Publishing, 1982). The original *In Search of Old Peking*, written by Messrs Arlington and Lewisohn in 1935, was reprinted by Paragon Book Reprint Corp. in 1967.

CHINA: A BRIEF HISTORY

The Dynasties

Xia (Hsia)	2205–1557 B.C.
Shang	1557–1122 B.C.
Zhou (Chou)	1122–770 B.C.
Spring and Autumn Period	771–481 B.C.
Warring States	481–246 B.C.
Qin (Ch'in)	246–206 B.C.
Han	206 B.C.–A.D. 221
Three Kingdoms	A.D. 221–265
Jin (Tsin)	265–420
Southern and Northern Dynasties	420–589
Northern Wei	386–534
Sui	589–618
Tang	618–907
Five Dynasties and Ten Kingdoms	907–960
Liao	947–1125
Jin (Chin)	1122–1234
Song (Sung)	960–1279
Yuan (Mongol)	1271–1367
Ming	1367–1644
Qing (Manchu)	1644–1911

China is the longest-running act on earth, the only one of the ancient civilisations not submerged by another, upstart culture. The recorded history of the Chinese nation begins some 3000 years ago, although the first recognisably Chinese societies started to emerge much earlier. Inscriptions have been found on tortoise shells which tell of events during the Shang dynasty, which had its capital near the city of Anyang in the valley of the Yellow River (regarded as the 'cradle' of Chinese civilisation), and ended sometime around 1122 B.C. The Shang was succeeded by the Zhou dynasty, and in the centuries that followed, the Chinese world, much smaller than that of today, was often divided into a number of independent states, all with a similar culture. They built long walls to protect themselves from each other and from the 'barbarian' tribes to the north. During the Warring States period (481–246 B.C.), these states fought among each other interminably, but eventually the kingdom of Qin, led by the man known to history as Qin Shi Huang (the 'First August Emperor' of the Qin dynasty), conquered the rest of the states in the Chinese world and created the first Chinese empire in 246 B.C. at about the time of the First Punic War between Rome and Carthage.

Qin Shi Huang is remembered for three things: he unified the country, joined together the various walls to make the first 'Great Wall' of China to keep the barbarians out, and burned all the books he could get his hands on except for technical manuals. He ruled the new Chinese empire for 35 years, but only four years after his death, his Qin (Ch'in) dynasty (probably the origin of the word 'China') fell, to be replaced by the Han.

The Han dynasty, which lasted over 400 years and roughly coincided with the Roman Empire, saw the first real flowering of Chinese culture. Buddhism was introduced from India, the borders were pushed back north and west into central Asia, and south towards present-day south China, and the ideas of Confucius, China's greatest philosopher, became firmly established as the ideological basis for Chinese society. The imperial civil service which ruled China for more than 2000 years was established and the Chinese writing system was formalised and has remained basically the same ever since.

When the Han dynasty collapsed in the year A.D. 221, China was plummeted into one of its periodic states of chaos. As before, the country was finally re-unified by a short-lived dynasty which gave way to a powerful, long-lived one – the Tang dynasty (618–907), considered to be classical China's 'Golden Age'. Tang-dynasty China was the most powerful state in the world at a time when western Europe was going through the darkest stretches of the Middle Ages. Its capital at Changan (today's Xi'an) was a cosmopolitan city of over a million people, and the starting point of the famous Silk Route across central Asia to Europe. The greatest of Chinese classical poetry and many of the greatest works of Chinese art were produced during this era.

At the beginning of the tenth century, the Tang dynasty fell, and

China
Urumqi
Aksu
Xinjiang
Turpan
Hami
Liuyuan
Dunhuang
Gansu
Wuwei
Xining
Golmud
Qinghai
Tibet
Qamdo
Sichuan
Lhasa
Xigaze
Emei Shan
Dali
Yunnan
Jinghong

Qiqihar
Heilongjiang
Harbin
Jilin
Jilin
Changchun
Erenhot
Liaoning
Fushun
Shenyang
Anshan
Dandong
Inner Mongolia
Hohhot
Beijing
Tianjin
Baotou
Datong
Yinchuan
Zhijiazhuang
Taiyuan
Hebei
Shanxi
Yanan
Yantai
Qingdao
Jinan
Tai Shan
Anyang
Shandong
Lianyungang
Kaifeng
Luoyang
Zhengzhou
Xuzhou
Shaanxi
Xian
Jiangsu
Hanzhong
Henan
Anhui
Bengbu
Suzhou
Shanghai
Xiangfan
Hefei
Nanjing
Ningbo
Hubei
Yichang
Wuhan
Hangzhou
Chongqing
Jiujiang
Huangshan
Jingdezhen
Zhejiang
Changsha
Nanchang
Shaoshan
Hunan
Jiangxi
Guiyang
Fuzhou
Hengyang
Fujian
Taibei
Guilin
Zhangzhou
Liuzhou
Wuzhou
Shaoguan
Xiamen
Tiawan
Guangxi
Guangzhou
Shantou
Nanning
Gaoxiong
Jiangmen
Guangdong
Zhanjiang
Haikou
Hainan Dao

China entered another period of partition. It was unified once more, by the Song (Sung) dynasty in 960, and enjoyed a renaissance of art, literature and science. Gunpowder, the compass and movable type were all invented, putting China well ahead of Europe in science and technology. In 1122, north China was seized by a barbarian tribe from Manchuria, and the Song dynasty retreated to the south of the country.

In the thirteenth century, the Mongols under the command of Genghis Khan invaded and conquered most of Asia and a large slice of Europe. China, too, became a subject, and Genghis Khan's grandson, Kublai Khan, founded the Yuan dynasty in 1271. The Mongols employed foreigners from different parts of their far-flung dominions as officials, and it was in that capacity that the well-travelled Venetian merchant Marco Polo lived in China for many years.

The Mongols were hated by the Chinese, and the incompetent rulers who succeeded the Great Khan slowly lost their grip on China. Finally, in 1367, a peasant revolt overthrew the Mongol dynasty and the last Yuan emperor fled back to Mongolia. The peasant leader, Zhu Yuanzhang, established the Ming dynasty (1367–1644), and China underwent another period of expansion. Armadas set out under the eunuch Admiral Zheng He to explore the south seas and to emphasise China's power to vassal states on its southern periphery. They went as far as the Persian Gulf and the coast of East Africa almost a century before Vasco da Gama made his way round the Cape of Good Hope. Unfortunately, these voyages were just part of a brief interlude, and China overall became increasingly isolationist.

Nevertheless, Europe began to impinge itself upon the Chinese consciousness. The Portuguese arrived in 1520 and set up the first foreign settlement on China's coastline at Macao in 1557. Next came the Dutch, who captured the island of Taiwan and made it a colony. Jesuit priests made their way to Peking in the hope of converting the emperor and his empire to Christianity.

In 1644, the Ming dynasty was overthrown by another peasant rebellion, which itself was crushed almost immediately by the armies of the Manchus, a powerful kingdom to the northeast of Peking. Sporadic Chinese resistance to this 'barbarian' regime continued, but as the Manchu forces moved in, the remaining Chinese forces fled to Taiwan, capturing the island from the Dutch. In their turn, the Manchus took the island a few decades later.

The Manchus formed their own dynasty, the Qing (Ching). Under the first few Manchu emperors – strong, capable men – the empire and classical Chinese culture briefly prospered again before sinking under the pressure of a new age. The court tried to control the foreigners by confining them and their trading activities to Canton, but by the early nineteenth century, the traders were getting restless. The British discovered that opium was a good selling item, and started to ship in tons of the drug from plantations in India. The Chinese tried to halt the imports, thereby sparking the first Opium War in 1839, which the British won easily. Under the Treaty of Nanking of 1842, China was forced to open up five ports to foreign trade and to cede Hong Kong island to Britain. Foreign influences were also largely responsible for the Taiping Rebellion (1850–64), led by a man who believed himself to be the younger brother of Jesus Christ. The Taiping rebels captured much of south China and almost took Peking, but were finally beaten when Britain and the other Western nations intervened on the side of the corrupt and malleable Manchu court.

The foreign powers, including Russia to the north and Japan to the east, continued to take advantage of China's helplessness, and forced the imperial government to agree to new leases and the creation of 'spheres of influence'. Popular anti-foreign feeling culminated in the Boxer Rebellion of 1900 in which the Legation Quarter in Peking, besieged by crowds supported by the imperial government, was only relieved when a foreign force marched on Peking. The strongest personality in China during the last decades of the empire was the Empress Dowager Ci Xi, who had first entered the Imperial Palace as a concubine and rose to power after she gave birth to a son for the emperor. She used any unscrupulous means necessary to keep her control, and almost certainly had the Emperor Guangxu killed the day before her own death in 1908.

With the demise of Ci Xi, the empire could not last long. After several abortive rebellions, an uprising in Wuhan in 1911 sparked the revolution, and the empire finally gave way to the Republic of China. Sun Yatsen was the leader of the republican movement, but when an old, powerful Manchu general named Yuan Shikai threatened trouble, Sun stepped aside and allowed Yuan to become the first president. Yuan decided to make himself emperor, but he died in 1916 before ascending the Dragon Throne.

The early republican governments were weak, and most of China was under the control of local warlords. The Chinese Communist

Party was formed at a secret meeting in Shanghai in 1922, and began collaborating with the larger, stronger Nationalist Party of Sun Yatsen. In 1925, Sun died, and his successor, Chiang Kaishek, mounted the Northern Expedition from Canton, re-uniting the country and establishing the capital of the Republic at Nanking. He also turned on his supposed allies, the Communists, and tried to exterminate them with successive military campaigns. The 1934 campaign almost succeeded, but the Communist guerrillas in southwest China escaped from the encirclement and set out on the famous Long March, which ended two years later in Yan'an in northwest China. Yan ' an became the base from which the Communist leaders, Mao Tse-tung, Chou Enlai and the rest, directed their gradual rise to complete power over the Chinese people.

Expansionist Japan occupied Manchuria in 1931, and invaded the rest of China in 1937. The Nationalist forces under Generalissimo Chiang Kaishek led the fight against the Japanese but they often seemed more interested in fighting the Communists than the invaders. The war went badly despite massive aid from the United States and the other allies, and when the Japanese surrender was announced in August 1945, the Japanese forces in China were still advancing. With Japan finally beaten, the Nationalists and Communists could now devote themselves wholeheartedly to their own feud. Civil war broke out and, despite an overwhelming superiority in armaments, numbers of soldiers and supplies, the Nationalists lost, both because of their corruption and their inability to institute meaningful land reforms. In 1949, the remnants of the Nationalist army fled to Taiwan, where they remain today.

On 1 October 1949, Mao Tse-tung declared the establishment of the People's Republic of China. The Communists began their rule on a sour note, killing large numbers of potential and actual opponents: in one unpublished speech, Mao estimated that 800 000 people had been executed in the first five years of the People's Republic. In spite of this harshness, much was achieved. The staggering inflation of the late 1940s was controlled; industrial production was slowly raised to pre-war levels; and, most importantly, the land was confiscated from landlords and handed over to peasants.

In 1953, the socialisation of the economy began. Having just gained control of their land, the peasants were told that it was to be 'collectivised'. Meanwhile, all major factories, banks and other enterprises were nationalised. The foreign diplomats and businessmen who had humiliated and used China for so long were expelled, and so were the rest of the foreigners, friends or not.

The 1950s are now viewed by the Communist Party as a 'Golden Age', and there certainly was an atmosphere of selflessness and idealism which has now largely dissipated; people worked hard to build the 'New China'. During its first decade, Communist China was also very closely allied to the Soviet Union, often officially referred to in those days as 'Big Brother', which gave them much valuable assistance in rebuilding China's industrial base, shattered after so many years of war.

In 1958, Mao launched the 'Great Leap Forward', his first serious mistake, and Chinese politics became polarised between the radical Maoists and the pragmatists, a division which has persisted until today. The Great Leap was a good example of Mao's overwhelming idealism in the face of all the evidence. He conceived it as a massive combined effort by China's people to transform the country at one stroke into a developed nation. It was, of course, an economic disaster of the first order, but Mao was just getting into his stride and brushed aside criticisms. He announced the establishment of the rural communes, in spite of protests from many in the Communist leadership that the move was too premature and would meet resistance among the conservative peasants. The dissenters were right: many peasants saw the communes as being new landlords, and huge tracts of land were left fallow that year. Just at that point, with industry and agriculture in chaos, nature stepped in to deepen the crisis. The harvests failed in 1959, 1960 and 1961 – now referred to as the 'Three Terrible Years' – and several million people died of starvation (the exact number has never been revealed).

The early 1960s were years of recovery. The pragmatists were in the ascendant, and Mao himself was pushed into the background. In 1966, he made his comeback by by-passing the Communist Party organisation, controlled by his opponents, and appealing directly to the masses. He called this new upheaval the Cultural Revolution, although it was very anti-culture. In fact, it is best viewed as a minor civil war. It is estimated that about one million people died violently during the ten years in which Maoist radicalism held sway in China, and tens of millions more suffered from persecution.

It was a crazy, frightening period. People disappeared into labour camps, or were declared to be counter-revolutionaries and deprived of their livelihoods. Mao was venerated as almost a god, and his followers claimed to be able to do almost anything, including heal sickness and reap bumper harvests, using nothing but 'Invincible Mao Tse-tung Thought' as their guide. During the late 1960s when the Cultural Revolution was at its height, countless books, paintings and ancient treasures were destroyed by Mao's storm-troopers, the Red Guards, whom he ordered to 'destroy the Four Olds'. Politics was placed 'in command'. Schools and colleges were shut, and most did not re-open for several years. China has still not recovered from this convulsion. One of the most amazing things about the Cultural Revolution is that so many people outside China were hoodwinked by it for so long, with Maoist groups springing up all over the world. (Some still exist, to the intense embarrassment of the present Chinese government.) Many people in the West really believed that Mao had created the perfect society.

But it was much more sordid than that. In 1971, the Defence Minister Lin Piao, Mao's official successor, was killed. The official version is that he attempted to assassinate Mao, and when the plot failed, fled towards the Soviet Union in a plane which crashed in Mongolia, killing all those on board. This seems highly unlikely, but there is no way of ascertaining the truth. In the early 1970s, Mao was at the height of his power, but his health was rapidly failing. His radical colleagues (including his wife), who had risen to power during the late 1960s, were unpopular with the ordinary people, and needed his support to survive. They attempted to have their prime opponents, Premier Chou Enlai and Vice-Premier Deng Xiaoping, purged, but in the end, they were not strong enough to win the game.

Chou Enlai died in January 1976, and the radicals had Deng Xiaoping purged in the wake of anti-radical riots in April of that year. But in September, Mao also died, and less than a month later, the leading radicals, immortalised as 'The Gang of Four', had been seized by the more moderate elements in the leadership, led at that time by Hua Guofeng. Hua had become Premier in April 1976, a surprise compromise after the pragmatists and the radicals both vetoed their respective candidates. After Mao's death, Hua was also made Communist Party chairman, an unprecedented concentration of power in the hands of one man. He even fashioned for himself a personality cult along the lines of Mao's, but despite some reforms, he was still too leftist for the real moderates.

Deng Xiaoping was finally allowed to return to active politics in 1977, and at a crucial Party meeting in November 1978, he supplanted

Hua as the real leader of the Chinese people. He has been fighting the remnants of 'leftism' ever since, and has been making steady progress. After a long, closely fought battle, Hua was finally toppled from power in 1981, and Deng consolidated his own hand-picked leadership with protégés Hu Yaobang as Party chief and Zhao Ziyang as Premier.

China today

China today is a poor, backward country of over 1000 million people with one of the most closely controlled societies in the world. In some areas, there is great poverty, but the poverty is nowhere near as widespread, and rarely as serious, as in, say, India. The Communist Party which rules China has made many disastrous mistakes since it came to power in 1949, and there is much about the present system which is unacceptable to bourgeois Western liberals (such as this writer) but, to be fair, there is no guarantee that any other government or system could have done a better job.

Thanks primarily to the efforts of Deng Xiaoping, China's present leader, the country is slowly emerging from the madness of the Maoist era. During the Cultural Revolution and after, the people of China had more than their fill of politics, political slogans and 'class struggle', and Deng has gone a long way towards de-politicising them. In other ways, things have not changed so much, especially for people living in the cities. Living conditions are still very cramped, and many basic foodstuffs and consumer products are still rationed. In the countryside, however, where 80 per cent of China's population live, there has been a real improvement due to the decision to dismantle the communes and divide the land up among the peasant households for them to farm on a contract basis. Farm output and household incomes have risen considerably.

Politically, China is more stable now than it has been for decades. Deng Xiaoping, aged 78 in 1983 and one of the greatest politicians of our age, has set himself the task of reshaping China: luckily for China and the rest of the world, his vision is far more rational and acceptable than that of his predecessor, Mao. Deng has been called a pragmatist, and he has done much to pull China out of the mire by adopting 'pragmatic' policies which have, in effect, desocialised a large part of the country's economy. Apart from the agricultural reforms, a small but significant private enterprise sector has been allowed to take root again, with shopkeepers, tailors and street hawkers working for themselves and keeping the profits. Meanwhile, industry is slowly pulling itself out of its traditional sluggish and wasteful inefficiency with the decision to place less stress on politics and more on management, technology, productivity and market forces.

Deng and his men may be economic pragmatists, but they are not liberals. They will not tolerate any challenge to the power and authority of the Communist Party, and have ruthlessly stamped on anyone involved in unauthorised political acts outside the official framework.

A measure of Deng's genius is the forthright manner in which he has addressed the basic problem facing any undemocratic system such as China's – that of political succession. He has made great progress in ending the 'gerontocracy' which has ruled China for so long, and has begun to institute reforms which will make retirement for Communist Party officials mandatory at a certain age. He has also tried to use his personal power to construct a system of collective leadership aimed at ending the debilitating power struggles which have cursed China during the decades of Communist rule. The longer Deng stays alive, the longer this system is likely to survive. However, my own guess is that in the long term, China is doomed to revert to some form of the 'emperor' system – rule by one man – and to see further power struggles. The traditions and instincts of 2000 years cannot be wiped out in a few years.

The most basic problem facing China, apart from the possibility of renewed political instability, is population growth. The country's grain output has increased sharply in the past few decades, but the population has grown faster, and per capita grain output is now slightly lower than it was in the pre-war years. The man responsible for this situation was Chairman Mao who rejected the policy of birth control in the 1950s, saying there was strength in numbers. The policy was changed in the late 1970s, and now the authorities are insisting that there should be no more than one child per couple. In the cities, the 'one child only' policy has proved relatively easy to implement, but in the countryside, there is widespread opposition. The peasants want sons, and lots of them, to help in the fields and to look after them in old age.

Controlling a country of 1000 million people is, of course, a daunting task for any government, but the extent to which the Chinese authorities interfere in the lives of ordinary people is staggering. You cannot move from your place of birth without permission; your profession is decided by a faceless bureaucrat with little or no regard for what you would like to do; the authorities tell you how many children you can have, what music you can listen to, what books you can read. To buy a bicycle or a television set or to travel from one city to another, you need the approval of your work 'unit' which also arranges weekly compulsory political study sessions. The Party activists in your work unit, your class or your neighbourhood are forever on the watch for unhealthy, unsocialist tendencies. And if you even so much as express an opinion opposing the Communist Party and the 'Socialist Road', you can, by law, be charged and convicted of being a 'counter-revolutionary'.

But you won't starve.

PEKING (Beijing, 'northern capital')

Peking . . . old, proud, secretive.
Juliet Bredon, *Peking*

Of all the cities of China, Peking has the most history and – despite the wanton vandalism, both official and unofficial, of the past 80 years – the best collection of historical buildings. As a result, it deserves more of the visitor's time than any other single place in the country. You could see the main sights of Peking in two or three rushed days, but you really need a week to do it properly.

Peking has been China's capital for most of the past 800 years, ever since the Mongols chose it as the headquarters of the Chinese portion of their empire in 1261. Marco Polo, employed by the Mongol emperor Kublai Khan 30 years or so later, spent ten pages of his *Travels* describing the city, which he said contained 'such a multitude of houses and of people, both within the walls and without, that no one could count their number.' The Ming dynasty, which succeeded the Mongols in 1368, first established their capital at Nanking, but the second Ming emperor decided to move back to Peking and there constructed the magnificent Imperial Palace. The Manchus, who conquered China in the seventeenth century, also made Peking their capital, as did the first weak republican governments after the downfall of the empire in 1911. The Nationalist Party of Generalissimo Chiang Kaishek moved the capital to Nanking in 1928, and renamed Peking as Peiping (northern peace), but the city became the capital once more in 1949 when the Communists established the People's Republic of China.

Peking is the political heart of the country. Decisions affecting just about every facet of the lives of the 1000 million Chinese are made here by the Communist Party leadership, and the Tiananmen Gate in the centre of the city is the dominant symbol of the People's Republic.

In fact, the whole country, including Tibet in the far west, operates on Peking time. The city has also become an important industrial centre in its own right, and now has a population of over nine million people.

It is a mixture of metropolis and village. The wide avenues and imposing buildings in the centre of Peking contrast strangely with the ramshackle, one-storey houses and winding alley-ways where most people live. Peking can be a very grey city at the best of times, and during the winter, when the green leaves have disappeared and the coal-dust pollution hangs heavy in the air, it becomes even more dreary. Like most north China cities, everything in Peking seems to have a wall round it, which makes it difficult for visitors to get a feel for the lives of the ordinary people. It is pleasant to wander round the back alleys of the city on summer evenings when the local residents flock out of their stifling homes to get some fresh air and talk with neighbours while the kids play about them. But in the winter, the alleys are virtually deserted as people hurry home to get out of the cold as quickly as possible.

The pattern of present-day Peking was established during the reign of the second Ming emperor who had the Palace placed at the centre, surrounded by an Imperial City containing the residences of court officials and government offices. Beyond that was the Tartar City and, to the south of the Palace, the Outer City. Walls were built around the Forbidden City, the Inner City and around the Outer City, too, with impressive gates placed at intervals along their lengths. To their eternal shame, in the late 1960s, the Communist government decided to pull down the city walls, and only one or two small sections survive.

The authors of the interesting, but slightly condescending, guide, *In Search of Old Peking*, published in 1935, warned readers that in some instances they may have problems finding some of the buildings mentioned in the book: 'This is not the fault of the authors but due to the indifference of the Chinese themselves, more especially of their authorities, towards the historical monuments in which Peking is so rich.' They spoke of acts of vandalism, 'such as converting historic palaces into modern restaurants and tea houses; famous temples into barracks and police stations; cutting down ancient cypresses to sell for firewood; defacing age-old walls and tablets with political slogans.' Unfortunately, this process of indifference and vandalism has continued under Communist rule during the past three decades and more although, to its credit, the present government of Deng Xiaoping has made some effort in recent years to preserve what is left.

A tour of Peking should begin with a visit to TIANANMEN SQUARE in the heart of the city. On 1 October 1949, Mao Tse-tung proclaimed the founding of the People's Republic from Tiananmen Gate (the gate of heavenly peace) where his picture still hangs; 'The Chinese people,' he declared, 'have stood up.' The square is one of the world's largest, with an area of 100 acres, and it can accommodate half a million people at once, as it did on several occasions during the Cultural Revolution. However, the square that Mao addressed in 1949 was much smaller: during the 1950s, when the Chinese were heavily under the influence of the Soviets, walls were knocked down and buildings demolished to widen it to its present gargantuan proportions. Consequently, the square and the two massive structures flanking it have a very Stalinist air about them. *(To get to the square from the Guanghua or Jianguo Hotels, walk south to Changan Avenue and take a No. 1 bus heading west.)*

On the western side of the square is the GREAT HALL OF THE PEOPLE where major political assemblies and meetings are held, while on the eastern side is the MUSEUM OF CHINESE HISTORY AND THE CHINESE REVOLUTION. Both were built in 1959. Between them is MAO'S MAUSOLEUM, an ugly building which looks very much out of place. The present leaders of China undoubtedly regret that it was built, but it would now be rather hard to get rid of it. Inside, Mao's embalmed body lies in a glass sarcophagus. In front of the mausoleum is the MONUMENT TO THE PEOPLE'S HEROES, a granite obelisk around which crowds calling for an end to the radical policies championed by Mao and his colleagues (the so-called 'Gang of Four') demonstrated in April 1976. The number of people who died around the monument when the militia was called in to break up the demonstration has never been revealed.

(Mao's mausoleum is sometimes open to visitors: enquire at the CITS office. The Museum of History is open most days; buy a ticket at the front gate. There are also tours of the Great Hall of the People on days when meetings are not being held. Check with CITS for times and tickets.)

TIANANMEN GATE itself was built in the seventeenth century. When an imperial edict was issued, officials would kneel at the foot of the gate, while the edict was lowered down to them in the mouth of a golden phoenix carved out of wood. The gate is the main entrance to the FORBIDDEN CITY, the home of 24 emperors of the Ming and

Manchu dynasties from the mid-fourteenth to the early twentieth century. Construction of the Palace began in 1406 and more than one million workmen were employed on the project, completed in 1420. Walking north from Tiananmen Square, you will first pass through Duan Men (main gate), and then come upon the imposing Wumen (meridian gate) which is the real entrance to the Forbidden City. Imperial criminals were always executed in the shadow of this truly 'forbidding' tower.

Beyond Wumen is a large courtyard through which flows a canal crossed by a number of beautiful marble bridges. Passing through the Gate of Supreme Harmony, the visitor comes upon the Hall of Supreme Harmony (Taihedian), the single most impressive piece of architecture in the Palace. Important ceremonies, such as those to mark the emperor's birthday or the pronouncement of important edicts, were held here. Next comes the smaller Hall of Central Harmony (Zonghedian) where the emperors rehearsed the ceremonies, and then the Hall of Preserving Harmony in which were held banquets and imperial examinations. These three halls constituted the outer palace. Beyond them, through the Gate of Heavenly Purity, is the inner palace where the emperor and his retinue lived. The area is a huge maze of courtyards and exquisite buildings which is a lot of fun to roam around.

The northeast corner of the Palace is now mostly devoted to museum displays, although the collection is not as interesting as it could be. In 1933, the Nationalist government of Generalissimo Chiang Kaishek had the entire Palace collection of treasures packed in crates and sent south to Shanghai and Nanking for safety in case of a Japanese invasion. From there, the treasures went to Taiwan with the Nationalists in 1949, and are now displayed in the Taipei Palace Museum, much to the ire of the Communists. (*A full tour of the Forbidden City can take a day or more; if you just walk straight through from Tiananmen to the back gate, it will take a couple of hours. There are taxis available at the northern entrance, or else take a bus down one of the streets on either side of the Palace, back to Changan Avenue.*)

Behind the Forbidden City is COAL HILL, the highest point in Peking, which provides an excellent view of the whole city. It is a man-made mound, constructed to protect the Forbidden City from the cold north winds and from evil spirits. The site of the hill was reportedly once a coal store, hence its name. The last emperor of the Ming dynasty is said to have hanged himself from a tree on the hill in

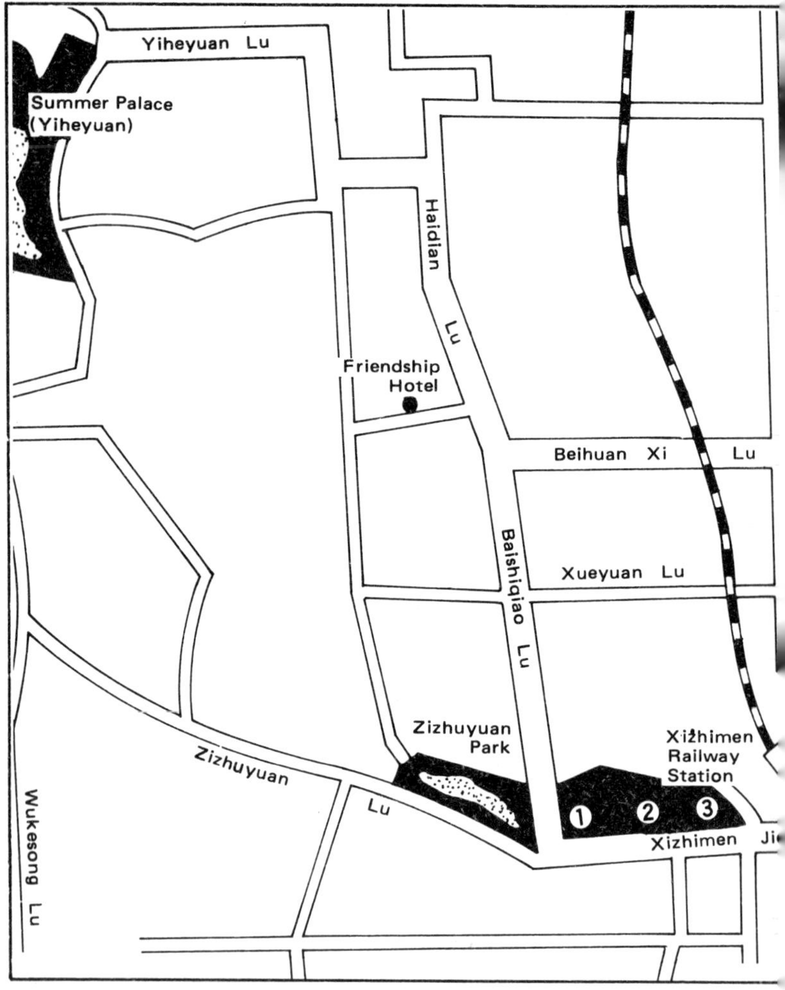

1 Capital Gymnasium
2 Beijing Zoo
3 Beijing Exhibition Center
4 Bell Tower
5 Drum Tower (Gulou)

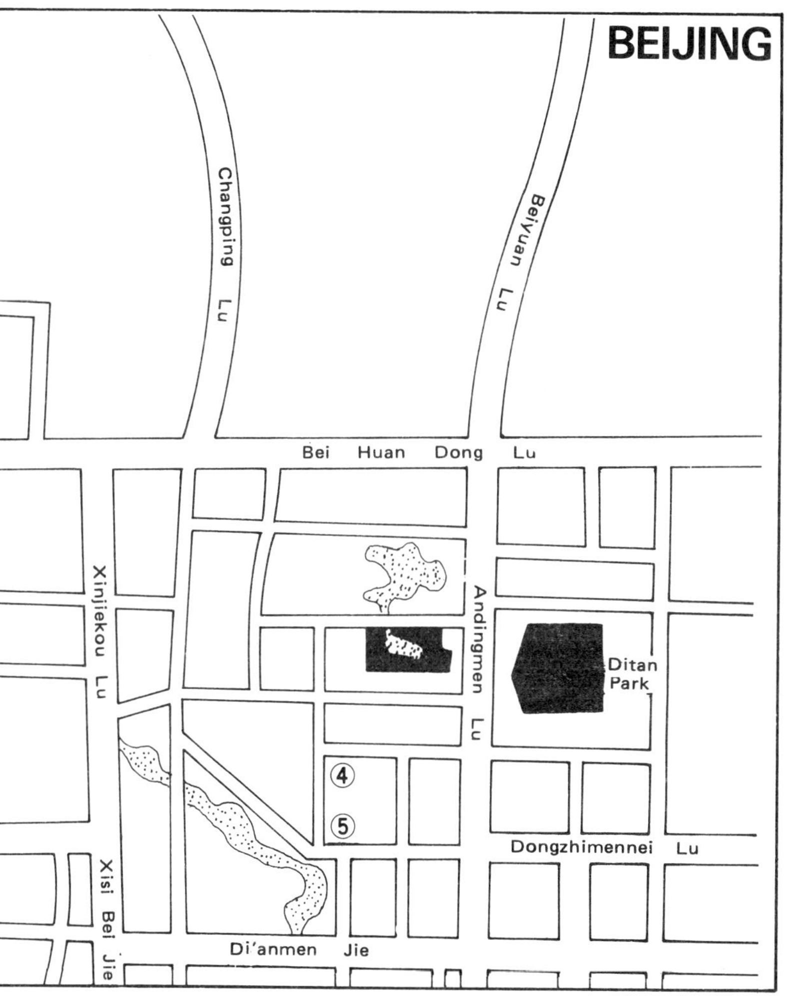
BEIJING
Changping Lu
Beiyuan Lu
Bei Huan Dong Lu
Xinjiekou Lu
Andingmen Lu
Ditan Park
4
5
Dongzhimennei Lu
Xisi Bei Jie
Di'anmen Jie

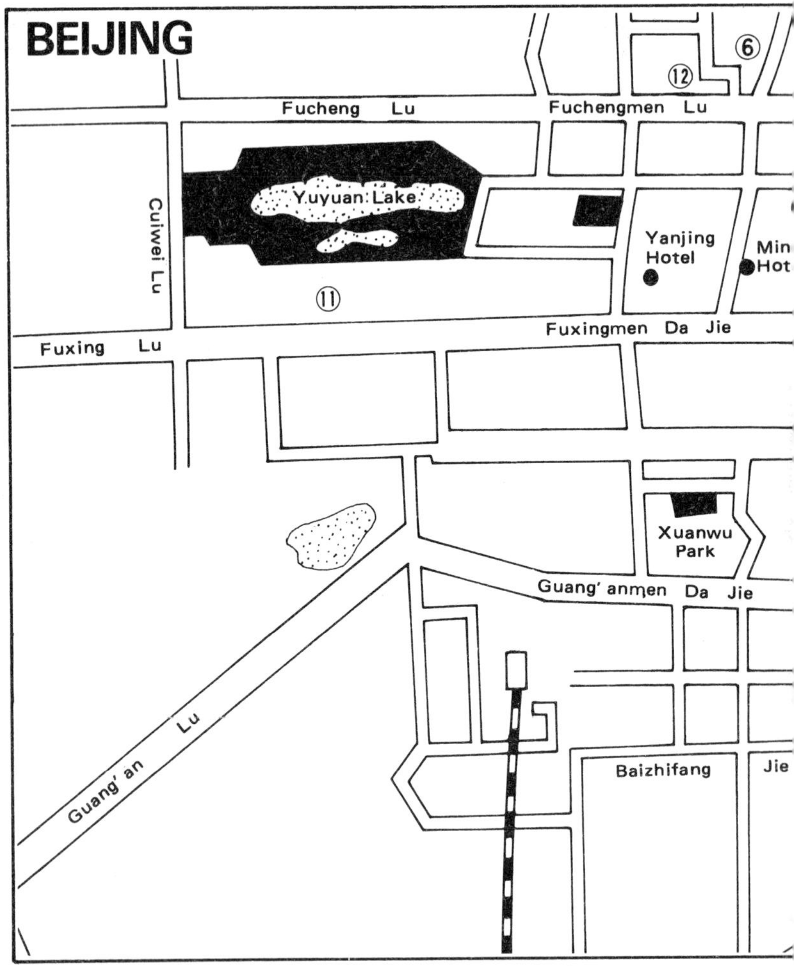

6 Temple of the White Pagoda
7 Xidan Market
8 Nationalities Cultural Palace
9 Beijing Post and Telecommunications Office
10 Beijing Library
11 Military Museum of the Chinese People's Revolution
12 Lu Xun Museum
13 Coal Hill (Jingshan)
14 National Art Gallery
15 Palace Museum (Forbidden City)
16 Tian' anmen
17 Great Hall of the People
18 Monument to the People's Heroes
19 Museums of the Chinese Revolution and Chinese History

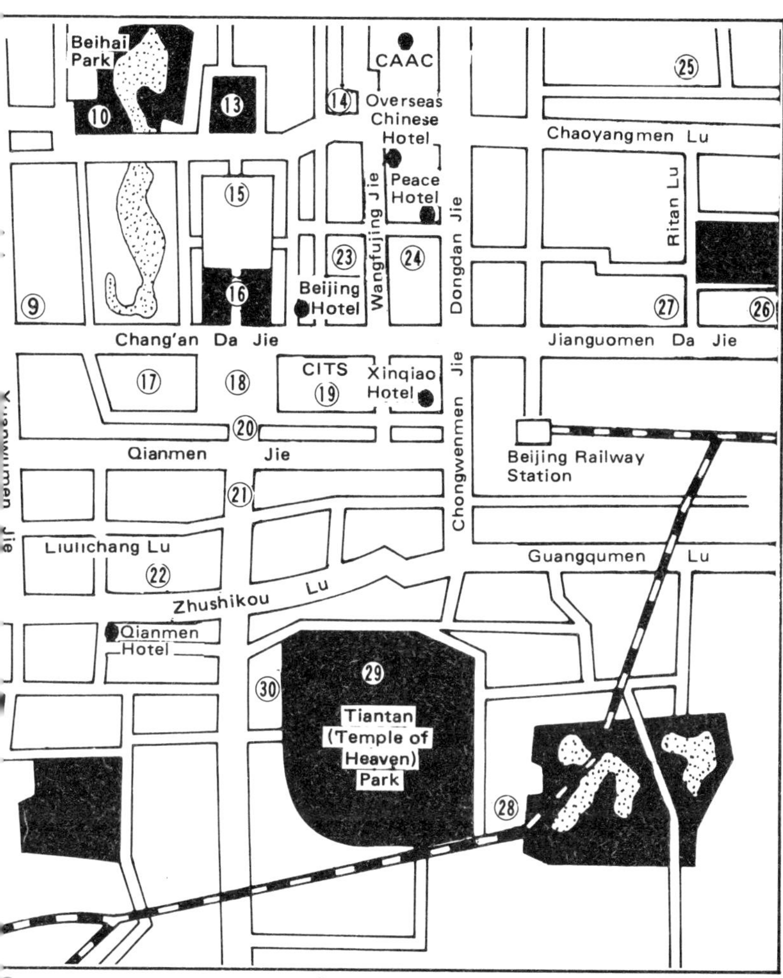

20 Mao Zedong Memorial Hall
21 Front Gate (Qianmen)
22 Shopping area for antiques (Liulichang)
23 Beijing Department Store
24 Capital Hospital
25 Workers' Stadium
26 Friendship Store
27 International Club
28 Beijing Gymnasium
29 Temple of Heaven (Tiantan)
30 Museum of Natural History

1643 rather than be captured by the peasant leader Li Zicheng who led the revolt against him.

Just to the right of Tiananmen Gate is the entrance to the PEOPLE'S CULTURAL PALACE, formerly the Tai Miao, or Imperial Temple, used by the imperial family to honour their ancestors. The halls were built in the fifteenth century, although they have been repaired and renovated many times. The spirit tablets of the emperors are gone, but the old cypress trees still grace the courtyards. On the left-hand side of Tiananmen, is the SUN YATSEN PARK named after the leader of the republican groups which overthrew the Manchu dynasty in 1911. In imperial times, the park was the Altar of Land and Grain where, twice a year, the emperor offered sacrifices.

To the west of the Forbidden City complex are three lakes, named the NORTH, MIDDLE and SOUTH SEAS where the court used to spend their summers. The lakes were constructed during the Ming dynasty and are fed by canals bringing water from the Western Hills (which are occasionally visible through the smog). The area around the Middle and South Seas (Zhong Nan Hai) is now the headquarters of both the Chinese Communist Party and the State Council, China's cabinet. During 1979, thousands of poverty-stricken peasants gathered outside the main southern gate to the compound, which faces on to Changan Avenue, pleading for assistance. Such demonstrations are no longer allowed, but are also less necessary due to the relatively liberal agricultural policies now in force.

The North Sea (Beihai) is now a public park. The Mongol emperor Kublai Khan reconstructed an earlier garden on the site and built a magnificent palace, described in glowing terms by Marco Polo, on a hill which is now an island in the lake. The palace collapsed in the sixteenth century after an earthquake and was replaced by a white dagoba, a Buddhist monument, which was rebuilt in 1741 by the emperor Qian Long. There is no entrance to the dagoba, but it is believed to contain Buddhist scriptures and other religious items. The main bridge to the island, just inside the park entrance, dates from the Mongol empire. During and after the Cultural Revolution, the park was closed to the public and only re-opened in 1978. It is said to have been used by Mao and his wife Jiang Qing as if it were their private garden. Just outside and to the right of the main south gate to the park is the CIRCULAR CITY, built originally by Kublai Khan. One of the pine trees in the small compound was granted the title of marquis by Emperor Qian Long in thanks for the shade it gave him.

Southeast of the Peking Hotel, the LEGATION QUARTER, the former foreigners' enclave, is interesting to walk round, and although it has changed immensely since the Communist victory in 1949, many of the old European-style buildings are still standing. In the days before the European powers forced their way into the Chinese empire, the only representatives of foreign states allowed in Peking were those from Burma, Annam (Indo-China), Korea and Mongolia, living in the 'Four Barbarians' Hostel' in what later became the Legation Quarter. The Russians obtained the right to open a church in Peking in 1727 and were given a plot of land just opposite these vassal embassies. In 1860, after the second Opium War, Britain and France forced the Chinese to allow them to open their own legations nearby, and other Western powers, and later Japan, followed suit. The area was beseiged by anti-foreigner crowds during the Boxer Rebellion of 1900, but the foreign powers used the rebellion as an excuse to strengthen their position in Peking, clearing the quarter of all Chinese houses, and building a wall round it to keep unwanted Chinese out.

The main street, running east to west through the quarter, was called Legation Street (today's Dongjiao Minxiang, although during the Cultural Revolution it was renamed Anti-Imperialism Road). The Catholic church opposite the former Belgian legation still stands, although the crosses on its steeples were knocked off during the Cultural Revolution. Just across the intersection as you head west is a large compound on the right in which stands a large mansion, rumoured to have been built in the late 1970s for the former Party Chairman Hua Guofeng. But he never lived in it, and it is now the Peking residence of the former Cambodian head-of-state, Prince Sihanouk. The grounds of the former British legation are now mostly occupied by the Ministry of Public Security, and some of the old legation buildings are still visible behind the high walls. An auditorium in the compound was used as the 'courthouse' when the 'Gang of Four' radicals and a few other leftovers from the Maoist era were put on trial in late 1980. The old French club is the Peking customs house, while the former United States legation and other mansions along East Qianmen Street are now used as foreign guesthouses. The Peking Hospital on the road running between Changan Avenue and the Xiunqiao Hotel, to the west of the Dongdan Park, was once the German Hospital, and is now an exclusive medical centre used by senior party officials. Chou Enlai reportedly died there.

Probably the most stunning piece of architecture in Peking is not the Forbidden City, in spite of its grandeur and size, but the TEMPLE OF HEAVEN (Tian Tan) in the south of the city. The round hall which dominates the temple is unique in Chinese architecture and a wonder to behold. It was designed and built during the Ming dynasty, but was virtually destroyed by fire in 1889 after being struck by lightning and had to be completely rebuilt. The large compound in which the temple stands is one of the nicest parks in Peking. To the west of the main altar is the Palace of Abstinence (Chai Gong), where the emperor used to change into his ceremonial attire and fast for a night before performing the annual rites. (The pavilions have now been turned into shops, including one rented by the French fashion designer Pierre Cardin and another by a Japanese department store.) The main altar, called the Qi Nian Dian (Hall of Annual Prayers), was visited by the emperor once a year, on the day of the winter solstice, to pray for good harvests. The last person to perform the rites was General Yuan Shikai, the first president of the republic who planned to declare himself emperor, although he died in 1916 before ascending the throne. There is a long walkway south from the main altar leading to a smaller but similarly designed hall, known as the Huang Qiong Yu (Imperial Vault of the Universe). This is surrounded by a circular wall, and anyone who stands next to a particular point on it is supposed to be able to hear clearly someone whispering at another point. The catch is that there are usually so many tourists whispering at the wall that no one can hear anything. To the south of the smaller hall is a huge circular altar called the Altar of Heaven. The number nine was considered to be the most powerful of the numbers, and the marble blocks that make up the altar are all in combinations of nine. *(To get to the Temple of Heaven from the Guanghua or Jianguo Hotels, take a bus along to the Dongdan intersection – to the east of the Peking Hotel – then take a No. 106 trolley bus south. The bus eventually turns right, and the park is on the left.)*

Other places to visit

WANGFUJING, the main shopping street of central Peking (known in the old days as Morrison Street after the famous London *Times* correspondent who lived there), runs north–south next to the Peking Hotel. Walking north along the street, you will pass the Xinhua Bookshop on the right, the largest in Peking and probably the whole country. Further up, a number of foreign shops have opened in the past few years, the first of which was a Seiko watch shop. On the left, is the Peking No. 1 Department Store, and on the right, the large Eastwind (Dongfeng) Market. Turn left at the next intersection, and you will arrive at the eastern gate of the Forbidden City. Continue on for one more intersection, and on the left will be a lane once home to some of the highest nobility of the Manchu court, including a Manchu lady who was accepted into the palace as a concubine and went on to become Empress Dowager Ci Xi. At the next major intersection on the left is the PEKING ART GALLERY.

Another interesting street to walk along is NANCHIZI (south pool) which runs along the eastern edge of the Forbidden City (two intersections west of the Peking Hotel). Number 15 used to be the bureau of Reuters News Agency, but the news service was temporarily suspended in 1967 when the then-correspondent Anthony Grey was attacked and imprisoned by Red Guards acting on orders from a particularly radical and xenophobic faction in the Foreign Ministry. They strangled his cat, and kept him in solitary confinement for two years in retaliation for the imprisonment of 13 Communist journalists in Hong Kong.

If you walk west from Tiananmen Square along Changan Avenue, you will pass the main entrance to the Communist Party headquarters, Zhongnanhai, on the right. Past the next intersection on the right is the Peking telecommunications building, built during the Great Leap Forward of the late 1950s along with the Great Hall of the People and a number of other structures. Just beyond is a length of wall, now shielded by advertising hoardings, which became world-famous in late 1978 under the name DEMOCRACY WALL. For a brief period, the Communist Party relaxed its grip and allowed a measure of free speech in China; people wrote posters on every conceivable subject, mostly about Chinese politics, and stuck them on the wall. Soon after it sprang spontaneously to life, strongman Deng Xiaoping declared Democracy Wall to be 'a good thing', thereby speeding its development. But it finally became clear that he was simply using the idealism and enthusiasm of the young activists for his political ends, and in December 1980, the crackdown came, the wall was 'closed', and many poster-writers were jailed for their views. The debates which took place around Democracy Wall helped to provide ammunition for Deng and his colleagues in the battle to oust former Party chairman Hua Guofeng and other leftists in the leadership. Once they had served their purpose, the Democracy Wall activists were gagged again. Many of them are still in jail.

Southwest of here is a large compound fronting on to West Qianmen Street which was once the IMPERIAL ELEPHANT QUARTERS. The area is now occupied by the official New China News Agency. The compound (which is, naturally, closed to outsiders) also contains a hall in which China's legislature used to meet in the early 1920s.

The OBSERVATORY, to the east of the city, was first constructed by the Mongol emperor Kublai Khan in the thirteenth century on a part of the city wall, and was moved to its present position in the sixteenth century. Most of the astronomical instruments displayed on the terrace were constructed by the Jesuit priest Ferdinand Verbiest on the orders of the emperor Kang Xi in 1674, although one of them is said to have been a present from Louis XIV of France. After the Boxer Rebellion, German troops carried off most of the instruments and had them set up in a park in Potsdam, but they were returned after the First World War, one of the few gains China made from the Treaty of Versailles. The observatory has been closed since the 1950s because of unstable foundations, a condition which led to its partial collapse in 1979. The structure has now been renovated and should open as a tourist attraction in mid-1983. (*The observatory is just south of Changan Avenue near one of the foreigners' compounds.*)

The LAMA TEMPLE (Yonghegong) at the northern edge of the old city is a large, beautiful structure re-opened in 1980 after a gap of nearly 20 years. It was built in 1694 as a palace for a Manchu prince who eventually became emperor, and his son turned it into a temple in his honour. One of the halls contains an extraordinary statue of the Buddha nearly 60 feet (18.3 metres) tall, carved out of a single sandalwood tree brought from Tibet. Another contains Buddhas in pornographic poses.

Across the road in a small lane is Peking's CONFUCIUS TEMPLE, now the municipal museum. Like all such places, the temple bears the scars of vandalism, particularly from Red Guards, but it is still in reasonable condition, and the museum exhibition is good. One statue of the Buddha on display was described by a British art expert as being the most beautiful piece of Chinese porcelain he had ever seen. Next door to the Confucius temple is the former HALL OF CLASSICS, now the municipal library, which once ranked as the highest seat of learning in the empire. The exquisite round building in the centre was where the emperor used to give lectures on the Confucian classics. (*To get to the Lama Temple area, take a No. 116 bus from Qianmen Gate.*)

Other temples and religious buildings worth visiting include:
WHITE DAGOBA TEMPLE (Baitasi), more beautiful than the more famous dagoba in Beihai Park. (*Take a No. 3 trolley bus from the railway station. The dagoba is on the right, to the west of Beihai park.*)
GREAT BELL TEMPLE (Dazhongsi), to the east of the Friendship Hotel in the northwest of the city, has a collection of ancient bronze bells in its courtyard. (*From Guanghua Hotel, take a No. 402 bus heading north, then change to No. 302 bus.*)
SOURCE OF THE LAW TEMPLE (Fayuansi): this beautiful temple is the headquarters of the China Buddhist Association, and accepts visitors every day except Wednesdays. (*Take a No. 10 bus from railway station to Niu Jie; walk down the street on the left, south of the mosque.*)
WHITE CLOUD TEMPLE and the PAGODA OF HEAVENLY REPOSE: the White Cloud Temple was the most important Taoist temple in China in the old days, but the compound has been occupied by the army for nearly two decades. At last report, it was being renovated. Taoism, China's only indigenous religion, has not been allowed to resurface in the past few years as have Christianity and Islam. The Pagoda of Heavenly Repose nearby is a beautiful pagoda overshadowed by a huge, dirty smokestack. The juxtaposition of the two makes an interesting photograph. (*Take a No. 307 bus from Qianmen Gate heading west.*)
TANZHESI TEMPLE: to the southwest of the city, this was opened to foreigners only recently, and makes a nice day's outing. Don't miss the stupas below the temple – the monuments built in honour of deceased monks by their disciples. (*Tickets for local bus tours can be bought at the kiosk opposite the CITS office.*)
NANTANG CATHOLIC CATHEDRAL: on West Qianmen Street, this is the oldest Catholic church in Peking, and the first to re-open after Deng Xiaoping's return to power in the late 1970s. Foreigners are welcome to take part in Sunday services, which are held in Latin. The Chinese Catholic church, under the supervision of the Communist Party, severed relations with the Vatican in 1957 and has missed out on all the liberalisations since.
NIU JIE (Cow Street) MOSQUE: one of Peking's two Moslem houses of worship, built in an interesting combination of Chinese and Islamic styles. (*Take a No. 10 bus from railway station.*)
The PEKING ZOO is the best in China and, of course, has a number of giant pandas in its collection. However, they are rather sad-looking animals and their living conditions are not as good as those in some zoos overseas. (*Take a No. 7 bus from Qianmen Gate.*)

The SOVIET EMBASSY compound in the northeast corner of the old city was once a Russian religious mission established in the eighteenth century. It was much enlarged during the 1950s when China and the Soviet Union were good friends, but a Soviet diplomat has said that there is now nothing but a few stones left of the old church. During the Cultural Revolution when the anti-Soviet campaign reached its hysterical height, the Chinese renamed the street leading to the embassy entrance 'Anti-Revisionism Road'.

To the north of the Forbidden City, the DRUM TOWER and BELL TOWER, traditionally found in all self-respecting Chinese cities, are impressive buildings. The Drum Tower was built in 1420, while the smaller Bell Tower to the north was built in 1734. The alley-ways to the southwest of the Drum Tower, leading to a stagnant lake, are interesting to walk round. (*Take a No. 204 bus from the railway station.*)

A worthwhile place to visit is the REVOLUTIONARY MILITARY MUSEUM on the western extension of Changan Avenue. The exhibits largely deal with the anti-Japanese war and the civil war against the Nationalists, and a couple of the halls are closed to non-Chinese. However, outside in the back courtyard are some old aircraft, including the wrecks of two American U-2 spy planes with Nationalist Chinese markings, shot down in the 1950s. (*Take a No. 1 bus along Changan Avenue. Entrance is free, but take your passport with you in case the guards want to see it.*)

At the other end of Changan Avenue, just before the Friendship Store, is the INTERNATIONAL CLUB, a complex run by the Chinese government for foreign residents in Peking. There is a mediocre restaurant, and recreation facilities including billiards, table tennis, tennis courts and a swimming pool open in the summer (to enter the swimming pool, you need a health certificate issued by the Capital Hospital). Close by the International Club are two of the three compounds in which foreign residents in Peking are forced to live. There are guards on the gates to stop unauthorised local Chinese from entering.

On the northeastern outskirts of the city are the remains of the old FOREIGNERS' CEMETERY, transferred from the Legation Quarter in the 1950s. The cemetery is now overgrown and most of the headstones have been lost, carried away during the Cultural Revolution by vandals or people wanting to use them as building materials. Foreigners who die in Peking are still sometimes buried there. (*Take a No. 402 bus to its terminus, walk across railway and turn left.*)

Excursions

The GREAT WALL, to the north of the city, is an absolute must for visitors. As the Chinese saying goes, you are not a real man until you have climbed on the Great Wall. Or to quote Dr Samuel Johnson, that eighteenth-century man of letters: the children of a man who had gone to view the Great Wall 'would at all times be regarded as the children of a man who had gone to view the Great Wall of China.' Or former American President Richard Nixon: 'It sure is a great wall.'

The wall, which has a total length of over 3500 miles (5600 kilometres), is a monument to China's traditional fear of the barbarians to the north. Construction began in the fifth century B.C. when China was divided into rival kingdoms. In the third century B.C., Qin Shi Huang unified China, and also joined up the sections of wall along the northern border to form the first Great Wall. It stretches around one-twentieth of the world's circumference and is said to be the only man-made object visible from space with the naked eye. The wall has been rebuilt and renovated many times over the past 2000 years, the last major repairs being carried out during the Ming dynasty (1368–1644). Most of the wall was about 25 feet (7.6 metres) high and 19 feet (5.8 metres) wide at the top, with about 25 000 towers about two arrow-shots apart so that the guards could cover its entire length. The concept which the wall represents – trying to enclose an entire country with a single man-made barrier – seems fantastic, and there is a continuing debate about whether the wall was, in the end, any use in keeping out the northern barbarians. Despite its existence, many groups of tribesmen over the centuries succeeded in breaking through and subjugating China.

The section of the wall shown to visitors is at Badaling to the north of Peking. Those who have visited this spot know something few others are aware of: the Great Wall is covered in graffiti. Over the years, thousands of Chinese tourists have found it impossible to leave without carving their initials into the brickwork for posterity to see. In the past few decades, the wall has also suffered greatly from vandalism on a much larger scale. Within the greater Peking municipality alone, over half of its length has been torn down over the past ten years, mostly by peasants wanting to use the bricks for building, and the destruction is still continuing.

Most people visiting the Great Wall also make a detour to the MING TOMBS, the barial place of 13 Ming dynasty emperors. The tomb area begins with an impressive marble archway erected in 1540 and, further on, the road is lined with stone animals and statues of officials. Most of the 13 tombs are in a dilapidated state and are virtually ignored by the tourists, but those that have yet to be restored are also the most peaceful and beautiful, and are very popular with foreign residents of Peking as picnic sites in summer. Two of the tombs are open as museums. Changling, the earliest and largest, dates from 1413. The other is Dingling, constructed in the sixteenth century for the emperor Wan Li who gave a party in his own funeral chamber to mark its completion. The tomb was excavated in 1958 and the treasures found inside are now on display. Nearby is the Ming Tombs reservoir, built in 1958 by 400 000 workmen in only six months. (*The cheapest way to see both the Great Wall and the Ming tombs is to join a local bus tour. Tickets, six yuan each, are sold in a kiosk next to the Xinqiao Hotel, opposite the main CITS office on East Qianmen Street; buses leave from Qianmen Gate. Book your ticket at least one day in advance. There is also a train which runs to the Great Wall every morning, leaving Peking station at 7.40 a.m. – also buy tickets in advance.*)

Another excursion is to the northwestern suburbs of Peking to the WESTERN HILLS. The large FRAGRANT HILLS PARK is nice to walk round and is a favourite spot in autumn when the leaves are changing colour. Next to the park is the TEMPLE OF THE AZURE CLOUD, dating from the fourteenth century, best known for its collection of 508 Buddhas, all different. (*Local bus tours are available – buy tickets at the kiosk opposite the CITS office. Otherwise, take the underground railway west to the end of the line at Pingguoyuan, then take a No. 318 bus to the Fragrant Hills.*)

The SUMMER PALACE (Yiheyuan) was built by the Manchu emperors as their playground. British troops who marched on Peking in 1860 during the second Opium War destroyed most of the original palace buildings, and it was rebuilt in 1888 on the orders of the Empress Dowager using funds meant for the construction of a modern Chinese navy. With delicious, if tragic, irony, she commanded that a marble boat be built by the shore of Kunming Lake, the palace's main focal point, and there it sits still, a ludicrous marble copy of a Mississippi paddle steamer. In 1900 when the foreign powers marched on Peking to relieve the Legation Quarter, under siege from the Boxer rebels, the palace was once again badly damaged. It was finally opened as a public park in 1923, although luckily it was closed for a while during the Cultural Revolution to protect the priceless treasures inside from the iconoclastic fervour of the Red Guards. One of the most interesting buildings is the Hall of Jade Ripples next to the lake shore, where the Empress Dowager placed young Emperor Guangxu under house arrest in 1898 after she discovered a plot to undermine her rule and institute much-needed reforms. Dominating the lake is the Pavilion of the Fragrance of Buddha which, for those who clamber up, provides a charming view of the whole palace area. Behind the hill is a quiet waterway called the Back Lake where people go in summer for picnics.

Near the Summer Palace is the OLD SUMMER PALACE, a once-beautiful collection of buildings, many of them designed by Jesuit priests in a pseudo-Grecian style. Only a few ruins still remain. The palace was destroyed by British troops in 1860 and was never rebuilt. (*From the Fragrant Hills Park, take a No. 333 bus heading for the Summer Palace, and get off at the first stop for the Reclining Buddha Temple [Wofosi]. There are local tours to the Summer Palace – tickets available at the kiosk opposite the CITS office, or take a No. 332 bus from the zoo.*)

One of the furthest excursions possible from Peking is the EAST QING TOMBS, the final resting place of some of the Manchu emperors, about 80 miles (130 kilometres) east of the city. Buried on the site are five emperors, 15 empresses, 100 concubines and one princess. The most impressive of the tombs are those of Emperor Qian Long (1736–1796), and the Empress Dowager who died in 1908. (*Local bus tours operate from Qianmen Gate on most days. Buy tickets at the kiosk opposite the CITS office. The bus trip one-way takes four hours which makes for a long day.*)

A less interesting excursion is to ZHOUKOUDIAN, the spot 30 miles (48 kilometres) southwest of the city where the remains of Peking Man were discovered in 1929. The bones disappeared during the Second World War when they were smuggled out of China for safe-keeping. During the 1970s, occasional reports as to their location, including a claim that they were buried in the rain forests of Tasmania, turned out to be hoaxes.

Also southwest of Peking but closer to town is the MARCO POLO BRIDGE (Lugou Qiao) which the intrepid Venetian traveller described as 'the most wonderful and unique bridge in the world'. The balustrades are covered with stone lions and it is said to be impossible to count how many there are: one estimate is 486. The bridge played a role in modern Chinese history as the place where on 7 July 1937, the Japanese engineered an incident (the circumstances of which remain obscure) which they used as an excuse to invade the rest of China.

(Buy tickets at the kiosk opposite CITS for a bus trip which includes both the Peking Man site and the Marco Polo Bridge. Bus leaves from Qianmen Gate.)

City life

Like many other Chinese cities, the ground under Peking is honeycombed by a network of *air-raid tunnels*, mostly dug during the late 1960s when the leadership feared a Soviet invasion. Entrances to the tunnel network are found in virtually all streets and courtyards in the central city area, and theoretically it should provide an escape route for most of the population out to the Western Hills in the event of an attack. I was once shown round the underground dormitories in one section of the network, but was surprised to find there were no beds. 'We plan to get some,' said the official. 'Anyway, it doesn't look like war is likely this year.' Sections of the tunnels are shown to tourists and visits can be arranged through CITS.

If you can get up early enough, you will see people all over the city performing the graceful shadow-boxing exercises known as *taiqiquan*. An especially nice place to watch enthusiasts doing these slow-motion callisthenics is the *Sun Altar Park* (Ritan Gongyuan) directly north of the Friendship Store. The park is also a rendezvous for old men who like to sing Peking opera arias to each other in the morning while their pet birds hop around in bamboo cages nearby.

Roller skating has become a favourite pastime in Peking in recent years, and there are a number of public rinks where skates can be rented. Try the one in the Sun Altar Park.

And after some energetic roller skating, or at any other time, why not sample the pleasures of a *Peking bath house*? At the Qinghuayuan Bath House on Wangfujing, you can have your nails cut, your hair done, have a massage and a long soak in a hot bath as well, all for next to nothing. (Walk north up Wangfujing and it's on the left, on the block after the Peking Department Store.) The Peking Hotel also has a massage service.

Free markets, where peasants can sell their produce directly to the consumer, have been set up all over China since 1979, and there are some very large ones around Peking which are well worth visiting. There's one on the northeast corner of the Temple of Heaven and another at Beitaiping Zhuang (take a No. 22 bus from Qianmen Gate to the end of the line).

It's always fun to try to get an idea of what life is like at the top. It is not known where Deng Xiaoping and other top leaders live, and the former residences of Mao Tse-tung and Chou Enlai in the Zhongnanhai complex to the west of the Forbidden City are not open to the public. However, two *residences of former top leaders* have been opened recently, which may give some clues to the living quarters of those in command today. The mansion which used to be home to Kang Sheng, Mao's secret police chief who died in 1974, has been opened as the Bamboo Garden Restaurant (located not far from the Drum Tower to the north of the Forbidden City). Soong Ching Ling, widow of the founder of the Republic of China, Sun Yatsen, lived in a huge mansion near the Back Lake, also near the Drum Tower, which is sometimes open to tourists. Check with CITS.

Bars or pubs are virtually unknown in Peking, but one place which almost rates is the *Peace Café* (Heping Canting), which sells beer and snacks and has an interesting clientele. The café became notorious in 1979 as a hang-out of hooligans, black-marketeers and the dissolute children of high officials, and was shut down by the authorities in early 1980. It re-opened again in mid-1981 with a slightly different atmosphere and a limit of one bottle of beer per customer. (Walk north up Wangfujing, turn right after the East Wind market, and the café is a few hundred yards down on the left, outside the entrance to the Peace Hotel.)

In winter, a common Peking pastime is *ice skating*. Beihai Park in the city proper and the Summer Palace in the northwestern suburbs both have large skate-able lakes and kiosks which rent out skates.

Transport

Peking is a relatively easy city to get around. *Taxis* operate from outside the main hotels and some other points, including the International Club and the back gate of the Forbidden City, but cannot be hailed on the street.

The *buses* are very crowded at peak times but, none the less, provide a fast and efficient service. Ticket prices are cheap. Stand near the conductor if you want help on where to get off. A few days on Peking buses will give you new insights into the afterlife of the sardine.

Most people in Peking have *bicycles*, and the streets are flooded with them all day long. Opposite the Friendship Store is a place that rents bicycles by the day. It's a great way to get round town in summer, but it has its disadvantages during the winter: apart from the cold, the exertion of peddling drives the coal-dust pollution deeper into your lungs.

Until the late 1960s, Peking was served by a fleet of three-wheeled *pedi-cabs*, but they were scrapped during the Cultural Revolution, presumably because they were a reminder of the 'old society'. This convenient form of transport, ideally suited to such a flat city as Peking, has been cautiously rehabilitated in the past few years, and a number of pedi-cabs are now available for rent outside the Peking railway station. Beware of over-charging.

The Peking *underground railway* is worth trying. The line runs east–west from the Peking railway station to the western suburbs, and was strictly out of bounds to foreigners until 1980. An around-the-city line, approximately following the course of the old city walls was built in the late 1970s, and was scheduled to open in 1979. The opening was supposedly delayed only until 1981, but by early 1983, there was still no word on when it would be put into service. Clearly, serious problems of some kind have been encountered.

Food

Peking has many good restaurants serving food in a variety of different styles. Here is a selection of the most interesting and unusual.

The most famous dish is Peking duck and there must be at least a dozen restaurants which serve it. The largest is called the *Peking Roast Duck Restaurant* on West Qianmen Street (tel: 334422). Better quality and atmosphere are found in the duck restaurant at 32 Qianmen Street, south of the gate (tel: 751379), and at a small restaurant just off Wangfujing, the main shopping street (tel: 553310). It is always best to book in advance. For cheap duck the way the locals eat it, try the restaurant at 32 Qianmen Street, or the *Bianyifang Restaurant* across the intersection to the east of the CITS office. Make sure you arrive early. The popular sections usually open at 4.00 p.m. for dinner.

In the winter, Peking people like to eat a Mongolian hot-pot dish called *shuangyangrou* – thin slices of mutton boiled in a pot on your own brass stove on the table. The dish is available at, among other places, the seventh floor restaurant of the *Peking Hotel*, or at the *Donglaisun Restaurant* in the Eastwind Market complex on Wangfujing.

Another kind of Mongolian food – barbecued mutton – is available at a couple of good restaurants. The *Koarouji* near the Drum Tower north of the Forbidden City once played host to former President Richard Nixon. Book a table on the balcony during the summer.

Peking's best vegetarian restaurant is south of the Xidan intersection at 74 Xuanwumen Jie. The vegetarian 'fish' and 'pork' shreds taste just like the real thing.

The *Fangshan Restaurant* in the middle of Beihai Park serves food cooked to recipes used in the old imperial kitchens, and is said to have been the favourite restaurant of Mao and his wife. The buildings are all Manchu dynasty, and the prices are high (tel: 442573).

Another restaurant with an 'imperial' menu is *Dongxinglou* on Dongzhimen Dajie (tel: 445972), not far from the Soviet embassy.

For Sichuan food (lots of hot chillis), try the *Sichuan Restaurant* (tel: 336356), situated in the residence of Yuan Shikai, the Manchu general and republican China's first president. It is one of the most beautiful courtyards open to the public in Peking, but can be costly. A cheap alternative is the *Xiangshu Restaurant* in the Eastwind Market on Wangfujing (walk in the southern gate and up to the first floor of the building at the end).

The *Jinyang Restaurant* (241 Zhushikou Jie), serving Shanxi food, is one of the best in Peking, and is famous for having been the 'Black Den' where former Peking mayor Peng Zhen and his cronies gathered in the days before they were all purged during the Cultural Revolution. The Shanxi-style duck and the onion cakes are especially good.

The *Russian Restaurant* in the Peking Exhibition Hall next to the zoo is cavernous and the borsch soup edible. It is one of the few Western restaurants open to local Chinese people.

The *Xinqiao Hotel* has a good Western restaurant on its top floor which serves what are undoubtedly the best chocolate sundaes in China. The *Minzu Hotel* also has pretty good Western food; try the baked Alaska. They also have something resembling Mexican tacos.

For Korean food, which features dog meat, try the *Yanji Noodle Restaurant* (tel: 662984).

In the middle of the Sun Altar Park near the Friendship Store is a restaurant lovingly called the *Jiaozi-ria* by foreign residents after its famous jiaozis – dumplings filled with meat. The spring rolls are good, too. On Dongdaqiao Road, one block east of the Friendship Store, is the *Phoenix Restaurant*, which has a relaxed, decadent feel to it compared to most Peking restaurants. Western rock music is sometimes played over the PA system. These two restaurants are reasonably cheap and within walking distance of the Guanghua Hotel.

Shopping

The *Peking Friendship Store*, China's largest, has a wide range of tourist items and foodstuffs, including some imported goods (Wrigley's chewing gum and Mars bars occasionally appear). There are some interesting shops on Wangfujing, the main shopping street, and on the road north of the Xidan intersection (west of Tiananmen Square). Just south of the Dongdan intersection (east of the Peking Hotel) is the *Theatre Shop*, an antique store which stocks a lot of knick-knacks, mostly over-priced but some are reasonable. Another excellent place for shopping or browsing used to be *Liuli Chang*, a street southwest of Tiananmen Square once lined with interesting old houses and antique shops. They were almost all knocked down in 1980, and new buildings are being put up to replace them. One shop that has remained open is *Rongbao Zhai*, which stocks paintings, prints and posters, some of them good value.

Where to stay

Peking now has a couple of dozen hotels, many of which were formerly used by officials until being pressed into tourist service when the foreigners started to flood in in the late 1970s.

The most prestigious is the *Peking Hotel*, but it does not accept individual tourists who walk in off the street; some tour groups do stay there. Even if you are not staying at the Peking, it is worth visiting. The ground-floor restaurant in the new building serves reasonable food at reasonable prices, and during the summer there is a roof-top café open on the top-floor balcony of the western building from which there is a nice view of the Imperial Palace.

Also on Changan Avenue to the east is the *Jianguo Hotel*, a joint venture between the Chinese authorities and an American/Chinese hotel operator named Clement Chen. China's only top-class hotel, the Jianguo is an exact copy of the Holiday Inn in Palo Alto, southern California, and is managed by the Peninsula Group in Hong Kong. Its coffee shop serves the best hamburgers in the country, while Charlie's Bar, another first for China, has live Western music on Friday and Saturday nights. The Jianguo is also the only hotel in China where it is possible to make a room booking in advance, either by telex or through the Peninsula Hotel in Hong Kong.

An even classier place to stay is *Diaoyutai* (Fishing Terrace), a large compound to the west of the city, south of the zoo, where some privileged tourist groups are put; virtually all heads of state visiting China stay there. The beautifully landscaped grounds contain a couple of dozen large guesthouses surrounded by quiet streams, lawns and trees. Guesthouse No. 17 figured in the sensational 'Gang of Four' trial when Madame Mao was accused of summoning her fellow radicals there in 1974, allegedly to plot the downfall of Deng Xiaoping.

Many tourist groups are lodged in the *Friendship Hotel* in the northwest of the city, a huge complex built in the 1950s to house experts from the Soviet Union. The Soviets have now gone, to be replaced mostly by Westerners and some Third World people. The main building is usually occupied by tourists. (To get into town from the Friendship Hotel, take a No. 332 bus to the zoo, then a No. 103 trolley.)

At the cheap end of the scale, most budget travellers stay at the *Guanghua Hotel* on Dong Huan Road. (Take a No. 9 bus from the railway station, and get off after it turns left. The hotel is on the right.) A two-bed room rents for 16 yuan, but the main attraction is that this is one of the main information exchanges on budget China travel.

Other cheap hotels, used mostly by Hong Kong travellers, include the *Beiwei Hotel* (take a No. 203 bus from the railway station, get off at Beiwei Lu and walk, hotel is on the right), *Xuanwumen Hotel* on West Qianmen Street opposite the Nantang Catholic cathedral (take a No. 9 bus heading west from the railway station) and the *Xiangyang Hotel*, five minutes' walk west of the railway station on East Qianmen Street. This last hotel was originally built to house pilgrims coming from the provinces to visit Chairman Mao's Memorial Hall, but with the change in political climate, the Maoist pilgrims have given way to bourgeois Hong Kong tourists.

Useful Peking telephone numbers

Airlines

Aeroflot 52-3581
Air France 52-3894
British Airways 52-3601
CAAC 55-8861
Japan Airlines 52-3457

Lufthansa 52-2626
Pakistan Airlines 52-3274
Pan American 52-1756
Philippine Airlines 52-3992
Swissair 52-3284

Hotels

Beiwei Hotel 33-8631
Friendship Hotel 89-0621
Huaqiao Mansions 55-8851
Jianguo Hotel 59-5261
Minzu Hotel 66-8541
Peking Hotel 55-2231
Xiangyang Hotel 75-7181
Xuanwumen Hotel 33-8531

Other telephone numbers

Capital Hospital 55-3731
CITS 75-7181
Public Security Bureau 55-3102

The Public Security Bureau (foreigners section), where you go to get visa extensions and travel permits, is located on Beichizi, a street parallel to, and west of, Wangfujing.

SHANGHAI

Life itself. Nothing more intensely living can be imagined.
Aldous Huxley, describing the city of Shanghai

Shanghai is an anomaly. The child of Western imperialism and the youngest of China's major cities, it is by far the largest, the most lively, the most productive, with one-eighth of China's total industrial output and almost a quarter of its exports coming from its factories. Above all, Shanghai is the only one of China's cities that really feels like a city: it hums like a metropolis should. Much of this is a holdover from the old days when Shanghai was the adventurers' paradise. It is still running on the vitality and momentum it built up when it was the greatest city in Asia. Shanghai was to the first half of this century what Hong Kong has been to the second – an international crossroads, a magnet drawing poor people from the Chinese hinterland, a place to get rich quick and lose it all just as fast. There are differences, of course. Even at its most risqué, Hong Kong cannot hope to match the sleaziness and decadence that was an integral part of life in Shanghai, and the extremes of rich and poor are less far apart in modern-day Hong Kong than they were in the old Shanghai.

The heart of the city is much as it was when the foreign magnates of the old China trade left it in 1949. The old banks lining the Bund, Shanghai's most famous street, facing on to the Huangpu River, and the department stores along Nanking Road are looking a little frayed now, but they are still the sturdiest structures in Shanghai. Around the central core of the city, housing has been built since 1949 to accommodate the huge influx of people that has made the city one of the world's most populous. But the endless housing estates look jerry-built and forlorn with many a cracked concrete wall and broken window. All over the city, fading political slogans from forgotten campaigns are still to be faintly seen, left to decay at nature's own pace. No one seems to care about the shabbiness. But it is all relative. The housing estates are at least better than the slums in which so many people lived in the old days.

Housing conditions can be appallingly cramped, but the Shanghainese still enjoy the highest standard of living in China. Their restaurants are excellent, their shops reasonably well-stocked. Prices are generally higher than in other parts of China, but then so are the wages. It is the dream of tens of millions of people in China to be allowed to move to Shanghai to live and work.

Before the foreigners came, Shanghai was just another fishing town near the Yangtse River. When the British moved in after the first Opium War in 1842, they created the basis for what quickly became the most important commercial centre in China, and its economic strength attracted hundreds of thousands of Chinese from other poorer rural areas of east China. The central city area was divided into the British-dominated International Settlement and the French Concession, and for many decades they were ruled entirely by the foreigners who even enjoyed 'extra-territoriality' – freedom from prosecution under Chinese law. During the Second World War, Shanghai was occupied by the Japanese, and in 1945, the Western powers agreed to dismantle the International Settlement and hand the administration of the city over to the Nationalist government. In May 1949, the Communist army marched into Shanghai and ended the rule of both foreigners and Nationalists.

The old pre-Communist Shanghai was really two worlds – the glitter and wealth of the upper crust, and the grinding poverty of the lower classes. The foreign Shanghai residents lived like royalty, as their sumptuous mansions, now proletarianised, attest. Meanwhile, in 1937 for example, the authorities in the International Settlement collected from its streets the bodies of 20 000 people who had died there of hunger and cold. To be fair, 1937 was a bad year, and the poverty of Shanghai was more a reflection of the conditions elsewhere in China than the fault of the city itself. But life there was cheap. In some textile mills, children were chained to their machines; gangland murders were as common as they are in Sicily today; prostitution was a major industry. The science fiction writer, J. G. Ballard, who grew up in old Shanghai, recalled going to the opening night of the film *The Hunchback of Notre Dame* and finding hundreds of hunchbacks outside the cinema, employed by the film's promotors to add atmosphere.

At the top of the Shanghai social scale were some of the great robber barons of the twentieth century. There was Victor Sassoon, born into a Jewish Indian family which became immensely rich after moving to

Shanghai. Sassoon had a great passion for horse-racing: 'There is only one race greater than the Jews, and that is the Derby,' he was once quoted as saying. There were gangland bosses such as Du Yuesheng, leader of the notorious Green Gang, who made millions out of opium, gambling, prostitution and extortion, and covered himself by establishing close ties with the Nationalists. There was a small but significant Chinese bourgeoisie, intent on learning Western ways and discarding any Chinese traditions which stood in the way. And below, there were the poor, the ordinary people struggling to get by.

At one stroke, the Communists killed the old Shanghai, exorcised the foreigners (who were either deported or else placed in a special camp for stateless persons) and began to transform the city. Opium dens were closed and the addicts weaned from their habit; the prostitutes were given medical treatment and taught a new trade. The worst of the slums were slowly cleared away. At first, the Communists promised those capitalists who stayed that their property would not be confiscated, a promise that was not kept – all factories were nationalised in 1953. Nevertheless, the transformation has not been total. Walking through the main downtown area, one could be in any one of a dozen Western cities. Only the ubiquitous Mao jackets and streams of bicycles remind you that this is China. The Shanghai people, too, have retained a cosmopolitan air and a disdain for the 'country bumpkins' from other parts of the country. They are also noted for their efficiency and a sense of style which surely has something to do with the city's decadent past.

The Shanghai of pre-1949 was full of colour and stories, but there was another Old Shanghai as well, that of the 1960s and early 1970s when Shanghai was the centre of radical Maoism, the base from which Mao began the Cultural Revolution and from where the leading radicals, later known as the 'Gang of Four' rose to prominence. How Shanghai could be both the most bourgeois place in China and, a few years later, the most radical, is something of an enigma. Probably the best explanation is that the Shanghainese are good at spotting a trend and leaping to its forefront.

With the Peking press firmly under the control of his opponents, Chairman Mao had to go to Shanghai in 1966 to get his Cultural Revolution moving, and he published the first articles of the campaign in the Shanghai newspaper *Wen Hui Bao*. The Red Guards, those millions of young people who believed they were fighting to uphold Chairman Mao's 'Correct Revolutionary Line', were quickly roused, and in August 1966, thousands of them from all over the country besieged the Shanghai City Hall, the old Hong Kong and Shanghai Banking Corporation headquarters. The mayor declared the Red Guards to be counter-revolutionaries and mobilised workers to ward off the siege, which they did after several days of fighting.

By the end of the year, students and workers in the city were gathering into mass organisations of up to one million people each, some leftist, some rightist, and clashes between the two became more frequent and bloody. The climax came at the beginning of 1967 with what was called the 'January Storm' when city life was virtually brought to a standstill. By the middle of the month, the leftist 'rebels' had taken control of the administration, and early the following month, the Shanghai Commune, modelled on the Paris Commune of the 1870s, was established, although it lasted only 18 days before being replaced by the Shanghai Revolutionary Committee. Shanghai was the first place in which the Maoists tried to take power, and their methods were repeated all over the country as the old guard was attacked by the Red Guards and replaced by radicals.

Once the new radical leadership was installed, they no longer needed the idealistic Red Guards, so millions of these young people were forcibly shipped off into the countryside, many of them to Xinjiang (Sinkiang) Autonomous Region in the far northwest. There have been constant problems over the years with exiled Shanghai youth wanting to return to the city, and these problems still continue. In 1980, an estimated 20 000 of them illegally returned from Xinjiang, although most were eventually shipped back to that largely barren region.

Right at the end of the Maoist period in 1976, Shanghai once more played a crucial political role. Mao died in September, and a struggle for the succession began between the radicals and the moderates. Shanghai was the base of the so-called 'Gang of Four' radicals, then commonly known as the Shanghai Gang, and plans were worked out for a military uprising in the city if the radical leaders in Peking, including Mao's widow Jiang Qing, were seized. Seized they were in early October but, for reasons never satisfactorily explained, the Shanghai uprising never took place.

Moving with the times as usual, Shanghai is now flirting once more with bourgeois pleasures. Most of the signboards along Nanking Road which used to bear quotations from Chairman Mao's Thoughts, now display advertisements for Sony tape recorders and the like. A local newspaper recently complained that some young female workers refuse to do menial tasks on the grounds that it might ruin their finger-nails.

To get a feel for Shanghai, you have to walk its streets. Start from the SHANGHAI MANSIONS, a huge hotel (known in the old days as Broadway Mansions) just over the bridge at the north end of the Bund. Take the lift to the top floor and walk out on to the balcony to get a stunning view of the whole inner city area. Just outside is the iron-girder bridge spanning Suzhou Creek, once called Garden Bridge, but now known as Waibaidu (outer ferry) Bridge. On the left bank is a large grey building which was formerly the Russian consulate, and now houses the Shanghai seamen's hostel. Straight ahead is the former BRITISH CONSULATE, a suitably imperial building set among green lawns. The main consulate building is now used by the Shanghai Foreign Trade Department, while one of the side buildings has been turned into the local Friendship Store. Opposite the British Consulate beside the river is Huangpu Park, formerly the public gardens of the old International Settlement. The regulations posted outside the park used to state (in separate provisions) that dogs and Chinese were not allowed in. After angry protests, the rules were changed to allow 'respectable' Chinese to enter but the ordinary natives were, naturally, still barred.

Further down the Bund, the present China Textiles Export Corporation was once owned by Jardin Matheson's, one of the original opium-trading companies. Just to the north of the Peace Hotel, the building now occupied by the People's Bank of China used to be the Bank of China, as operated by the Nationalist government. This bank was under the control of T. V. Soong and H. H. Kung, two relatives by marriage of Generalissimo Chiang Kaishek who, by their devious financial dealings, were largely responsible for the waves of inflation which swept through Shanghai in the late 1940s, fatally weakening the Nationalist government.

Next is the PEACE HOTEL, opened in 1930 as Sassoon House after the family which built it. It contained the Cathay Hotel, in its day one of the grandest hotels in the Far East. Noel Coward is supposed to have finished off his play *Private Lives* while staying there. The silver milk jugs and toast trays used in the Peace Hotel's splendid restaurant still bear the emblem of the Cathay. On the other side of the street is the south wing of the Peace Hotel which used to be the Palace Hotel.

Further down, topped by a tall clock tower, is the old Customs

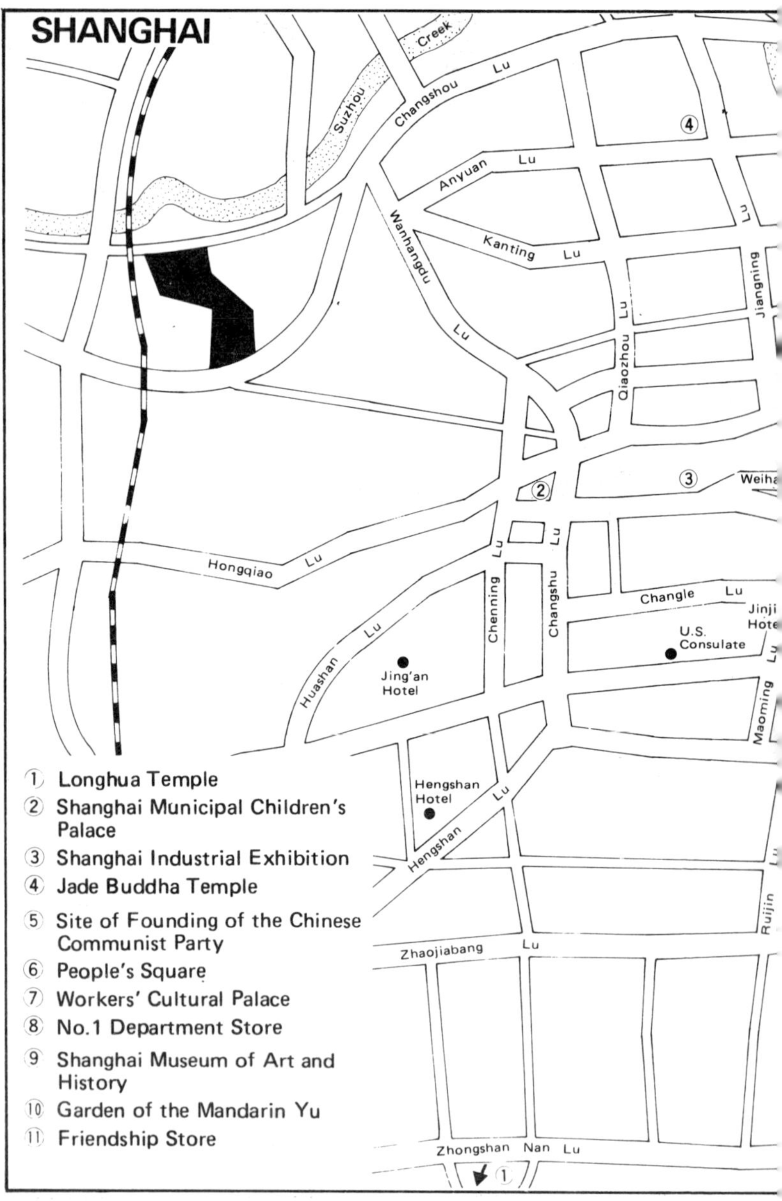
SHANGHAI
Suzhou Creek
Changshou Lu
Anyuan Lu
Kanting Lu
Wanhangdu Lu
Qiaozhou Lu
Jiangning Lu
Weihai
Hongqiao Lu
Chenning Lu
Changshu Lu
Changle Lu
Jinji Hotel
U.S. Consulate
Huashan Lu
Jing'an Hotel
Maoming
Hengshan Hotel
Hengshan Lu
Ruijin
Zhaojiabang Lu
Zhongshan Nan Lu
1 Longhua Temple
2 Shanghai Municipal Children's Palace
3 Shanghai Industrial Exhibition
4 Jade Buddha Temple
5 Site of Founding of the Chinese Communist Party
6 People's Square
7 Workers' Cultural Palace
8 No.1 Department Store
9 Shanghai Museum of Art and History
10 Garden of the Mandarin Yu
11 Friendship Store

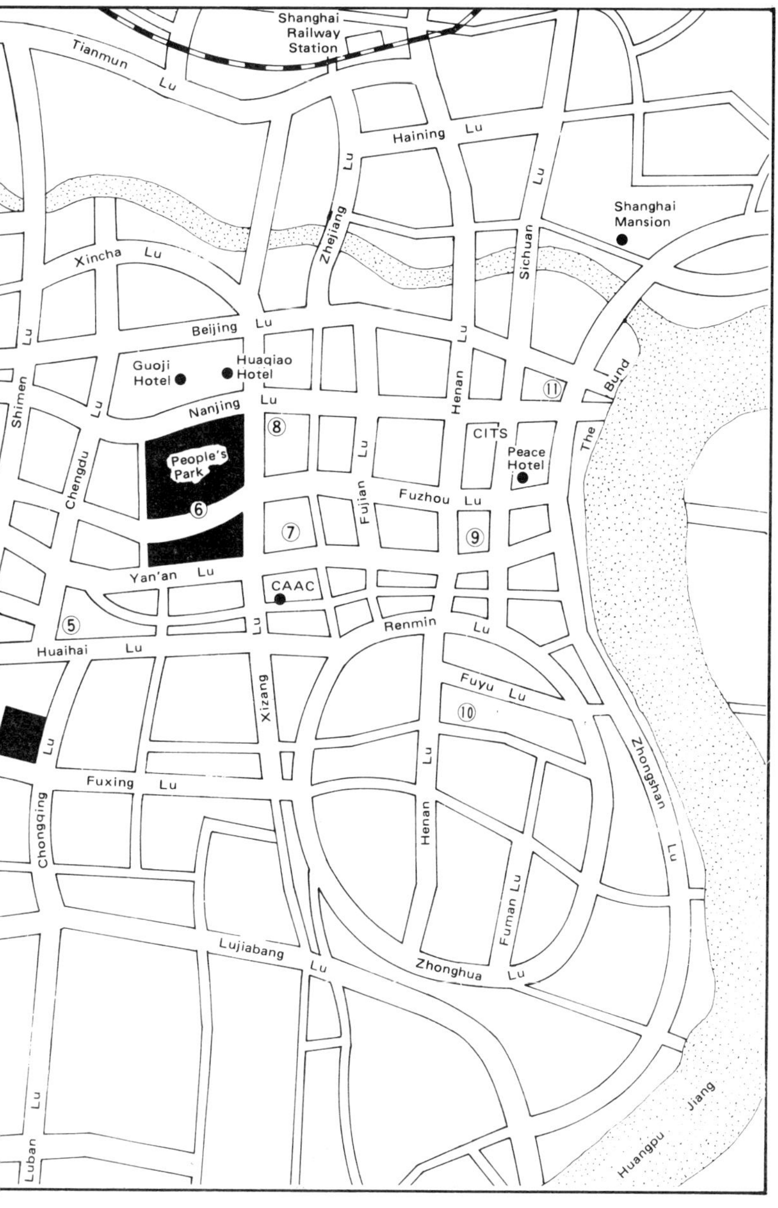

Shanghai Railway Station
Tianmun Lu
Haining Lu
Zhejiang Lu
Sichuan Lu
Shanghai Mansion
Xincha Lu
Beijing Lu
Shimen Lu
Guoji Hotel
Huaqiao Hotel
Nanjing Lu
Henan Lu
The Bund
Chengdu Lu
People's Park
CITS
Peace Hotel
Fujian Lu
Fuzhou Lu
Yan'an Lu
CAAC
Renmin Lu
Huaihai Lu
Xizang Lu
Fuyu Lu
Zhongshan Lu
Fuxing Lu
Chongqing Lu
Henan Lu
Fuman Lu
Lujiabang Lu
Zhonghua Lu
Luban Lu
Huangpu Jiang

House, the headquarters of the foreign-run administration which collected China's customs duties on the grounds that the Chinese government was not efficient enough to do it itself. Next door is the SHANGHAI COMMUNIST PARTY HEADQUARTERS (city hall), built in 1921 as the headquarters of the Hong Kong and Shanghai Bank. The two large bronze, very British lions which used to sit outside the bank's entrance have been replaced by a People's Liberation Army guard, but the lions reportedly still exist. A bank employee told me that they re-appeared one day a few years ago when a film was being made about old Shanghai.

A little further down is the DONGFENG HOTEL, which in the old days was the Shanghai Club, a re-creation of the exclusive London club atmosphere which British colonials all over the world seemed to need so badly. The club claimed to have the longest bar in the world; this still exists, although it has been partitioned into three sections. The building is now used mostly for wedding receptions, and the old bar, where once British bankers lingered over their port undisturbed by the teeming masses outside, is now a public café.

Walk back north to the Peace Hotel, and turn west into NANKING ROAD, the premier shopping street of old (and new) Shanghai. The Wing On and Sincere Department Stores, both of which still maintain shops in Hong Kong, were among the most splendid shops in Asia. Wing On is now the No. 10 Department Store; Sincere is the Shanghai Clothing Store. (There are still beggars to be seen in this area, far fewer than in the old days, but they are there nevertheless.)

Just south of Nanking Road on Jiujiang Road is the PEIGUANG MIDDLE SCHOOL, which in the old days was the Laozha police station. In 1925, this was the scene of an incident which caused massive strikes and boycotts of foreign goods right across China. A Chinese worker was killed in a fight with the management of a Japanese-run textile factory and a demonstration was organised to protest. The police arrested 23 students and took them to the Laozha police station outside which crowds gathered, demanding their release. The situation turned ugly and the British officer in command ordered his men to fire on the demonstrators. Dozens were killed and injured.

One block south of Nanking Road is FUZHOU ROAD, once famous for its brothels and 'sing-song girl' teahouses, as well as its second-hand bookshops. The brothels disappeared in 1949 when the Communists came, and although the bookshops lasted a bit longer, they too were closed during the Cultural Revolution of the late 1960s. Most of the books were probably pulped to produce copies of the Little Red Book of Chairman Mao's thoughts. (A couple of bookshops are still open, but there are few books of interest on offer.) On the corner of Fuzhou Road and Henan Road stands a large building which used to be the headquarters of the International Settlement Municipal Council, described by one writer as 'the citidal of Western, and particularly British, power in Shanghai'.

Further along Nanking Road, you come upon the PARK HOTEL, formerly the International Hotel, which overlooks an area once occupied by the Shanghai race track. Half of the race course is now People's Square, a vast expanse of concrete; the other half has been turned into People's Park. The race course club house, with its impressive clock tower, is now the municipal library. The grandstand also still exists and is sometimes used for meetings.

The street south of Fuzhou Road, YANAN ROAD, marked the dividing line between the International Settlement and the French Concession. Huaihai Road, formerly called Avenue Joffre, was full of interesting little cafés and was known for its tailors' shops. The French authorities generally maintained a tolerant attitude towards shady political activities, and in a building just off the old Avenue Joffre (at 76 Xingye Lu), the Chinese Communist Party was established in 1921. Mao Tse-tung didn't attend; he said he couldn't find the address.

The old French Club, now the JINJIANG CLUB, is a magnificent art deco structure built in the early 1920s. The club was opened for tourists in 1979 and has a very good restaurant. Above the room now used for video games is a vast ballroom, while at the end of the corridor is a beautiful, well-preserved indoor swimming pool. The club was reportedly used by Chairman Mao as his Shanghai residence for many years.

Directly across the road is the JINJIANG HOTEL, consisting of blocks of luxury apartments built by the French. In the one-storey block in the centre of the compound, President Nixon and Premier Chou Enlai signed the Shanghai Communiqué in 1972 in which the Americans agreed that there was only one China. (It was another eight years before they further agreed that the capital of that China was Peking and not Taipei.)

Diagonally across the intersection from the old French Club is the Shanghai Art Theatre, opened in 1931 as the Lyceum, home of the Shanghai Amateur Dramatic Club.

Back to the Bund, walk south from Yanan Road and you will come to the oldest part of town, the CHINESE CITY. Renmin and Zhonghua Roads now mark where the old, roughly circular city wall once stood. The narrow lanes, usually crowded with pedestrians, are pleasant to walk through and contain some interesting specialist shops selling items such as chopsticks. The best area is the northeast section of the old city, where there is a market, and an old-fashioned teahouse set in a tepid pool. Nearby is the YU YUAN, an extremely cluttered garden built in 1577 which is popular with both locals and tourists.

On the corner of Yanan and Henen Roads, just north of the Chinese City, is the SHANGHAI ART AND HISTORY MUSEUM, one of the best in China. Two or three intersections further west, on the corner of Tibet Road and Yanan Road and marked by a tall white pagoda rising from its entrance, is the SHANGHAI YOUTH PALACE, once a pleasure house known as the Great World. The writer Pan Ling, in her excellent book *In Search of Old Shanghai*, quotes at length from a description of the place written by a 1930s Hollywood director who visited it:

> The establishment had six floors to provide distraction for the milling crowd, six floors that seethed with life and all the commotion and noise that go with it, studded with every variety of entertainment Chinese ingenuity had contrived. On the first floor were gambling tables, sing-song girls, magicians, pick-pockets, slot machines, fireworks, bird cages, fans, stick incense, acrobats and ginger. One flight up were the restaurants, a dozen different groups of actors, crickets in cages, pimps, midwives, barbers and earwax extractors. The third floor had jugglers, herb medicines, ice cream parlours, photographers, a new bevy of girls, their high-collared gowns slit to reveal their hips, in case one had passed up the more modest ones below who merely flashed their thighs. The fourth floor was crowded with shooting galleries, fantan tables, massage benches . . . the fifth floor featured girls whose dresses were slit to the armpits, a stuffed whale, story tellers, balloons, peep shows, a mirror maze, two love-letter booths with scribes who guaranteed results . . .

Because it is such a young city, Shanghai has few of the temples and towers which form the bulk of the tourist attractions in other cities in China. One of the few Buddhist temples which are still open is the JADE BUDDHA TEMPLE (Yufosi) on Changshou Road to the northwest of the city centre. The temple contains two exquisite jade statues of the Buddha, one seated, the other lying, which were brought from Burma in the early years of the century.

In the Hongkou district to the north of the city is the HOME OF LU XUN, one of modern China's greatest writers, who died in the 1930s.

The Communists have adopted him as their own, but my favourite quote of Lu Xun's is a damning indictment of the vast bulk of the so-called literature produced in China since 1949: 'To my mind, any kind of literature that can be used for the goal of political propaganda is devoid of persuasive force. Good literature always refuses to be ordered from outside, it never cares about practical considerations, it spontaneously springs from the heart.'

City life

Any foreigner walking along the Bund usually attracts at least a couple of young Chinese wanting to practise their English. But if you want more of the same, there is a place in the People's Park where people go on Sunday mornings to practise: in the 'English corner', only English is spoken.

A *haircut and massage* can be an interesting experience, and prices for the service are cheap. Try Mr Ti in his salon in the Peace Hotel, who gives a haircut and wash followed by a brisk head and neck massage for only 3.20 yuan. Alternatively, just round the corner there is the Xinxin barber on East Nanking road where it is even cheaper.

The Huangpu River plays a vital part in Shanghai life, and a *ferry trip* is a good way to see it. There are public ferries running from the Bund across to the east bank, a largely uninteresting industrial area. China Travel Service also operates *cruises* which go down to the mouth of the Yangtse River which pass by warships of the East China Fleet as well as the usual ferries, tugs and barges.

Pumpkin Lane, a former slum area, is interesting to visit, although it has to be arranged through China Travel to be really worthwhile. In a corner of the post-1949 model housing estate stand a group of mud huts preserved in their pristine ramshackle state to prove how bad things were in the 'bad old days' before the Communist Party came. This little museum of poverty is kept hidden behind iron gates, and is only shown to foreigners who specifically ask to see it. Old residents are wheeled out to describe in gory detail how dreadful things were. 'I was a beggar for 15 years and a rickshaw puller for 27 years before that,' said one old man who acts as a sort of custodian. He pointed at the small huts, perhaps four feet (1.2 metres) wide, six feet (1.8 metres) long and covered with a bamboo mat. 'It was not easy to find a place like this in the old days in Shanghai. You had to bribe the local tyrants who controlled the land before they let you move in.' 'Dead babies,' added an old woman who also lived in the infamous Pumpkin Lane. 'There were children's bodies everywhere in the old days. When your baby died, you just rolled it up in straw and threw it away.'

Shanghai is full of *factories*, and a visit to one of them is not hard to arrange through the China Travel Service. One interesting one, I think, is the Shanghai toothpaste factory, a tiny place which churns out one quarter of China's total toothpaste supplies. The key question, of course, was: How many people in China brush their teeth? 'My own personal estimate,' said the vice-director, 'is that about one-third of China's population brush their teeth.'

Food

Shanghai cuisine is recognised as one of the great schools of Chinese cooking, and Shanghai's restaurants are among the best in China. The seafood and European food are particularly good.

Probably the most authentic Shanghai cooking is available at the *Rongshun Restaurant* (242 Fuyou Lu, not far from the Yu Garden in the Chinese City), also known as the Shanghai Lao Fandian – the 'old Shanghai restaurant'. For Cantonese food, try the *Xinya Restaurant*, a famous three-storey place (719 Nanking Road). Another Shanghai-style restaurant is the *Yangzhou Restaurant* (306 Nanking Road).

For European food, try any of the major hotels, or else the *Red House* (37 Shaanxi Road, near the Jinjiang Hotel) which, before the Communist take-over, was called Chez Louis. The baked Alaska is excellent.

Nightlife

The coffee bars at the Peace Hotel and Shanghai Mansions both used to feature jazz bands composed of musicians from the dance bands of the 1940s, pulled out of retirement to play those old Glenn Miller tunes once again, this time for the benefit of the Four Modernisations. Then in mid-1982, with a mounting campaign against so-called 'bourgeois liberalism' sweeping the land, the bands were forced to stop. Hopefully they will be allowed to strike up the music again soon. It was so nice to sit amidst the 1930s decor of the Peace Hotel coffee shop, sipping an Irish whiskey and listening to the scratch band in the corner play 'I Wonder Who's Kissing Her Now', just slightly out of tune. Real atmosphere.

Hotels

The *Peace Hotel*, conveniently located on the Bund, is expensive but well worth the price. Everything from the lobby to the plumbing recalls another era. Visitors may find they are woken early by the honking of cars and the hooting of ships, but in Shanghai you should get up early anyway. Some rooms now feature colour television sets and awful video movies. Such is progress. (Take a No. 65 bus from the railway station.)

The *Jinjiang Hotel* is the largest in Shanghai and the most luxurious. Heads of state visiting the city usually stay in one of the suites in the south block. It's quieter than the Peace Hotel and close to the Jinjiang Club and the Red House, two good restaurants, but it is rather isolated from the main action down on the Bund. The main block has a dormitory, although it can be hard to get a bed. (Take a No. 41 bus from the railway station.)

Most budget travellers stay at the *Pujiang Hotel*, close to the Shanghai Mansions, where dorm beds cost five yuan. (Take a No. 65 bus from the station, get off at Nanking Road, cross the bridge over Suzhou Creek and turn right past Seamen's Hostel.) Another budget hotel is the *Sang Chiang Hotel* (740 Hankow Road).

TIANJIN (Tientsin)

With a population of about five million, Tianjin is China's third largest city after Shanghai and Peking, although it matches neither Shanghai's vitality nor Peking's history. Tianjin began life about 800 years ago as a market town, and has remained a centre of commerce ever since. Its development received a big boost after it was made a Treaty Port in 1858 and was opened to the 'foreign devils', who established 'concessions' along the river to the south of the Chinese city. It became a major industrial city, partly thanks to its port facilities, and partly to the large coal deposits nearby.

The former British and French concessions are still the centre of town, now called the HEPING DISTRICT. The streets are lined with large, sturdy buildings, built in the early twentieth century as banks, post offices and trading houses. Walking round this area is one of the most interesting things to do in Tianjin. Tianjin suffered badly in the 1976 Tangshan earthquake, although not as badly as Tangshan which was completely flattened (see p. 131). The former foreign banks and trading houses appear to have weathered the tremors better than many of the structures that followed them. For several years after the quake, the streets of the city were covered in shacks hastily built by the many thousands of people who had been made homeless. Work on rehousing them went very slowly, but was finally completed, more or less, in late 1981 after some heavy prodding by the central government.

The Chinese city is also worth walking around, although everything seems to be hidden behind large, high, grey walls in the manner traditional for cities in north China. The old city consists of a maze of alley-ways and old-style Chinese houses, most of which seem to have miraculously escaped destruction in the earthquake. There used to be a city wall, but it was knocked down by foreign troops in 1901 as part of their retaliation for the anti-foreign Boxer Rebellion.

Tianjin has little else to interest the visitor. There are few historical or cultural sites, and no spectacular views. The highlight of most guided tours is the Tianjin No. 1 Carpet Factory, which says it all.

There are three Tianjin institutions, however, worth visiting: the first of which is a large, sprawling restaurant named *Gou Bu Li* (Shandong Lu, Heping District) which, roughly translated, means 'God, Take No Notice'. The story behind the name goes like this: the restaurant, famed throughout China for its steamed buns, was established over 200 years ago by a gentleman whose nickname was Gou Bu Li. According to one waiter, people in the old days often took such nicknames in the hope that the gods, when looking for someone to take off to the other world, would pass over them as being unworthy of attention, thereby ensuring a long life. The buns are delicious, but if you want to eat with the ordinary Chinese be sure to arrive early. There is also a foreigners' room at the back.

Then there is *Keissling's* (Zhejiang Lu, Heping District) which is one of the best restaurants in China serving Western food to the Chinese. It was originally run by two Austrians, Keissling and Bader, and inside it has the look of a rundown 1930s nightclub. You can sit by the long kidney-shaped balcony on the second floor and watch the passing scene below as you devour such un-Chinese delicacies as beef stew and fish and chips. Again, there is a room where the staff like to quarantine foreigners, but it is much better to sit outside, even though the service is atrocious, and the standards of hygiene leave something to be desired. The restaurant is also famous for its coffee-flavoured toffees, on sale on the ground floor. There are two kinds, wrapped in either red or white paper: buy the white ones.

The last place of interest is the former British Club, now called the *Tianjin Club*. For many years, it was the playground of senior Communist officials, but it is now somewhat less exclusive. There is a restaurant on the ground floor which is open to both foreigners and Chinese. After lunch, you might care to go upstairs and have a game of snooker on the excellent tables which the British were forced to leave behind when they were kicked out by the Communists in 1949.

How to get there and where to stay

Tianjin is connected to most important cities by air, and there are also direct flights from Hong Kong. The train ride from Peking takes about two hours. The city makes a good day-trip from Peking, but if you want to stay, there is the *Friendship Hotel* on Shengli Lu (Victory Road), or the *Tianjin Hotel* (Jiefang Bei Lu), which was built in the French concession in 1927. It's a gloomy place, but the fittings, from the door-handles to the toilet fixtures, are all veritable antiques.

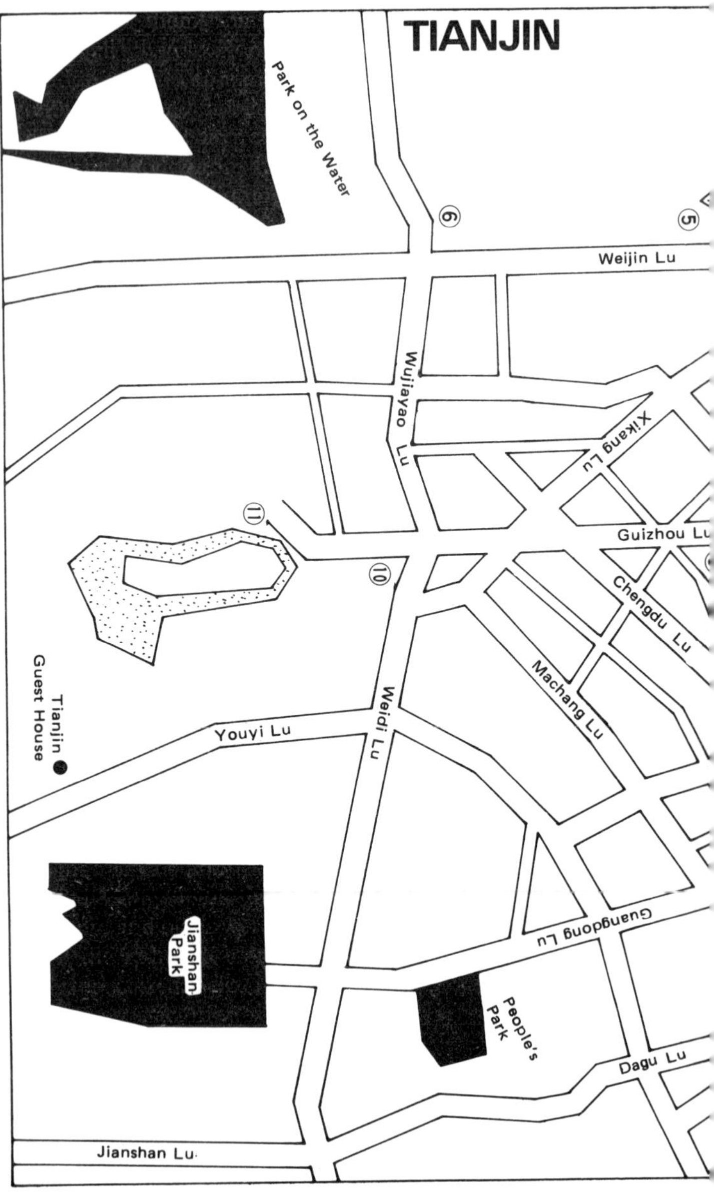
TIANJIN
Park on the Water
6
5
Weijin Lu
Wujiayao Lu
Xikang Lu
11
Guizhou Lu
10
Chengdu Lu
Machang Lu
Tianjin Guest House
Youyi Lu
Weidi Lu
Jianshan Park
Guangdong Lu
People's Park
Dagu Lu
Jianshan Lu

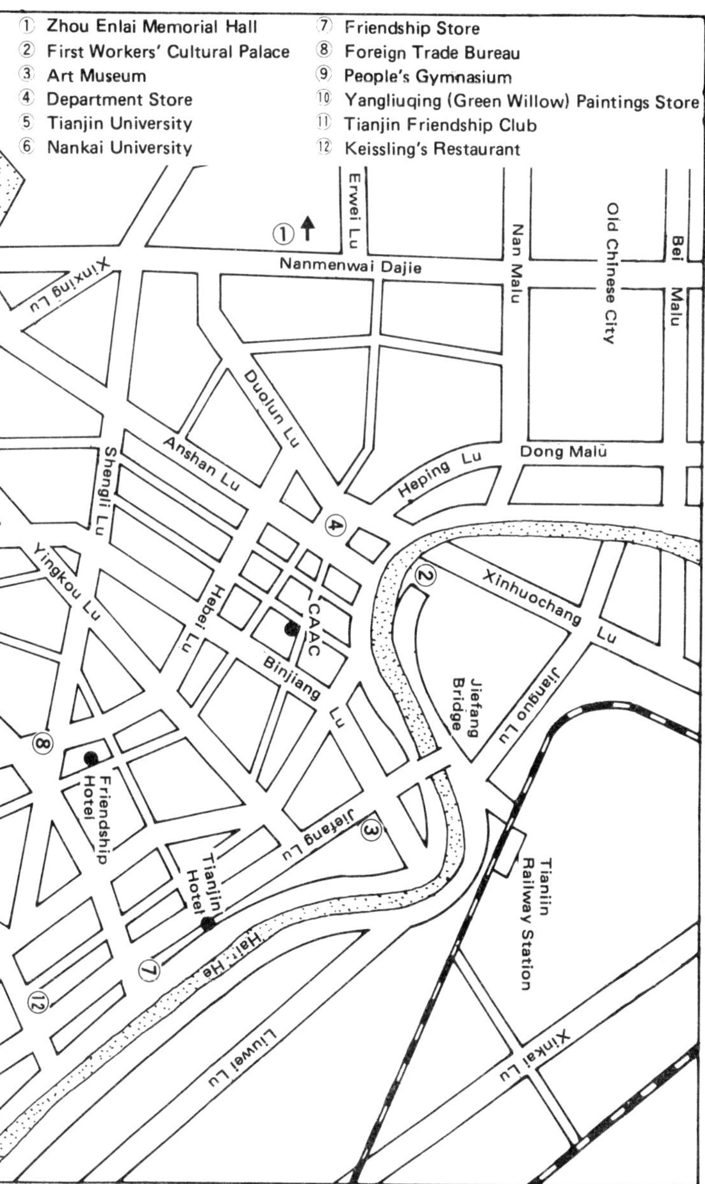

1 Zhou Enlai Memorial Hall
2 First Workers' Cultural Palace
3 Art Museum
4 Department Store
5 Tianjin University
6 Nankai University
7 Friendship Store
8 Foreign Trade Bureau
9 People's Gymnasium
10 Yangliuqing (Green Willow) Paintings Store
11 Tianjin Friendship Club
12 Keissling's Restaurant
Erwei Lu
Nan Malu
Old Chinese City
Bei Malu
Nanmenwai Dajie
Xinxing Lu
Duolun Lu
Anshan Lu
Heping Lu
Dong Malu
Shengli Lu
Yingkou Lu
Hebei Lu
CAAC
Binjiang Lu
Xinhuochang Lu
Jiefang Bridge
Jianguo Lu
Friendship Hotel
Jiefang Lu
Tianjin Hotel
Hai He
Tianjin Railway Station
Liuwei Lu
Xinkai Lu

ANHUI PROVINCE

Anhui Province has the reputation of being one of the poorest in east China. There has been an increase in the number of beggars on the streets of Shanghai in recent years, and most of them seem to come from here.

Anhui is cut in two by the Yangtse River, and with no bridges along its path through the province, travel from one part to the other is difficult. There is a railway line south which joins the river opposite the city of Wuhu on the southern bank. Most of Anhui's tourist attractions, most notably Huang Shan mountain, are in the southern part of the province, and are more easily approached from Shanghai and Hangzhou than from Hefei, the capital.

Hefei

Hefei, the province's capital, is a rather nondescript town with little to recommend it to the tourist. It used to be a quiet market town, but has been built up since 1949 as an industrial centre. The local PROVINCIAL MUSEUM (268 Anqing Lu) is quite good, and contains a jade burial suit composed of slabs of jade sewn together with silver thread.

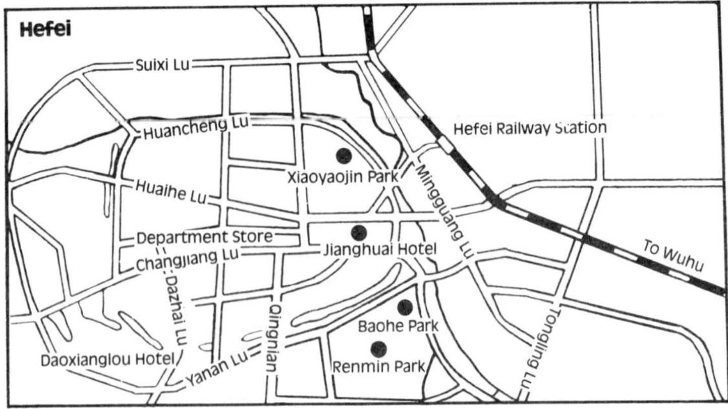

How to get there and where to stay

There are a couple of flights a week to Hefei from Peking and Shanghai, and the city is also served by trains from Peking.

The main hotel in Hefei is the *Daoxianglou* (fragrant straw hall) *Guesthouse*, on the corner of Dazhai Lu and Yan'an Lu. Another is the *Jianghuai Hotel* (86 Changjiang Lu).

Huang Shan

This mountain in the southern part of the province is generally considered to be the most beautiful peak in China and its crags and abysses, trees and streams have been an important influence on Chinese art. Huang Shan is, in fact, the collective name for a whole range of mountains, but the main ones are Guangming (bright), Lianhua (lotus flower) and Tiandu (heavenly capital) peaks. According to one Chinese saying, loosely translated, if you've seen Huang Shan, there's no point in bothering with any other mountains. From the foot of the southern slope of Huang Shan, it should take about four or five hours to climb to the top. It's steep but well within the capabilities of most people, and the stunning vistas which are revealed along the way make the effort well worthwhile. It looks like one enormous Chinese painting.

The best time to go is in spring or autumn but, except at midsummer, it gets chilly up on the peak, so take an extra layer of clothing. Also be warned that, in season, you can hardly see the vistas for the crowds of Chinese tourists.

There are hot springs at the bottom of the mountain, the waters from which have been diverted into private baths for visitors.

How to get there and where to stay

Most people approach Huang Shan from Hangzhou in the east, via Tunxi, a former grain-trading centre south of the noble peak. It is also possible to get there from Wuhu, a railway junction to the north on the banks of the Yangtse River. Either way, the trip involves a long drive.

There are hotels at the village of Tangkou, including the *Huang Shan Guesthouse* and the *Yuping Lou* (jade screen mansion), a former temple. If you want to spend the night on the mountain and watch the sunrise, there is the *Beihai Guesthouse* at the top which is spartan but adequate.

FUJIAN PROVINCE

Fujian Province on the southeast China coast opposite the island of Taiwan is one of the most fascinating places in China, but unfortunately most of the interesting areas are closed to foreigners. More than 80 per cent of the province is mountainous, and only the thin coastal strip and three or four ports along it are open to outsiders. The huge, mysterious interior, where the people are very poor, is out of bounds. Thanks largely to its ruggedness, there are 140 distinct dialects spoken in the province. People from Fuzhou and Xiamen (Amoy), the two main cities of Fujian Province cannot understand each other if they speak their respective languages. It may be an apocryphal story, but it is said that a group of young Red Guards who penetrated one particularly isolated area in Fujian in the late 1960s were asked by the locals who the current emperor was.

For the present, we have to make do with the coast which is very beautiful, with a rich and lush countryside and a climate that is humid but pleasant. Paddy-field green is probably the most beautiful colour in the world, and there's plenty of it here. Throughout the rural areas can be seen the distinctively designed Fujian farmhouse, much larger than those in other parts of China and accommodating whole clans under one roof.

Fujian was the first area, after Guangdong Province to the south, to meet with the red-haired, big-nosed 'foreign devils' who appeared on the scene in the 1830s and 1840s selling opium. Partly because of this early contact with the outside world, and because of the traditional backwardness of the region, Fujian became a major source of Chinese emigrants to other parts of east Asia; most people in the Chinese communities of Singapore, Indonesia. Malaysia and the Philippines are descendants of Fujian migrants. These overseas Chinese still maintain links with their ancestral homes, and the local government is trying to encourage them to invest in the province in order to speed up economic construction. (Most of the people on Taiwan are also descended from settlers from southern Fujian.)

Almost all foreign visitors to Fujian fly into Fuzhou city and then travel by road south through Butian and Quanzhou to Xiamen, better known in the West as Amoy. I will deal with them in that order.

Fuzhou (Foochow)

Fuzhou, the capital of Fujian Province, is a city with a long history and has been known by its present name for at least 1000 years. Marco Polo, who visited it towards the end of the thirteenth century, described it as being an important commercial centre but heavily garrisoned by the central government due to frequent rebellions staged by the local people. He said that the city was a major staging point for Indian and Arabian goods unloaded at the port of Quanzhou down the coast and then brought up to Fuzhou by smaller ships for distribution throughout China. Marco also reported the existence of a 'Christian' community in the city, who must have been Nestorian Christians, a sect from Syria who spread along the Silk Road and established colonies in most major settlements through central Asia and China. He claimed that there were 700 000 'Christian' households in Fujian Province, probably an exaggeration. (For further details of Nestorian Christianity in China, *see* Xi'an, p. 194.)

Fuzhou was one of the four ports which China was forced to open to foreign trade under the terms of the Treaty of Nanking at the end of the first Opium War, and the first foreign traders moved in to do business in 1844.

With its distinctive wooden houses and lively streets, Fuzhou is a nice place to walk around. The huge square in the centre of the city is dominated by an absolutely massive statue of Chairman Mao erected to commemorate the 'glorious' Ninth Congress of the Chinese Communist Party, the meeting in 1969 at which Maoism was enshrined as the state 'religion' of China, and at which the late Defence Minister Lin Piao was named as Mao's heir-apparent.

Landing at Fuzhou airport gives you a good view of some of the MiG-17s and MiG-19s which form the backbone of China's air force. Fujian has always been considered the 'frontline' province in the battle to 'liberate' Taiwan, the island 100 miles (160 kilometres) off the coast held by the Nationalist Chinese. Peking is now taking a different tack in its attempts to re-unite Taiwan with the motherland, and no longer refers to 'liberation' of the island, but Fujian remains one of the best-defended parts of the Chinese mainland.

There is not much in the way of regular tourist sights in Fuzhou.

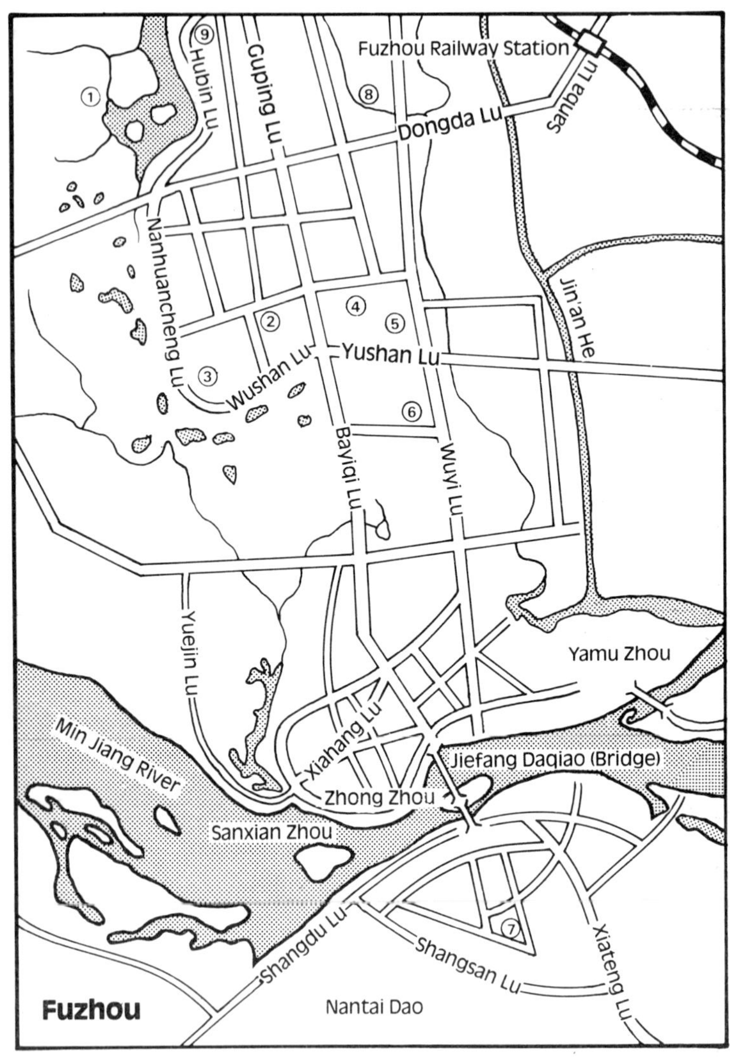

1. Xihu (West Lake) Park
2. Wu Ta (Black Pagoda)
3. Wu Shan
4. Bai Ta (White Pagoda)
5. Yu Shan
6. Wuyi Square
7. Renmin Park
8. Overseas Chinese Hotel (Huaqiao Daxia)
9. West Lake Guest House

The best area to walk round is down by the river (take a No. 2 bus from the Overseas Chinese Hotel to the end of the line, then keep walking). Across the bridge is *Nantai Island* where the foreigners lived and worked in the Treaty Port days, and some of the old buildings are still standing. There is a LACQUERWARE FACTORY which can be visited for those interested in such things, and XIHU (west lake) PARK is pleasant. A few miles outside town on Gu Shan (drum hill) is the YONGQUAN (bubbling spring) TEMPLE which is the proud owner of what is said to be a tooth of the Lord Buddha.

How to get there and where to stay

There are regular flights to Fuzhou from Shanghai, Canton and Hong Kong, and a railway line that runs inland links Fuzhou with the Shanghai–Canton railway. The main hotel is the *Overseas Chinese Hotel* (Huaqiao Daxia; take a No. 2 bus from the railway station and get off at third stop). Two others are the *Fuzhou Hotel* (36 Dongda Lu), and the *West Lake Guesthouse* (Xihu Binguan), situated beside Fuzhou's nicest park.

Butian

On the road between Fuzhou and Xiamen (Amoy) is the county seat of Butian, a deceptively sleepy place which was the centre of intense factional fighting during the last years of Mao. In April 1980, some of the first foreigners to visit Fujian for many years rolled into Butian – a group of foreign correspondents of whom I was one. Whenever I think of the incident, I still have to laugh. It was a classic confrontation between The Press and The Communist Official.

We were ushered into a reception room in the local Communist Party headquarters by the deputy chief of the county, Li Bangying. He was probably ready to reel off his usual speech about how excellent the situation in Butian was, but the pack of foreign journalists did not want to know. What they wanted were precise details of what happened in Butian in the mid-1970s. Shocked by this sudden assault of sensitive questions, the official metaphorically backed into a corner, parrying and blocking as best he could, protesting that he was just a commercial official. On reflection, we may have been too aggressive. It was a hot day, and the provincial officials with us had gone out of their way to be unhelpful on a number of occasions. But it was nice to see a Communist official suddenly brought face-to-face with the reality of the Western press in all its fact-finding ferocity.

What we discovered at that meeting, and later, was this: There was a school teacher in Butian named Li Qinglin who wrote to Chairman Mao in the early 1970s, complaining of the hardships he had to endure as a father whose sons had all been sent to do farm work in other parts of the country. The Chairman personally wrote a reply to this teacher, commiserating with him, and enclosed 300 yuan to tide him over. Based on this minor contact with the Great Leader and Teacher of the Chinese People, Li built himself a political career. He aligned himself with the powerful radicals and, according to a later report, was contacted by Mao's wife, Jiang Qing, further bolstering his power in the Butian area. He is said to have declared that he had 'an antenna' on his hat which linked him directly to Madame Mao in Peking.

In February 1976, as Mao was sinking towards death and China towards chaos, 'Li and his gang issued a notice to seize power in Fujian Province,' the Butian official said, as a result of which the whole provincial bureaucracy was paralysed and schools and factories closed down. Li then 'released counter-revolutionary prisoners from the jails and used them as a social force to help him seize power,' and 'organised militia commanding centres as an alternative armed force to engage in fighting, robbing and looting.' There were armed clashes, apparently between Li's forces and People's Liberation Army units, in which, according to the Butian official, four people died, including one soldier.

After Mao's death in September 1976 and the arrest of the radical 'Gang of Four' the following month, Li and his comrades seem to have taken to the hills to continue the fight against the 'capitalist roaders', and he was not captured until nearly a year afterwards, in July or August 1977. The Butian official declined to say how many supporters Li had had or how many had been arrested with him.

He was tried in 1979 before a huge rally and sentenced to death, although the sentence was commuted to life imprisonment because he 'confessed his crimes in a relatively good way'.

So ends the story of School Teacher Li from Butian.

Quanzhou

This town to the south of Butian is only a shadow of its former self, but is still very interesting. It was once the largest port in China and, in Marco Polo's estimation, one of the two biggest ports in the world at the end of the thirteenth century (Alexandria was the other); he referred to the city as Zayton, and said that all the merchant ships from India docked there. Trade of one sort or another continues – on a trip there in 1980, I was surprised to find black-market Dunhill menthol cigarettes for sale on the street. But the port has silted up over the centuries and is now of minor importance.

There is a cemetery to the east of the city at LINGSHAN where foreigners who died in Quanzhou were buried. The first two interred at the site were disciples of the prophet Mohammed, sent to China to propagate the teachings of Islam in the seventh century A.D. Their tombs are halfway up the hill, below a small pavilion.

The most impressive temple in town is the KAI YUAN TEMPLE, founded in the seventh century. It features two pagodas which were originally erected at that time, but rebuilt in the thirteenth century. There is also an interesting mosque built about 1000 years ago by Quanzhou's once-large Muslim community. Near to the Kai Yuan Temple is a museum housing the remains of a ship from the twelfth or thirteenth century that was uncovered recently, in the cabin of which were found herbs and spices.

Quanzhou experienced great disruption during the Cultural Revolution, although there are few details available of what exactly happened. The town is also the ancestral home of most of the overseas Chinese from Fujian Province, a fact which accounts for the free-wheeling economic activities there. The main street of Quanzhou is one of the liveliest in China.

The *Overseas Chinese Hotel* is centrally located, not far from the bus station. Take a pedi-cab.

Xiamen (Amoy)

This is the most interesting 'open' city in Fujian. Its name causes some problems: the two characters which make it up are pronounced 'Xiamen' in the national Chinese dialect (Mandarin) and 'Amoy' in the local dialect.

The town was established in the fourteenth century, and became of crucial strategic importance in the mid-seventeenth century when the Chinese forces still resisting the invasion of the Manchus gathered there under the command of Zheng Chenggong, a brilliant strategist known in the West as Koxinga. Using the city as a base, Zheng fought a long war with the Manchus, and at one point was on the verge of capturing Nanking. But in the end, he was forced to retreat back to Xiamen, and in 1661 set sail from there with his fleet and attacked

Taiwan, then under the control of the Dutch. He set upon the main Dutch settlement, Casteel Zeelandia, not far from today's Tai'an on the west coast, and besieged it for six months before the Dutch finally surrendered.

Zheng hoped to use Taiwan as a stepping stone to restore the Ming dynasty and drive the Manchus out of China, but it was not to be. He died in 1663, and the Manchus finally conquered Taiwan a couple of decades later, making it an integral part of the Chinese empire for the first time. The parallel with the Nationalist Chinese is remarkable. They were also driven from mainland China, retreated to Taiwan, and hope one day to return in victory. But, as with Zheng Cheng-gong, it is almost certainly a dream which will never be fulfilled.

Xiamen was one of the four Treaty Ports opened to foreign trade under the terms of the Treaty of Nanking in 1842, and developed into an important trading centre, which it remains today.

The city is lively and bustling, and the downtown area is a great place to walk around, especially in the evening. It seems to have more nightlife than the rest of China put together. People stroll around the streets, eat at stalls by the side of the road, go to the cinema or to one of the many restaurants and wine shops. The architecture of the central city area is all pre-1949 – two-, three- and four-storey buildings with colonnaded walkways underneath, very much like the China-towns of many Southeast Asian cities. When the foreigners moved in during the 1840s, they built their little colonial quarter on an island next to Xiamen, called GULANGYU. Foreign powers controlled it until the end of the Second World War. Full of old-style European man-sions and consulates, it can be reached by ferry from Xiamen.

Not far away is another island, QUEMOY, which the Nationalist Chinese have managed to hold on to. It is a fortress, honeycombed with underground tunnels and caves which house an estimated 50000 troops, all pledged to fight the Communist 'bandits', as the Nationalists still call them. The Nationalists on Quemoy and the Communist batteries on the mainland used to shell each other reg-ularly, at first with live ammunition and later with shells filled with propaganda leaflets. But even that stopped in 1979.

In 1981, Xiamen was named as a Special Economic Zone, one of four or five in south China in which investors get special benefits. The city is also being developed for a bigger role as a tourist destination, and an airport is due to open in mid-1983.

Of the tourist sights in Xiamen, the best is probably Gulangyu. In addition to the European buildings, there is also the ruin of the castle used by Zheng Chenggong while preparing for his invasion of Taiwan. The ZHENG CHENGGONG MEMORIAL HALL is nearby. Xiamen itself has a couple of nice parks, both in the northwest part of the city – the WANSHI (ten thousand stones) PARK, and the ZHONGSHAN PARK which contains several temples. A few miles outside Xiamen to the southeast is one of China's oldest temples, the NANPUTUO TEMPLE built in the ninth century A.D.

How to get there and where to stay

Xiamen is linked to the national railway network, and there are buses north to Fuzhou. An airport has been under construction for some time, and should be open by the end of 1983. A local steamer also makes regular trips to Hong Kong.

The main hotel used by foreigners is the *Overseas Chinese Hotel* (Huaqiao Daxia) on Zhongshan Lu (take a No. 3 bus from the railway station, get off at fifth stop and keep walking; the hotel is on the left, the tallest building in Xiamen). A nicer place to stay is the *Gulangyu Guesthouse* (25 Huangyan Lu) on the island but, apparently, it is occasionally used for conferences, during which times it is closed to foreign tourists.

GANSU PROVINCE

Lanzhou

Lanzhou, the capital of Gansu Province, has long been a strategically important link on the Silk Road, and has been used for centuries as a garrison town and supply post. A railway line linking the northwest more firmly to China proper was constructed through Lanzhou in the early 1950s, and the city quickly became an important industrial centre. One unfortunate side-effect of this is that Lanzhou has become arguably the most heavily polluted city in China, admittedly in the face of stiff competition. The city, built in a valley on the upper reaches of the Yellow River, now has a population of over two million people.

There is little to see in the way of formal tourist attractions. On the north bank of the river is BAITA SHAN (white pagoda mountain) which can be climbed to the small temple on top. A panoramic view of the city and its blanket of chemicals awaits those who bother.

The PROVINCIAL MUSEUM is on Xijin Lu, opposite the Friendship Hotel.

However, as in many other cities, probably the most interesting thing to do in Lanzhou is walk round the streets and people-watch.

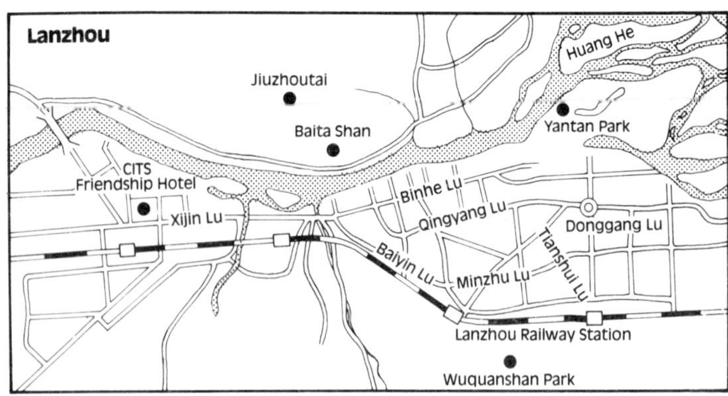

There are also some interesting free markets here and there.

The main excursion from Lanzhou is to BINGLINGSI up the Yellow River where there are spectacular Buddhist statues, dating from the Tang and Song dynasties, carved into the rock cliffs facing the river. To get there, you have to hire a boat, which can be expensive, but the carvings are magnificent.

How to get there and where to stay
Lanzhou is accessible by air from Peking, and is a major rail junction. Railway lines go northwest towards Xinjiang, southeast towards Xi'an and northeast along the Yellow River towards Baotou and Huhehot in Inner Mongolia.

Most people stay in the *Friendship Hotel* (Yonyi Binguan), a typical Soviet-style structure on Xijin Lu to the west of the downtown area. (Take a No. 1 bus or No. 3 trolley from the railway station. The hotel is on the right.)

Dunhuang

Near this desert town in Gansu Province is a Buddhist shrine which has become the centre of the most bitter debate in central Asian archaeology, a debate similar to that which surrounds the Elgin marbles, originally from the Parthenon but now in the British Museum.

Dunhuang was the last stop for caravans heading out of China on the Silk Road linking China with central Asia and, at the other extreme, Europe. Fifteen miles (24 kilometres) to the southeast of the

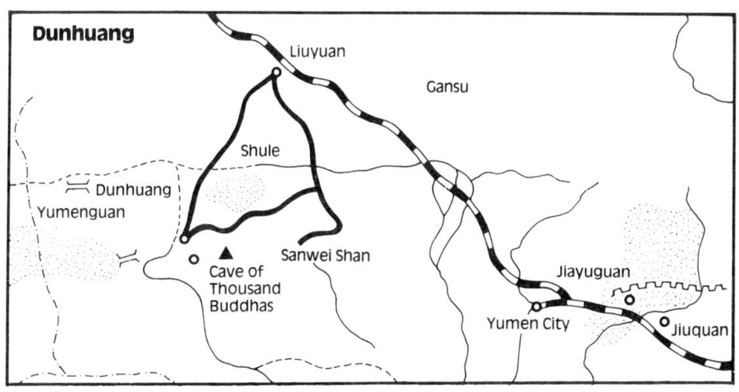

town of Dunhuang is the CAVE OF A THOUSAND BUDDHAS, a shrine at which travellers would either pray, or give thanks, for a safe journey, depending on the direction in which they were going. Like other oases and townships along the Silk Road, Dunhuang flourished as a centre of Buddhist culture in the fourth and fifth centuries A.D., and several hundred caves and grottoes were cut out of the sandstone cliffs and elaborately decorated with Buddhist statues and murals.

These priceless works of art alone give Dunhuang a place in history, but what really makes it stand out was the hoard of Buddhist paintings, documents, books and manuscripts found in one of the caves in 1900. The hidden library was found by accident by a Taoist monk named Wang Yuan, in a small room that had apparently been bricked up in the eleventh century to prevent the contents falling into the hands of invading barbarians. There they had lain for 800 years, protected by the bricks and by the dry desert air which prevented the delicate paper from disintegrating.

When he passed through Dunhuang in 1907, the famous British/Hungarian explorer Sir Aurel Stein happened to hear a rumour about this hoard and decided to try to find it. After a long wait, he finally found the monk Wang Yuan and gradually gained his trust to the point where Wang allowed him to inspect the contents of the secret library.

In his book, *On Ancient Central Asian Tracks*, Sir Aurel described how the priest opened the rough door leading to 'the rock-carved recess where the great trove lay hidden':

> The sight disclosed in the dim light of the priest's little oil lamp made my eyes open wide. Heaped up in layers, but without any order, there appeared a solid mass of manuscript bundles rising to ten feet from the floor and filling, as subsequent measurement showed, close on 500 cubic feet.

Stein eagerly began examining this archaeological gold mine, consisting largely of Buddhist texts in Chinese, Tibetan and many other central Asian languages, some known, some unknown. There were also paintings on silk and linen, and what may be the earliest printed book still in existence, printed in the year 868. An incredible haul. Stein convinced the monk to part with a large section of the library in return for a donation, amounting to £130, towards the restoration of some of the grottoes. For that sum, he carried away 24 packing cases of manuscripts and five others filled with paintings, embroideries and other art relics, all of which he deposited in the British Museum.

A French explorer who passed by Dunhuang the following year also bought a quantity of the manuscripts from the monk but, soon after, news of the discovery filtered back to the imperial court in Peking which ordered that the remainder of the library be transported to the capital. Stein, who was of course anxious to defend himself against the charge of theft, said that the priest had told him later that the manuscripts had been taken away in carts 'packed in a very perfunctory manner. A good deal of pilfering occurred while the carts were still waiting at the Dunhuang Yamen [government office], for whole bundles of fine Buddhist roles were, in 1914, brought to me there for sale.' Stein said that, on his return in 1914, the priest expressed regret at not having accepted Stein's original offer for the whole collection *en bloc*.

Stein's removal of this huge hoard of manuscripts has earned him the hatred of many Chinese people who see him as a symbol of all the foreigners who humiliated and plundered China in the waning years of the Manchu dynasty. But there is the question of what would have happened to the library if Stein had left it where it was. A large part of it would probably have been looted by local Chinese and sold off or destroyed. According to Peter Hopkirk in his interesting book, *Foreign Devils on the Silk Road*, it took the world's greatest experts in the British Museum seven years, using techniques akin to brain surgery, to restore some of the Buddhist paintings.

Some say the manuscripts should now be returned to China. Others say the manuscripts are likely to be better preserved in the British Museum than in their country of origin, and are available there for study by a far greater number of scholars than they would be if they were returned. The debate continues.

There are just under 500 caves and grottoes in the Dunhuang complex, but only 40 of them are open to visitors. Photographs of the murals inside are sometimes forbidden and sometimes allowed after the payment of huge sums of money. Cave No. 17 is the place where the manuscripts were found, while No. 462, known as the Mizong Cave, has erotic Buddhist art murals on its walls. The latter is closed to all except the most privileged visitors, but give it a try.

Dunhuang may be famous and its history fascinating, but many visitors find it a disappointment. For a start, it can be expensive to get to, and the three-hour drive from the train station is very uncomfortable. Once there, most of the caves are out-of-bounds and the ones that are open are dark inside, in some cases making it virtually impossible to see any of the murals and statues clearly.

Getting to the caves can be difficult. There is sometimes a local bus leaving from the traffic circle at 8.00 a.m. You can rent bicycles from the hotel, but the ride would be murder in the heat of summer. You can also rent a taxi or a jeep from the hotel. All foreigners are supposed to leave the cave area at lunchtime and return to the guesthouse, primarily, it would seem, to allow the local hawk-eyed custodians a chance to have an afternoon nap. However, there is a noodle shop at the caves where you may be able to get something to eat if you insist on staying.

Close by the town is an area of sand dunes, and a beautiful lake (although one person who swam in it said the bottom is covered with broken glass).

How to get there and where to stay

An important preliminary fact: Dunhuang is 'closed' to tourists from November to 1 April.

An airport has been built near Dunhuang, and scheduled flights now link the town with Lanzhou twice a week. The traditional way of getting there, however, is by road from Liuyuan, the closest stop on the Urumqi–Lanzhou railway line, about 100 miles (160 kilometres) to the north. There are two local buses a day from Liuyuan to Dunhuang, one at about 7.30 a.m. the other at about noon, from the local bus station (along the main street and on the left). For the return trip to Liuyuan, you should buy your ticket in advance at the bus station. Alternatively, it costs about 75 yuan to rent a jeep to take you to Dunhuang town. There is a small, dirty hotel in Liuyuan if you decide to stay overnight. Another possibility is to take the bus to Dunhuang from Jiuquan (passing through Jiayuguan) which takes about 11 hours (for details of where to get the bus in Jiayuguan, see the next entry).

The main hotel in Dunhuang is the *Dunhuang Guesthouse* (left out of the bus station, then right) where a bed costs six yuan.

Jiayuguan

For centuries, this town marked the northwest extremity of China and the beginning of the central Asian unknown. The Great Wall once extended beyond Jiayuguan, but the present fortress was built in 1372 during the Ming dynasty, and has from then on been considered to be the end of the wall. In their book, *The Gobi Desert*, two intrepid missionaries who lived in this barren area of northwest China for many years in the 1930s, Mildred Cable and Francesca French, gave a fascinating description of Jiayuguan as it was in those now far-off pre-Communist days. The book has been long out of print, and is worth quoting at length.

The two nuns described the three main gates to the fortress, one of which faces east towards the oasis of Jiuquan (spring of wine) about ten miles (16 kilometres) to the east.

> Every day, soldiers were galloping through the gate and over the plain to fetch supplies of pleasant food for the Governor and his ladies. Their horses clattered through the little crooked street but the old residents, sitting at their counters, exchanged not a word with the youthful riders. News of matters outside their own gates meant nothing to them, nor had they any requirements which were not met by their own meagre supplies. Even the opium from the poppy patch by the side of the stream was sufficient for their dope.
>
> The most important door was on the farther side of the fortress, and it might be called Travellers Gate, though some spoke of it as the Gate of Sighs. It was a deep archway tunnelled into the thickness of the wall where footsteps echoed and re-echoed. Every traveller toward the northwest passed through this gate, and it opened out on that great and always mysterious waste called the Desert of Gobi.
>
> The long archway was covered with writing and anyone with sufficient knowledge to appreciate Chinese penmanship could see at once that these were the work of men of scholarship who had fallen on an hour of the deepest distress. Who were the writers of this Anthology of Grief? Some were heavy-hearted exiles, others were disgraced officials, and some were criminals no longer tolerated within China's borders. Torn from all they loved on earth and banished with dishonoured name to the dreary regions outside, they stood awhile within the tomb-like vault, to add their moan to the pitiful dirge of the Gate of Sights.

Travellers setting out would throw a stone at a part of the fortress wall to test their luck. If it rebounded, it was believed the traveller would return safely. If it did not . . .

How to get there and where to stay

Jiayuguan is situated on the main railway line from Lanzhou to Urumqi, about 500 miles (800 kilometres) from Lanzhou. The city has grown considerably in the past 30 years, but there is little to see except for the old fort. There is only one hotel, in which rooms can be rented for five yuan a day. A bus for the fort leaves from in front of the hotel every day at 9.30 a.m. and returns at 11.30 a.m.

There is a bus to Jiuquan from a bus stop just north of the traffic circle next to the hotel. For the bus to Dunhuang, walk east from the hotel, then north to a major intersection of several roads. The Dunhuang bus terminus is on the left.

GUANGDONG (Kwangtung) PROVINCE

The people of Guangdong Province, known to the outside world as the Cantonese, have always been independent-minded and proud of their distinctive dialect and customs, often very different from those of north China. The exotic eating habits of the Cantonese are, for many northerners, conclusive evidence that they are the products of intermarriage with the snake-eating 'barbarian' natives who once inhabited the area. The province has been a source of rebellion for centuries, and the appearance of large numbers of Europeans off the Guangdong coast in the early nineteenth century served to make it even more volatile.

The first European settlement on the China coast was established by the Portuguese in 1557 at Macao, to the south of Canton, the provincial capital. Then came the opium traders and the first Opium War in 1839, a result of which Canton, or Guangzhou as it is known in China, was opened up to foreign trade and Hong Kong island was ceded in perpetuity to Britain.

Guangdong was the starting-point for the biggest uprising to occur in China in the nineteenth century, the Taiping Rebellion, led by a peasant born in the province named Hong Xiuquan, who proclaimed himself to be the younger brother of Jesus Christ and wanted to establish a 'Kingdom of Heavenly Peace' in China. The rebellion was finally crushed in 1864 only with the help of the foreign powers who decided that they would prefer to deal with the corrupt and weak Manchu dynasty than with the unpredictable Taipings, even though they did claim to be Christians.

Another famous revolutionary born in Guangdong was Sun Yat-sen, the leader of the revolt which toppled the Manchu dynasty in 1911 and established the Republic of China.

Guangdong is the ancestral homeland of most Chinese people living overseas. The Cantonese have been emigrating for a century and a half, mostly to Southeast Asia and North America, but just about every country in the world seems to have a Chinese community these days, and virtually all of them are composed of Cantonese people.

South China was once settled by aboriginal tribes who were systematically driven out or killed by the Chinese as they advanced down from the north more than 1000 years ago. Pockets of these people still exist in remote areas of south China, including some in Guangdong.

The province saw some of the most furious factional fighting during the Cultural Revolution of the late 1960s, during which period it was virtually sealed off from the British colony of Hong Kong. However, after 1978, with the rise of Deng Xiaoping and the decision to adopt an 'open door' economic policy, contacts between Hong Kong and Guangdong began to multiply once more. Almost every family in the southern portion of Guangdong has relatives in Hong Kong, and huge sums of money are remitted back into China by them every month.

In addition, many Hong Kong people make regular trips into China and bring with them consumer goods not readily available on the mainland, including colour televisions, jeans and cooking oil, to give to their relatives. 'Bourgeois' influences are therefore very strong in the area. Hong Kong television has a large audience in south China despite numerous attempts by the provincial authorities to pull down the 'fish-bone' TV antennae people suspend over their houses to catch the latest episode of *Dallas* or *Charlie's Angels*.

Many Guangdong people see Hong Kong as a sort of paradise or refuge, and hundreds of thousands have escaped to the British colony over the years in the hope of building better lives there. There was a particularly large surge in the number of refugees in 1979 and 1980, when an estimated 500 000 Guangdong people moved to Hong Kong, either legally or illegally.

Canton (Guangzhou)

This is the first city that most travellers to China visit, but to really appreciate how extraordinary Canton is in the context of China, it should really be left to the very end of the trip. The heavy influence of capitalist Hong Kong, apparent in just about every facet of the city's life, along with the innate 'different-ness' of the Cantonese, makes Canton something special.

Generally speaking, Canton is a messy, dilapidated city. Most of the buildings seem to be pre-1949, or else sub-standard post-1949, and everything looks in need of repair and a coat of paint. The city's saving grace is its colour and vitality (that is, by the standards of China; compared to Hong Kong, life in Canton crawls along at a snail's pace, which many consider to be one of its attractions).

The best thing to do in Canton is just to walk round the streets as much as possible and soak in the atmosphere. Watch a street barber in action, people queueing for coal, women washing clothes under public water pumps, cyclists on the crowded streets, sampans on the Pearl River, the large free markets, the hawkers selling their wares – there is something happening wherever you look. If you are in the right place at the right time, you may see some black-marketeering in progress – suspicious young men offering foreign cigarettes or calculators for sale. I once came upon a few youths operating a gambling stall near a ferry terminal – three cards face down, place a yuan on the one you think is the king and, if you win, you get your money back and the same amount again. I won two yuan.

The best streets to walk round are down by the river. The small island of SHAMIAN (sandbank) is interesting. It was the foreigners' enclave in the old Canton, and is filled with houses of worship and once-elegant villas, churches and mansions which are now looking ramshackle but proletarian. There are two bridges leading to the island, both of which in the old days were closed to Chinese not actually working there. A thick undergrowth of waist-high ferns along the centre of the main street on the island used to be a favourite haunt of young couples in the evenings until the unromantic city authorities chopped them all down.

Near Shamian is the CULTURAL PARK, a wonderful place to visit in the early evening. You pay a small sum to get inside and can then wander about, listen to a variety performance, watch people roller skating or playing chess, stroll through art exhibitions or just people-watch. The park is full of people every evening, and provides a welcome centre of entertainment in a very crowded and amusement-starved city. Make sure you go early – it closes at 9.00 p.m. Also close to Shamian is the QINGPING MARKET, famous for the wide variety of wildlife on sale, including at least one endangered species – the pangolin (a sort of Chinese armadillo).

Apart from walking, the best way to see Canton is by bus. These are usually crowded, but if you get on at the terminus, you can be sure of

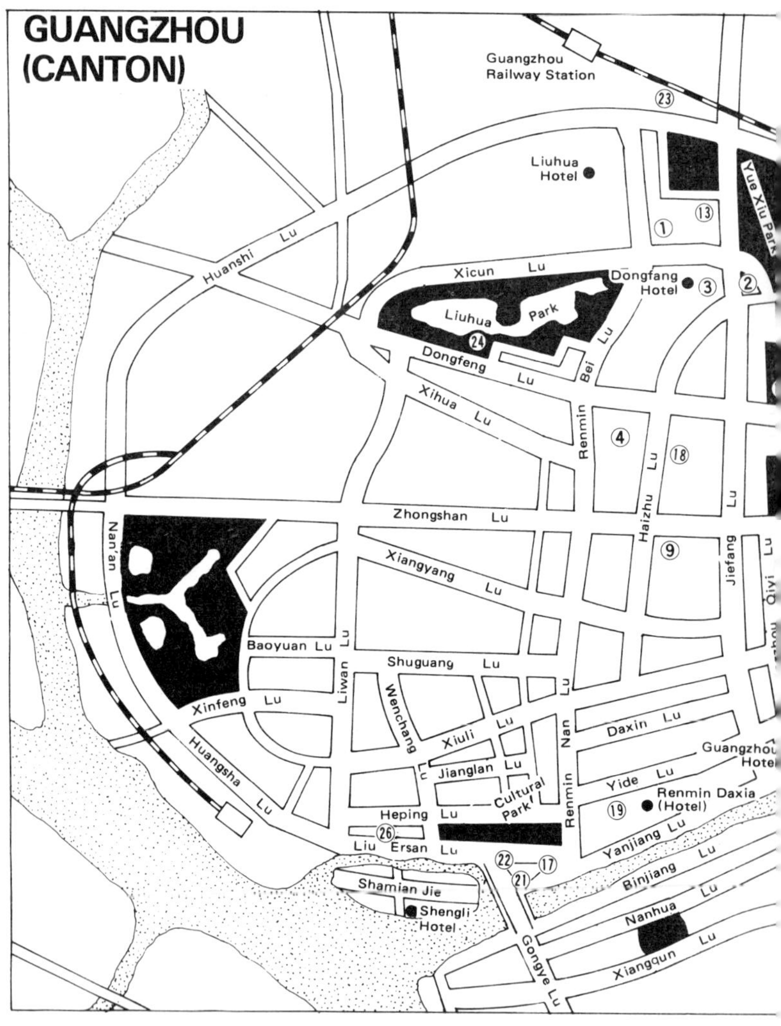

1 Chinese Export Commodities Fair
2 Civil Aviation Administration (CAAC)
3 Public Security Bureau (Foreign Affairs Section)
4 Guangzhou No. 1 People's Hospital
5 Guangzhou Zoo
6 Zhenhai Tower and Guangdong Historical Museum
7 Statue of Five Goats
8 Haizhu Square
9 Huaisheng Mosque
10 Guangzhou Uprising Memorial
11 National Peasant Movement Institute
12 Sun Yat Sen Memorial Hall
13 Guangzhou Gymnasium

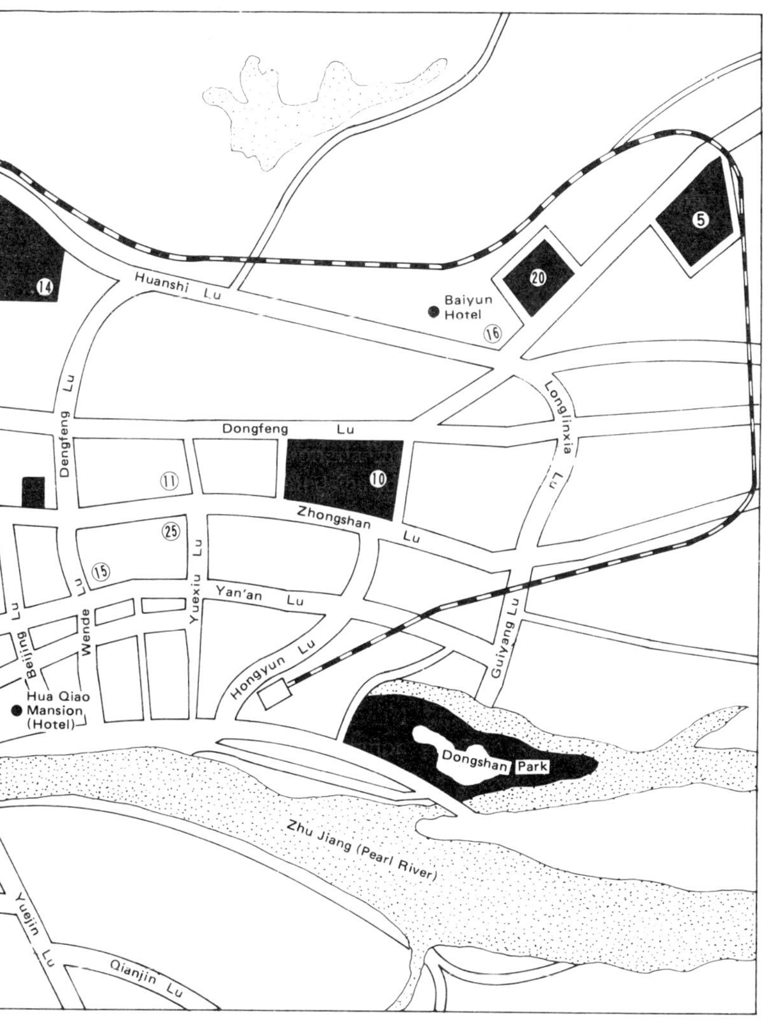

14 People's Stadium
15 Antique Shop
16 Friendship Store
17 Nanfang Department Store
18 Temple of the Six Banyan Trees (Liurong Temple)
19 Roman Catholic Church
20 Mausoleum of the 72 Martyrs (at Huanghuagang)
21 Guangdong Post Office
22 Guangdong Cable Bureau
23 China International Travel Service (CITS)
24 Children's Palace
25 Guangdong Provincial Museum
26 Qingping Market

a seat. There are also ferries crossing the Pearl River to other parts of the city.

No matter which hotel you stay in, a visit to the DONGFANG HOTEL is an absolute must. It has become a symbol of the new New China, of the 'open door' economic policy and of the more tolerant attitude towards 'decadence', although the hotel's management would probably be appalled at such a description. The Dongfang's nightclub and its Hong Kong-style restaurant have to be seen to be believed. And surely no trip to Canton would be complete without a few rounds of Space Invaders in the games room. You can have your hair done in the exclusive hairdressing salon, or else relax in a real sauna. In 1981, the management even installed some poker machines to keep guests amused, but they were removed after only a couple of weeks when someone realised that they constituted a form of gambling.

Close by the Dongfang Hotel, opposite the entrance to Yuexiu Park is another smaller park called the PUYUAN (orchid) GARDEN which, apart from being very beautiful, has a connection with Mao's wife, Jiang Qing. In the early 1970s, Madame Mao decided she wanted to tell her personal story to someone, and chose the American Sinologist and academic Roxanne Witke. She granted Ms Witke a series of audiences in the Puyuan Garden which is filled with thousands of orchids, and reminisced about her long life as an actress in Shanghai, her journey to Yan'an, her meeting there with Mao and her rise to power in the 1960s at the extreme radical end of the political spectrum. Ms Witke eventually wrote a book called *Comrade Chiang Ching*, based on these interviews, in spite of the intense pressure from the Chinese leadership to stop its publication.

Of the regular tourist sights, the most interesting are the GUANGDONG HISTORICAL MUSEUM, which is in the five-storey pagoda on the top of a hill in Yuexiu Park, and the SIX BANYAN TREE TEMPLE. The trees have disappeared, but the temple stands, apparently the place where a Buddhist monk named Hui Neng delivered the Platform Scripture, the most significant Chinese contribution to the Buddhist canon. The temple is to the south of the Dongfang Hotel, near Haizhu Road.

Canton is, of course, famous for its Cantonese cuisine although, these days, the best Cantonese food is available not in Canton, but in Hong Kong. There are a number of very pleasant garden restaurants around the city where you can sit and eat a meal, or have a morning tea with Cantonese dim sum, dumplings and delicacies which come in dozens of different varieties. The best are the *Nanyuan Restaurant*

(120 Qianjin Lu), the *Beiyuan Restaurant* (439 Dengfeng Bei Lu) and the *Banxi Restaurant* (151 Xiangyang Yi Lu). If you want to eat in the classy foreigners' sections, you should always book in advance. If you want to rough it with the locals, go early.

Cantonese food may be better overall in Hong Kong, but Canton still beats the British colony in the field of exotic dishes, mostly because of a lack of legal inhibitions, which prohibit the sale of dog meat and other such items in Hong Kong's restaurants. If you like to try some unusual foods, the best place to go is the *Wild Game Restaurant* (Ye Weixiang, 249 Beijing Lu) where the menu reads very much like a zoo guide.

Always book before you go: the restaurant is very popular, especially with Hong Kong Chinese. Dog meat is the speciality, and the menu, thoughtfully printed in both English and Chinese, includes such mouth-watering dishes as 'grainy dog meat with chilli and scallion sauce' and 'dog meat ready to be cooked in earthen pot over charcoal stove at table'. If you're unhappy at the idea of canine cuisine, there are plenty of other things to go for – braised python, civet cat, bear's paw, 'steamed old cat' or perhaps 'braised guinea pig (whole)'. Most meals at the Wild Game Restaurant begin with Dragon-Tiger-Phoenix Soup, a concoction of snake meat, cat meat and chicken. Monkey dishes are a regular item, and for those with hearts of stone, it is possible to go and view the ingredients cowering in cages near the main door. Just in case you ever have a spare monkey and feel like having a go, one waiter said that the animal should be drowned and then boiled for three to four hours. Cantonese cuisine used to be famous for live monkey brains served straight out of the monkey's skull on to your plate, but it is now rarely heard of. 'Eating live monkey brains is very cruel,' the waiter said. 'But we do serve them boiled.'

Other tourist sights of interest are: the NATIONAL PEASANT MOVEMENT INSTITUTE (Zhongshan Lu) where Mao taught for a few months in 1926, the CANTON ZOO (Xianlie Lu), the CATHOLIC CATHEDRAL (in a back street close to the river, east of Renmin Nan Lu) and the HUAISHENG MOSQUE (Zhongshan Lu).

The most common excursion from Canton is to the town of FOSHAN (Buddha mountain), about 20 miles (32 kilometres) to the west. Visitors are usually shown a ceramics factory, an arts and crafts workshop and a large ancestral temple which is now purely a tourist spot.

Another excursion is to the CONGHUA HOT SPRINGS about 50 miles (80 kilometres) north of Canton. The springs are in a pleasant mountain area in which a number of tourist hotels and villas have been built. It is said that China's present leader Deng Xiaoping spent several months here after he was purged for the second time in April 1976.

People travelling on their own will need to know that the Public Security Bureau is on Jiefang Lu. That is where you have to go to apply for your travel permits and visa extensions.

Bus and trolley bus routes

* The No. 3 trolley bus travels between Yuexiu Park in the north of the city to the Cultural Park near the river.
* The No. 31 bus starts near the railway station and heads south, passes the Cultural Park and crosses the river via the People's Bridge.
* The No. 7 bus starts near the railway station and heads southeast down Jiefang Beilu and Beijing Lu, ending up at a river wharf at the eastern end of town.

How to get there and where to stay

Canton is probably the city with the best connections in China. There are planes, trains and hoverferries to and from Hong Kong, and if you are really pushed for time and are willing to pay the price, it is possible to rent a taxi to take you to the border. The China Travel Service operates daily buses to and from Zhuhai, a little town within walking distance of the Portuguese territory of Macao.

The best hotel in town is the *Dongfang Hotel*, favoured by businessmen because of its wide range of facilities and its location just opposite the Canton Export Commodities Fair building. The hotel has dormitories as well as luxury suites. (Take a No. 7 bus from the railway station, and get off at the second stop.) Other hotels regularly used by foreigners include the *Baiyun* (on Huanshi Lu) and the *Renmin Daxia* (people's mansion; 207 Changdi Lu).

Budget travellers usually stay at the *Liuhua Hotel* directly opposite the railway station, where a dormitory bed rents for six or eight yuan, depending on which wing you choose. The Liuhua is a good place to meet other budget travellers and to gather the latest information on the China travel situation.

Shenzhen

Just across the border from Hong Kong, Shenzhen is being developed as a 'special economic zone' to attract foreign investment, and is also becoming a major destination for day-tours organised by the China Travel Service in Hong Kong, for which no visa is required. People who join one of the tours and think they are going to see China might as well not bother. Shenzhen is trying so hard to emulate Hong Kong economically and socially that it hardly seems like a part of mainland China any more.

A large amount of construction work is under way in the town. Several hundred Hong Kong companies have signed manufacturing deals, making use of the cheaper, socialist labour.

For the casual tourist, there is not much to do in Shenzhen except to look at the chaotic bustle of the town, have a meal and then cross the border back into Hong Kong. But at least you can say, if you do it, that you have been to China.

How to get there and where to stay

Shenzhen can be reached by train from Hong Kong or Canton. There is only one hotel which takes foreigners – the *Bamboo Garden* which is a joint venture with the Hong Kong company, Millie's. But it's not really worth staying. You might as well continue on to either Hong Kong or Canton and spend the night there.

Hainan Island

Hainan, lying off the south coast near Vietnam, is the second-largest Chinese island after Taiwan. For centuries, it has been a place of exile, and even today it is suffering from economic neglect, a scruffy sub-tropical backwater with coconut palms, beaches, picturesque mountain tribesmen and poverty.

The first inhabitants of Hainan were presumably the ancestors of the mountain people, the Li and Miao tribes, who have been retreating ever since the first Han Chinese appeared from the mainland. The traditional attitude of the Hans towards minority peoples is probably best summed up by the fact that, in the 1920s, a batch of the Li people were rounded up and displayed in cages in a park in Canton. Despite such abuse, the minorities have managed to retain their own separate cultures and languages.

The Li people, who number about 800 000, have seven different dialects but no writing system. Traditionally, they had a very easy-going code of sexual morality. Young people moved out of home early and had free sexual relations, and girls only married when they became pregnant. The Chinese Communists have imposed their puritanical moral code on the Li people during the past 30 years, but the more permissive sexual customs continue to some extent. Another Li custom was the tattooing of women's faces. One local told me that there were two explanations for this: some people say that it was considered beautiful, others say that the tattoos were first put on attractive girls to discourage Han Chinese from kidnapping them.

The Miaos, who number only 40 000, live in the remote mountain areas of central Hainan. Some are Protestants, most are apparently nomads, moving from one place to another in search of wild game. Most of the Han Chinese on Hainan seem to have immigrated to the island from Fujian Province a couple of centuries ago. Another wave of more than a million migrants arrived in the 1950s, many of them Cantonese people brought in to administer the island. Hainan's population in mid-1982 was 5.6 million people.

The Japanese occupied Hainan during the Second World War, and slaughtered thousands of people suspected of being sympathisers or members of the Communist guerrilla bands who formed the main resistance force. Monuments have been placed near some of the mass graves around the island. The most famous guerrilla band was the Red Detachment of Women which became the inspiration for one of Madame Mao's appalling 'revolutionary operas' during the late 1960s. After the war, the Communists continued to fight the Nationalists, and parts of central Hainan were 'liberated' as early as 1947. The main Communist forces, under the command of Marshal Lin Biao, invaded the island in 1950, and the remainder of the Nationalist garrison was evacuated to Taiwan.

Despite its excellent geographical location, varied natural resources and pleasant climate, Hainan is desperately under-developed. The island used to be covered by large tracts of virgin forest, but huge areas have been short-sightedly chopped down, leaving much of the centre of the island barren and highly susceptible to soil erosion. In 1978, the average annual income of peasants there was about 50 yuan, one of the lowest in China, and although the authorities claim that this tripled to 150 yuan by 1982, the people on Hainan are still very poor. In 1980, the island administration was given permission to start soliciting foreign investment, and a number of projects were started, including an oil palm plantation and a duck farm set up by an Australian company.

The authorities have big plans for tourism on Hainan, and obviously see it as China's future Hawaii. At present, things are very primitive and development is likely to be slow, but the potential is there. There are some beautiful white-sand, palm-fringed beaches on the south coast near Sanya, and some of the mountain scenery in the centre of the island is magnificent. One problem for tourist development, however, is the presence of large numbers of military (particularly air and naval) bases on the island, both to watch Vietnam and to patrol the South China Sea, full of islands claimed by China and other countries. The whole western coast of Hainan is supposed to be off-limits to foreigners, and military units are very much in evidence almost wherever you go.

Travel around the island is not difficult. There is a comprehensive local bus network, and there are towns at regular intervals along most of the main roads. The local Chinese hotels along the way range from basic to filthy, but they are cheap, while the China Travel Service operates hotels in some places.

HAIKOU is the island's main city and the site of the only civilian airport on Hainan. The centre of town is cluttered and frenetic, and probably resembles the Hong Kong of 40 years ago. Private enterprise seems to have taken over the streets, with hawkers selling all sorts of things – incense, clothes, door charms to drive away evil spirits, 'decadent' music tapes imported from Hong Kong, peanuts, coconut sweets, mangy bits of meat covered with flies. Transport around the town is easy. There are motorised pedi-cabs everywhere which are cheap and fast, but agree on a price before getting in. The streets are still alive in the evenings, and there are a couple of large markets where you can eat at food stalls.

Just outside Haikou is the TOMB OF HAI RUI, a Ming dynasty official who unwittingly sparked off the Cultural Revolution. A vice-mayor of Peking, Wu Han, wrote an opera in the early 1960s called *Hai Rui Relieved of Office* in which an official spoke up for the people before the emperor and was exiled. Chairman Mao interpreted the opera as a personal attack on himself (as it almost certainly was) for purging the former Defence Minister Peng Dehuai in 1959. An article published in 1966 criticising the opera is generally seen as the first shot in the Cultural Revolution, during which the opera's author, Wu Han, was persecuted to death and Hai Rui's tomb almost completely destroyed by vandals. It is now being restored.

Down the east coast, there are the towns of WENCHANG and JIAJI, and the XINGLONG STATE FARM inhabited largely by overseas Chinese and Vietnamese–Chinese refugees who fled from Vietnam in 1978. The state farm guesthouse features a huge villa built in 1970 on the orders, it is believed, of the late Marshal Lin Piao. The villa, designated Building No. 1, contains the biggest bed you've probably ever seen and a superbly decadent marble bath that is large enough to hold a party in. You can rent the villa if you want. Mao's wife, Jiang Qing, visited the farm in 1970, and stayed in Room 202. The Vietnamese refugees there are a sad bunch of people, many of them angry and frustrated at landing up in China while many of their relatives are busy building new lives in the United States. Life is very hard in Hainan and they are very poor but, after all, they are refugees and are being treated much like ordinary Chinese peasants. Their tragedy is that they know that life can be different.

On the south coast is SANYA, the location of a large naval base, but also the prime potential site of Hainan's future tourist industry. The Dongfang Hotel in Canton is planning to build a branch hotel here, but the best place to stay will always be LUHUITOU, a resort a few miles outside town which features nice old villas, large rooms, a good restaurant and a beach a few minutes' walk away. Building No. 1 is where the Communist leaders, including Liu Shaoqi, have stayed over the years on their visits to this far-flung corner of their empire. Another good beach nearby is at DADONGHAI.

From Sanya, a road leads north through the mountains back to Haikou, passing through the minority-populated areas. Many of those in the main towns, BAOTING and QIONGZHONG, are Li people, but they are already very Han-ised. The real minorities live up in the mountains. In Qiongzhong, the hotel is close to the river. The local department store sells nice machine-made Li material very cheaply, the hand-made variety seems to be very expensive, at least for foreigners.

How to get there and where to stay

Most foreign tourists fly into Haikou from Canton, and direct flights from Hong Kong may be possible sometime soon. There are also ferries from Canton and from Zhenjiang, a town north of Haikou on the mainland. The Canton ferries leave from the Zhoutouzui ferry terminal southwest of the People's (Renmin) Bridge and take about a day to get to Haikou.

In Haikou, you may be able to get a room at the *No. 1 District Guesthouse* (Qu Yi Suo) on Fuhai Lu inside the local Communist Party headquarters. Accommodation there is spartan, but the grounds are very peaceful and beautiful. Otherwise, there is the *Overseas Chinese Hotel* closer to the centre of town which is cheap and dirty. There are plans to build a large modern hotel just outside Haikou called the *Qiongzhou Hotel*, complete with swimming pool and some sort of horse-racing track, and the first 200 rooms in this project are scheduled to be open by early 1984.

GUANGXI PROVINCE

Nanning

This pleasant, tree-filled town in southwest China is the capital of Guangxi Province, and in some ways feels more like Southeast Asia than China. The climate is semi-tropical, the countryside round about lush and green. The Guangxi area is populated by many minority races or 'nationalities' who controlled the area before the arrival of the Chinese from the north and for several centuries before the Mongol invasion in 1253, a kingdom based in northeast Thailand had control of most of the region. Nanning was provincial capital from 1914 to 1936 when local officialdom moved briefly up to the resort town of Guilin, but the capital was shifted back to Nanning after the Communist victory. Since then, the city has grown enormously and now has a population of over half a million.

During the early part of the Cultural Revolution of the late 1960s, Nanning and several other places in Guangxi were the scenes of pitched battles between rival political factions, and later between Red Guards and the army units sent in to restore order. Similar fighting occurred in many parts of China, but in Guangxi it was exacerbated by the fact that the various factions looted the trains taking guns and ammunition to North Vietnam for the war effort, and used the arms to attack their opponents. One resident told me that the entire area of Nanning in front of the railway station was virtually destroyed during artillery battles fought by the Red Guards.

Nanning again served as an important staging area for men and supplies during China's own Vietnam War in early 1979, when the Chinese army launched what was called a 'self-defence counter-attack' into Vietnamese territory. The Chinese troops seized a strip of territory along the border, several miles deep, reportedly at a huge cost in lives, to teach the Vietnamese a 'lesson' but they withdrew after a month. The border has remained tense ever since with both sides reporting a constant stream of armed clashes, mostly of a minor nature.

To the south of Nanning, on the Vietnamese border, is the ironically named FRIENDSHIP PASS where the war started. Until the 1950s, the pass had another name, one which perhaps illustrates the traditional attitude of the Chinese empire towards the people in Indo-China. It was called Zhennan Guan – 'Suppression of the South Pass'.

The majority race in Guangxi is the Zhuang, which numbers 13.3 million, according to the 1982 census. They have some cultural and linguistic ties with the Thais, but illiteracy is a major problem as the Zhuang language has no set writing system.

Guangxi cooking uses a lot of weird animals, and weird parts of animals, much in the same way as Cantonese cuisine. The most famous local alcohol, known as Hejie Jiu, features a large, pickled lizard floating in each bottle. Snakes, turtles and pangolins (a sort of

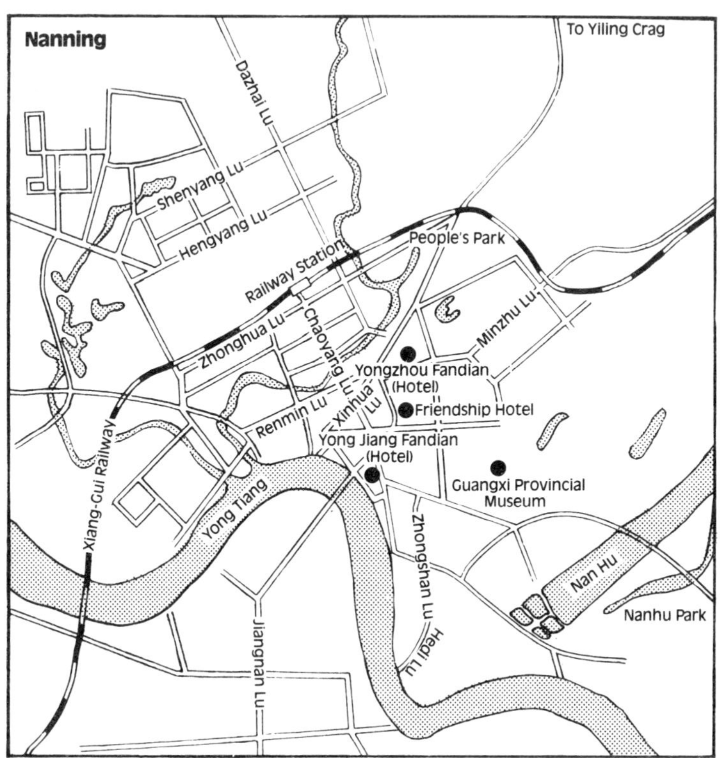

Chinese armadillo which is an endangered species) are all considered delicacies, but the most exotic Guangxi dish is called Chia San Jiao, literally 'Eat Three Squeals'. It consists of live rat embryos laid out on a plate. The dish's name is said to have originated from the fact that the animal squeals once when picked up with chopsticks, a second time when dipped in the accompanying sauce and a third (and last) time when it is popped into the mouth. Mmmm!

How to get there and where to stay
There are flights to Nanning from Canton, and it is also accessible by train from Liuzhou and Guilin to the north. There are three main hotels: the *Yongjiang Hotel* (Chaoyang Lu; take a No. 5 bus from the railway station) and the *Mingyuan Hotel* and *Youyi Hotel* (both on Minzhu Lu). If you are on your own, probably the best way of getting to the hotel is by a pedi-cab from the station. Agree on a price with the driver before starting out; at last report, the going rate was about 1.50 yuan to any of the hotels. Rooms in all three hotels can be rented for about 18 yuan a night.

Guilin (Kweilin)

With its picturesque limestone hills rising out of the rice paddy fields in imitation of a million Chinese paintings, Guilin is China's best-known tourist resort. It has been a favourite holiday spot for centuries, and any number of poets have composed ditties while meditating on the wonders of nature here displayed. 'The river forms a green silk ribbon, the mountains are like blue jade hairpins,' wrote one poet 1200 years ago. 'I have been to many famous places in the world, but none is more beautiful than Guilin,' said former US President Richard Nixon, also famous for his comment on the Great Wall (*see* p. 65).

Guilin is situated on the banks of the Li Jiang (Li River) and has a population of more than 300000. It was a centre of Chinese resistance during the Second World War, and Japanese bombing raids damaged large sections of it; however, there are still some picturesque streets left in the north of the town. A number of industries were established after the Communist victory including machine tools and electronics and, by the 1970s, were operating so successfully that the Li Jiang was becoming seriously polluted and the extraordinary crags that leap out of nowhere were being eroded by the heavy chemical pollution in the air. Steps have since been taken to clean up the offending factories.

There are many lovely sights to see in and around Guilin. Some of the best known are: REED FLUTE CAVE (Ludi Yan) in the northwest of the town, containing huge technicolour stalagmites and stalacites; FOLDED BROCADE HILL (Diecai Shn) and FUBUO SHAN in the northern part of the town next to the river; SEVEN STAR CRAG on the eastern bank of the river; and ELEPHANT TRUNK HILL to the south of the town.

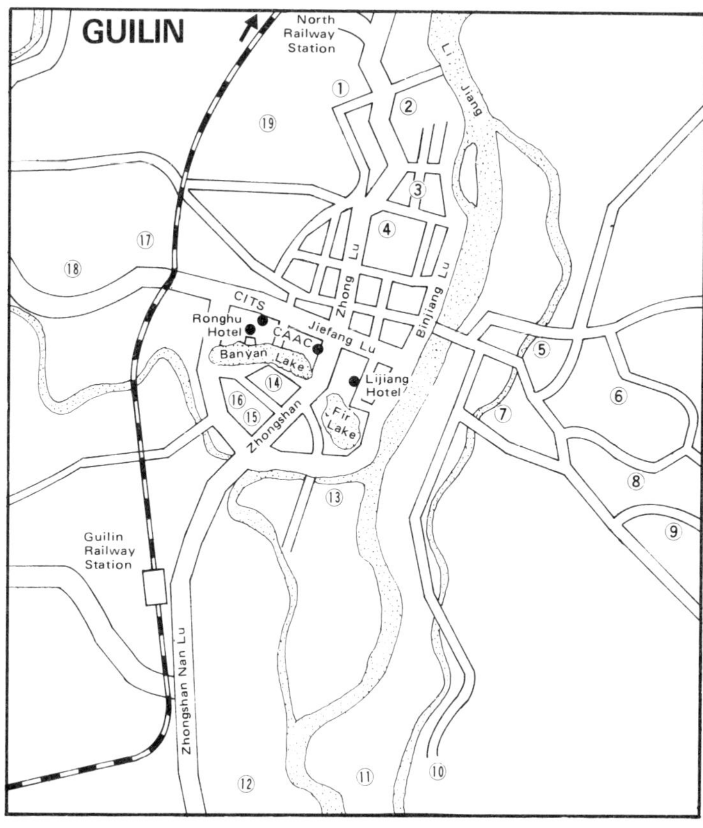

1 Treasure Hoard Hill (Baoji Shan)
2 Folded Brocade Hill (Diecai Shan)
3 Fubo Hill
4 Duxiu Peak
5 Flower Bridge
6 Seven Star (Qixing) Park
7 Crescent Moon Hill (Yueya Shan)
8 Zoo
9 Potted Landscape Area
10 Tunnelled Hill (Chuan Shan)
11 Pagoda Hill (Baota Shan)
12 South Creek Hill (Nanxi Shan)
13 Elephant Trunk Hill (Xiangbi Shan)
14 Friendship Store
15 Department Store
16 Antiques Store
17 Hidden Hill (Yin Shan)
18 West Hill (Xi Shan)
19 Old Man Mountain (Laoren Shan)

For budget travellers without a CTS guide and car, the following bus tour is suggested: take a No. 3 bus to Reed Flute Cave (which is the route terminus); from there, a No. 13 bus, get off at the fourth stop for Folded Brocade Hill; return to the same bus stop and go one more stop for Fubuo Shan; from there, take a No. 2 bus and get off at the third stop for Elephant Trunk Hill. For the Seven Star Park, take a No. 11 bus to its terminus.

The Friendship Store is on the main street (119 Zhongshan Zhong Lu), close to most of the city's other main shops.

Guilin is famous for its exotic foods, and most of the main hotels can provide a meal consisting of various strange beasts. The *Yueya Lou* (Moon Tooth Hall) *Restaurant* in the Seven Star Park also serves wild game meals; always book in advance. Another of Guilin's specialities is fermented beancurd. One shop that sells it is at 12 Zhongshan Zhong Lu.

No visit to Guilin would be complete without a cruise on the Li Jiang. CTS arranges five-hour boat trips every day from Guilin south to YANGSHUO, an interesting town about 30 miles (48 kilometres) south. Buses take passengers back to Guilin at the end of the day. The boat ride is expensive – 40 yuan a head – but the scenery is gorgeous. A tip for budget travellers: you might try taking a bus to Yangshuo and taking the boat (which costs only six yuan) back to Guilin. There is a small hotel in Yangshuo if you feel like spending the night there. One person I spoke to who had stayed there described its location as being 'down the main street on the left'.

How to get there and where to stay

There are flights to Guilin from Canton and Hong Kong, and trains from anywhere else on the China railway network.

The list of hotels is long, as befits an important tourist resort. The *Li Jiang Hotel* (1 Shahu Bei Lu) is a huge, modern hotel in the centre of the city with all mod-cons, but the restaurant is terrible. The *Ronghu Hotel* (17 Ronghu Bei Lu) is cheaper and is situated beside the two lakes in the south of the city. The *Guilin Hotel* (25 Zhongshan Zhong Lu; the hotel sign says 'Kweilin Hotel') is the one at which budget travellers usually stay. The dormitory is on the sixth floor.

If you're with CTS, getting from the railway station to your hotel is no problem. If you're by yourself, none of the hotels is more than half an hour's walk, but if you have a heavy load, take a No. 1 bus from the station and get off at the second stop for the Guilin Hotel.

Liuzhou (Liuchow)

This town in southwest China is a major rail junction and stopping-place on the way to or from such places as Nanning, Guilin and Sichuan Province. The countryside around the town is very pleasant, as is the countryside in the whole of southwest China.

The main tourist attractions are the DULE (pronounced Doo-luh) CAVES (take a No. 9 bus from opposite the Liujiang Hotel; the trip takes about 45 minutes), and the YUFENGSHAN PARK which provides an excellent view of the whole town (take a No. 9 bus from opposite the Liujiang Hotel; get off at the ninth stop, Renmin Nan Lu, then walk south for five minutes).

How to get there and where to stay

Liuzhou is only accessible by train. There are three or four hotels, all reasonably priced, the two main ones being the *Liuzhou Hotel* (1 Wenge Lu), and the *Liujiang Hotel* (72 Gongyuan Lu). Both hotels have special buses waiting to pick up passengers from some trains, and there are pedi-cabs at the station. A pedi-cab ride to one of the hotels should cost about 2.50 yuan.

GUIZHOU PROVINCE

Guiyang

A Chinese proverb says of this city in the mountains of southwest China: no three feet of earth are flat, no three days are sunny, and no one as three taels of silver. Like most Chinese proverbs, it doesn't translate very well, but the idea is that Guiyang, the capital of Guizhou Province, is hilly, wet and poor.

One well-travelled Hong Kong Chinese described Guiyang as being 'one of the two poorest cities I have seen in China' (the other being Baoji, a railway junction in western Shaanxi Province). Hong Kong Chinese are just about the only people who are able to make such a comparison: because of its poverty and backwardness, the whole of Guizhou Province including Guiyang city is off-limits to foreigners. However, there is a railway which passes through the city, joining Chongqing in Sichuan Province with Liuzhou in Guangxi Province to the south.

On the off-chance that Guiyang is opened up to tourism in the near future, I include the following information.

The city itself has little to offer in the way of tourist sights except for a couple of parks. One of them, known as DIXIA GONGYUAN (underground park), has a waterfall with a cave behind it which, it is claimed, was the home of the mythical Monkey-King of Chinese folklore who features in the classical novel *Xi You Ji* (Travels to the West). The best English version of this excellent fairy story is, by the way, *Monkey*, translated by Arthur Waley and available as a Penguin paperback.

There is one good excursion from Guiyang, and that is to see another waterfall, China's largest, about 60 miles (97 kilometres) west. The HUANGGUOSHU (yellow fruit tree) WATERFALL is situated close to the town of Anshan, and a tourist bus leaves from Xinlukou Zhan in Guiyang every Sunday morning; tickets for the round-trip cost eight yuan. Check the local branch of the China Travel Service for times.

How to get there and where to stay

I repeat, Guiyang is closed to foreigners at present, but it is connected to a number of other cities by plane, and there are regular trains.

There are two hotels in Guiyang. The *Yunyen Binguan* (1 Beijing Lu) is quite a distance from the railway station. If you're on your own, take the No. 1 bus, get off at the museum (buowuguan) stop and walk north for about three minutes. A room with a bathroom costs about ten yuan, and a dormitory bed four yuan. For the second hotel, the *Jinqiao* (gold bridge) *Fandian*, also take the No. 1 bus and get off at the Daximen (west gate) stop. Double rooms rent for nine yuan a bed.

HEBEI PROVINCE

Shijiazhuang

Shijiazhuang, a real challenge of a place-name for non-Chinese speakers, is the capital of Hebei Province, and ranks as one of the most featureless cities open to foreigners in China. The city owes its existence to the decision of the railway builders in the early twentieth century to make what was once a small village a stop on the north–south railway line to Peking. It now has a population of over 500 000, and a host of industries, including textiles.

It became the provincial capital by default. Tianjin always used to be the capital of Hebei, but the Peking government decided in the late 1960s that it was necessary to bring Tianjin more closely under central control and separated it from Hebei. The next largest city in the province was Shijiazhuang which therefore took on the honour of becoming capital.

Probably the most interesting place in the city is an orphanage which accommodates all the orphans from the 1976 earthquake in Tangshan. The FOSTERING THE REVOLUTION ORPHANAGE originally had 500 children under its care, and about 300 were still there in 1981. All the children have to go back to Tangshan, the place where their parents died, when they leave the orphanage, unless they pass the entrance examinations to some college or university. They all study very hard, and are not allowed to mix with children outside the hostel. Three baby girls found among the rubble after the earthquake could not be identified, and were given the surname 'Party'. The three, whose names roughly translate as 'Seedling fostered by the Party', 'Revolutionary Redness fostered by the Party' and 'New Generations fostered by the Party', sing songs for visitors with lyrics such as 'The Party is the sunlight and I am a flower.'

Close to Shijiazhuang is the village of XIBAOPUO from where Chairman Mao directed the civil war against the Nationalists in 1947–48. There is a memorial hall there, and according to the official city guide published in the late 1970s, 'China's wise leader, Chairman Hua, wrote an inscription for the Memorial Hall.' As Hua has now fallen from power. One can assume that the inscription is no longer there.

About 30 miles (48 kilometres) north of Shijiazhuang is a town called Zhengding which contains what are reputed to be the oldest monastery buildings still standing in China, the LONG XING MONASTERY, constructed around the eleventh century.

How to get there and where to stay
Shijiazhuang is the junction of four major railway lines. It is about 150 miles (240 kilometres) south of Peking, and the train trip from there takes about four hours.

The hotel used by foreigners is the *Shijiazhuang Guesthouse* on Yucai Jie in the southeast of the city.

Tangshan

Until 28 July 1976, Tangshan was just another north China coal-mining town with a population of about one million. There was nothing much to see there, especially for tourists. After 28 July 1976, there was even less.

Tangshan had the misfortune to be almost on top of the epicentre of one of the most powerful earthquakes to shake the earth's crust this century. The town was razed in a couple of minutes, and a total of 242 000 people died, most of them in Tangshan.

The Tangshan quake measured 8.2 on the open-ended Richter scale. Apart from destroying Tangshan, it shook a large part of north China, causing heavy damage in the cities of Tianjin and Peking as well. It was a major disaster by any measure, although the death toll was still small compared to an earthquake in Shanxi Province in 1556 which reportedly killed 830 000.

The best descriptions of the earthquake were obtained by an American seismologist named Cinna Lomnitz and his wife Larissa who visited China in May 1977. They were told that just before the quake hit at 3.42 a.m., the sky over Tangshan lit up 'like daylight' with multi-coloured bursts of light, mostly red and white, waking many people who thought their bedroom lights had been turned on. Then came 'a huge jolt from below' that threw people up against the ceiling. The earth began to churn and sway, demolishing buildings as if they were made of cards. Thousands of sinkholes, looking like bomb craters, appeared throughout Tangshan, some of them probably caused by the collapse of the coal mine shafts below. About 10 000 coal miners were believed to have been underground when the quake hit, although Chinese news reports at the time claimed that most of them were rescued.

There were some foreigners in Tangshan on that fateful day, and a couple of them died there. In Peking and other north China cities, the authorities ordered all residents on to the streets in case of further after-shocks, and people lived there, camped beside their homes, for several weeks before the all-clear was announced.

The first foreign travellers to visit Tangshan almost a year after the quake gave a frightening description of what they saw: 'Tangshan is a wreck. The city centre is just an enormous heap of rubble. At first glance it is impossible to distinguish buildings from rubble, but on closer inspection some wrecks that were factories and tenement blocks can be distinguished. It looked like the worst pictures of bombing after World War II.'

However, China, still under the influence of Maoism, seemed to want to pretend that nothing at all had happened. A couple of months after the travellers quoted above visited Tangshan, the official New China News Agency issued the following report: 'With everything in order, Tangshan is as lively and vigorous as any other Chinese city . . . The number of shops and stalls now operating is 30 per cent more than before the quake . . . all schools and colleges are open.'

Obviously, things did not go as smoothly as the Chinese tried to suggest. The army was immediately sent in to take control of the area and begin the rescue and clean-up operation, but there were still reports of disease and looting, although there is no evidence that either occurred on a large scale.

The earthquake was a severe shock to China in other ways, too. At the time, it was clear that Chairman Mao would not last much longer (he died six weeks later), and suspicious peasants were watching closely for signs that the Mandate of Heaven was about to be shifted. The Tangshan earthquake fitted the bill exactly.

In the mid-1970s, the Chinese were also trying to pretend, almost as a matter of national honour, that they had virtually solved the problem of earthquake prediction. The seismologists, and the politicians backing them, however, came out of the Tangshan quake looking rather silly. Not only did they fail to predict the tremor, but they forecast a second strong earthquake in the vicinity of Peking shortly afterwards which failed to materialise.

Early in 1983, more than six years after the quake, Tangshan had still not been officially re-opened to foreigners, although a number have been there. In March 1982, the Chinese press announced that one-third of Tangshan's surviving residents had been re-housed, indicating that two-thirds of the population were still in make-shift shacks.

How to get there
Tangshan is closed, unless you happen to be a lucky seismologist. However, trains running from Peking to the seaside resort of Beidaihe pass through the city, and it is still possible to see signs of the destruction caused on that summer night in 1976.

Beidaihe (Peitaiho)

Four hours by train east of Peking is the tiny seaside resort of Beidaihe, the summer retreat of the Chinese leadership. Until 1979, this little socialist Lyme Regis-*sur*-Behai Gulf was strictly out of bounds to all foreigners except diplomats resident in Peking, but it is now open to just about everyone, and is well worth a visit just to catch a glimpse of the Chinese Communist Party on holiday by the sea. When the heat of summer makes the Chinese capital unbearable, many senior Communist officials with their families go to Beidaihe where they can temporarily put aside such things as ideological problems and line-struggles.

The resort was first built around the turn of the century for foreigners resident in Peking and Tianjin – the diplomats, missionaries and businessmen. Around the shores and up in the hills are quaint little bungalows, which in their day were owned by the cream of foreign society in China. It was a resort for an élite, and the natives were, of course, kept very much in their place. Every summer, a substantial Royal Navy ship would anchor off Beidaihe township to relay any important messages to and from the British diplomatic staff ashore.

Beidaihe's charms also appealed to the new élite which came to power in 1949, the year the People's Republic of China was proclaimed by Chairman Mao. The foreigners were, naturally, cleared out, and the bungalows and villas either reserved for senior party officials or given to the ordinary Chinese to live in.

Chairman Mao visited Beidaihe regularly and even wrote one of his obscure classical poems in honour of the place. China's present leaders, Deng Xiaoping, Hu Yaobang and the others, also reportedly maintain villas in the hills at a discreet distance from the foreigners' area.

The DIPLOMATIC CONVALESCENCE HOSTEL, where most foreigners stay in Beidaihe, is symbolic of one of the more weird aspects of life in China. The Communists, who came to power determined to wipe out the privileges which foreigners enjoyed, have continued them, selectively, for their own purposes. Diplomats and their families, towels over their shoulders, saunter down from their hillside residences, past the guards keeping away local Chinese, and make their way to the foreigners-only beach. An audience of perhaps a couple of dozen local Chinese gentlemen sometimes gathers on the perimeter of the beach to observe the foreigners at play, and to ogle the foreign women in their revealing bikinis.

Up in the village behind the hostel is KEISSLING'S RESTAURANT, a charming place opened by an Austrian entrepreneur in the old days, which probably serves the best bread and ice cream in China. The terrace of the restaurant is, naturally, for foreigners only. The village itself is less segregated. On the pavements, diplomats and foreign tourists mingle with the increasing number of ordinary Chinese tourists.

Meanwhile, officials glide by in their sleek black 'Red Flag' limousines, although the curtains in the car windows prevent the occupants from having to go through the agony of being recognised. Movie stars would sympathise – they have the same problem at St Tropez.

Beidaihe's other claim to fame is that it was the centre of operations for Lin Piao, the late defence minister who allegedly tried to assassinate Mao in 1971. The assassination attempt, as revealed at the sensational 'Gang of Four' trial in 1980, was a farcical comedy of errors. Chairman Mao was to travel by rail from Shanghai to Peking, and Lin Piao and his men 'plotted to attack Chairman Mao's train with flame throwers and 40mm bazookas, dynamite the Shuofang railway bridge near Suzhou, bomb the train from the air or blow up the oil depot in Shanghai near which the special train would pull up.' The other alternative considered, according to the prosecution, was just to murder him. But as Lin Piao and his wife sat waiting in their villa in Beidaihe, their subordinates botched the job, and Mao made it safely to Peking. Panic stricken, the diminutive Lin Piao is said to have requisitioned a British-made Trident jet waiting at the nearby airfield and took off with his closest lieutenants, heading northwest, apparently towards the Soviet Union. The plane crashed on a hillside in Mongolia. There are other theories as to what might have happened, including speculation that Lin Piao was murdered in his Beidaihe villa and his body put on the plane, but the Chinese are unlikely to shed any further light on the incident.

Lin Piao's former residence in Beidaihe, surrounded by an imposing wall and other fortifications, is occasionally used as a guesthouse and can sometimes be visited. Chairman Mao's dragon-like wife, Jiang Qing, also had a villa in Beidaihe, which is now known as Villa No. 125.

During the 1950s a large number of convalescent homes were opened in the area, especially for coal miners from the nearby Kailuan mines, among the largest in China. A whole beach and several guesthouses are also traditionally reserved for model workers.

The sedate atmosphere of the village and beach is unlike anything else in China. It is one of the most restful places in the country, although the weather can sometimes be very muggy and oppressive.

How to get there and where to stay

Beidaihe is only open during the summer months and is only accessible by train from Peking. The *Diplomatic Convalesence Hostel* is the largest and most expensive hotel in Beidaihe with rooms renting for up to 50 yuan a day. Whole bungalows are also available for rent by the month for larger parties. In the village, there are two or three smaller and cheaper hotels which take in foreigners when there is room.

The seafood is fresh and delicious and not to be missed. And what could beat having an ice cream and coffee while sitting on the terrace of Keissling's as the sun goes down?

Shanhaiguan

Shanhaiguan (the pass between mountains and sea) is the gateway on the Great Wall of China, which stretches away to the west, ending 1500 miles (2400 kilometres) away in the desert at Jiayuguan. Shanhaiguan itself is *not* the end of the Great Wall, which juts into the sea, but that part of it is, alas, closed to foreigners; however, there is a photograph of the end of the wall in the hall above the gateway. The town has always been a strategically important point on the road from central China and the northeast, or Manchuria as it used to be called. The most famous aspect of the gate itself (which was built in 1639) is a huge name board inscribed in striking calligraphy with the words 'Tianxia Di Yi Guan' – 'the first pass under heaven'. Also in the hall above the gateway are a few museum pieces, including some Manchu guard uniforms.

A few miles north of Shanhaiguan is the ZONGNU TEMPLE built in honour of a women whose fiancé, according to legend, was carried away by soldiers on their wedding day to work as a slave on the construction of the Great Wall. She went to find him, and is said to have waited for many weeks on the spot now occupied by the temple, hoping for some news. When she was finally told that her love had died, she began to cry and a long section of the wall instantly collapsed.

Most visitors to Shanhaiguan get there by bus from the seaside resort of Beidaihe to the south. Tours are organised almost every day during the summer.

Chengde

Five hours north of Peking by train is the former summer resort of the Manchu emperors, once known by its Manchurian name of Jehol and now called Chengde. Its full title is Bi Shu Shanzhuang, 'Mountain Hamlet for Escaping the Summer Heat'. The valley in which it is situated, 150 miles (240 kilometres) north of Peking, enchanted the second Manchu emperor, Kang Xi, and he ordered the construction of a palace for him to retire to during the hot summer months. Work began in 1703 and was completed in 1790 by the emperor Qian Long. The resort was virtually abandoned by the court in 1820 after Emperor Jia Qing died there after being struck by lightning.

The palace includes miniature replicas of famous structures in other parts of the country. The seven-mile-long wall which surrounds the former deer park palace looks like a small version of the Great Wall, while around the small lakes are causeways and bridges reminiscent of those in Hangzhou in eastern China. Outside the palace grounds are eight temples, one of which resembles the Potala Palace in Tibet. At the southern point of the resort park are the Four Palaces, the main living quarters of the emperor and his attendants, while the lakes are to the northeast of these.

Unless you are in a rush, Chengde is worth more than just one day of your time. During the summer, there are pleasant walks among the old palace buildings or you can strike out into the controlled wilderness of the walled deer park, almost deserted except for courting couples necking behind trees and no doubt cursing the lumbering, inquisitive foreigners.

There are two guesthouses, one just opposite the entrance to the resort, and another about 20 minutes' walk away. The food in both is reported to be very good.

HEILONGJIANG PROVINCE

Harbin

Harbin is just about the northern-most city that visitors to China can visit. In the winter, it is bitterly, bitterly cold, conjuring up images of the Siberian wastes which lie to the north. In the summer, however, it is as hot as just about anywhere else in the country. Travel to Harbin is most pleasant, therefore, during the warmer months, but as far as I'm concerned the northeast of China is only really the northeast during the winter, and that's when visitors should go, weighed down by padded coats and three pairs of socks to really experience what the word 'cold' means.

The city of Harbin is one of the most distinctive in China due to the heavy Russian influence still apparent in the architecture. The city once had the largest European population of any city in Asia, and was often known as the Paris of the Orient for its sophistication and the Moscow of the East for its large number of Russian residents, many of them refugees from the Bolshevik Revolution. It was founded in 1898 by the Russians on the site of a small fishing village, and grew as an important junction on the Trans-Siberian Railway.

'The long afternoons and evenings are gay with dinners and parties and the nightlife rivals that of Shanghai,' said one guidebook writer in the 1920s. Walking around, it is not hard to imagine what a splendid place it must have been.

The middle of the town is full of impressive Russian-style houses, shops and hotels, many of them ornamented with the iron lattice-work which was so popular in that by-gone age. Ancient trams continue to trundle along the streets of the city, many of them still cobbled. Overall, central Harbin looks, perhaps, like a tatty replica of nineteenth-century St Petersburg. A few Russian Orthodox churches still exist, including one magnificent bronze-domed cathedral (in the alleys west of Diduan Lu and north of Tiandi Jie) which dominates the centre of the city. None of them is now used for religious purposes. The cathedral was obviously ransacked and closed during the Cultural Revolution, and is now in a very sorry state, with bricked-up windows and a gaping hole in the roof. When I visited the church, there was a sign on the padlocked back door which read: 'No urinating allowed here. Offenders will be fined 10 yuan.'

Since the Communist victory in 1949, Harbin has become a major industrial centre and the home of nearly two million people. The White Russian population, which in the 1920s numbered over 100 000, has evaporated over the years, leaving only 57 still living in the city in 1982. The others died or emigrated, mostly to Australia or Brazil. A few of those left live in the Foreigners' Old People's Home in the suburbs of Harbin, which also houses a number of other people washed up in China by the tides of history, including a number of old Japanese women left over from the occupation, and two stateless American women, Marjorie and Seraphine Fuller, who say they are waiting for the Euphrates River to dry up as a sign that the end of the world is imminent.

Apart from the architecture, there appears to be little Russian influence left in Harbin now, unless you count a park named after Joseph Stalin down by the river and the borsch soup served by a

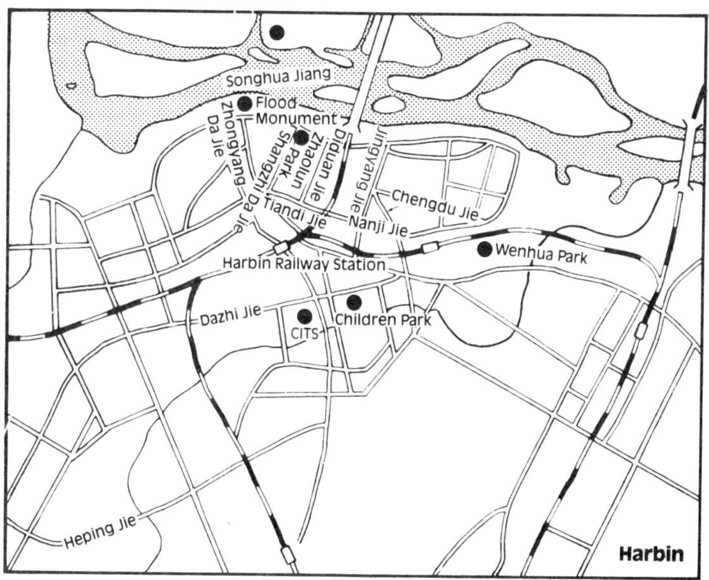

number of hotel restaurants. But the old buildings, mostly painted pale yellow, remain as evidence of a more glorious past, glorious at least for the foreigners who were part of the glamorous Harbin social whirl. The Chinese citizenry presumably suffered the usual deprivations to keep the foreigners in the style to which they were accustomed.

During the Japanese occupation of China up to 1945, a village, Pingfang, 20 miles (32 kilometres) south of Harbin became the home of a secret Japanese germ warfare establishment where prisoners of war, including some European (and probably some British) soldiers were subjected to horrors probably unparalleled in human history except for the Nazi concentration camp atrocities.

The Japanese 731st regiment experimented on live human beings, or 'logs of wood' as those involved called them. The Japanese 'doctors' injected cholera, syphilis and plague germs into their victims to monitor the effects, and froze people alive under observation in order to explore the workings of frostbite. They exposed their captives to prolonged X-rays, and carried out hundreds of dissections on living people. The horror of it all is hard to grasp. The full details of Regiment 731's deeds have never been revealed, and much of the information is in Washington where it was taken at the end of the war by the Americans, who hoped to make use of it.

According to a book published in Japan recently, *The Devil's Gluttony*', the research carried out in Harbin was indeed important. The regiment succeeded in mass-producing penicillin several years before their counterparts in the West and did pioneering work on the effects of vitamin and nutrition deficiency – by systematically starving the camp inmates, of course. In the search for a substitute for human blood, they drained one prisoner and pumped him full of horse blood.

One of the former regiment officers interviewed by the book's author, Masaki Shimozato, recalled a prisoners' revolt just before the end of the war in 1945: 'The Russians had broken out of their chains. We all ran to the cells with our pistols. There were 40 or 50. All of them were killed.'

At the end of the war, some sort of deal was struck between the regiment's commanders and the Americans whereby all their data would be handed over in return for freedom from prosecution. Many of those involved went on to become prominent doctors and medical researchers in Japan. The compound at Pingfang, has since been razed to the ground, and there is nothing to see.

To get to downtown Harbin from the International Hotel, take a No. 16 bus. The best streets for walking round are Zhongyang Jie and Shangzhi Jie, both of which have a number of good restaurants along their lengths. Close to the river, the No. 16 bus passes ZHAOLUN PARK, one of the city's biggest, which in winter becomes a fairyland of ice sculptures. Meanwhile not far from the No. 16 bus terminus is the SONGHUA RIVER and a monument to people who died in a river flood in the 1950s. During the winter there are ice slides down from the promenade on to the frozen river surface. You can also rent skates and glide about above the fishes.

There are not many excursions possible or worthwhile from Harbin. There are trains to DAQING, China's largest oilfield northwest of the city, but there's little to see there except for the vast, dismal expanses of the Manchurian plain dotted with oil rigs. To the north is the city of QIQIHAR, but few foreigners are allowed to go there. Winter sport enthusiasts might try applying to visit QINGYUN, the biggest ski centre in China, which opened in late 1982.

How to get there and where to stay

There are direct flights to Harbin from Peking, and also daily trains. Harbin is not on the regular tourist route, and there are few hotels open to foreigners. Most people stay in the *International Hotel* (Guoji Fandian; take a No. 1 trolley bus or a No. 16 bus from the station), which is a pleasant, comfortable old place left over from the Russian era. Just outside the hotel is a large roundabout on which once stood a Gothic-style Russian Orthodox church made of wood. By all accounts, it was one of the most beautiful churches of its kind in the world, but unfortunately it was burned to the ground by those contemptible zealots, the Red Guards.

HENAN PROVINCE

Zhengzhou

Zhengzhou is a fairly nondescript central Chinese city with a population of just over one million and very little in the way of interesting things to visit. It is a major rail junction and has largely been built, or re-built, since 1949 with wide, tree-lined streets and featureless brick buildings of the functional, socialist style which, these days, tends to make all Chinese cities look much the same. But Zhengzhou does serve as an excellent base from which to see two or three interesting places nearby including the Shaolin Monastery, renowned as the Mecca of Chinese kung fu.

In Zhengzhou itself, there is a distinctive monument known as the FEBRUARY 7 PAGODA built in the early 1970s to commemorate a strike organised by workers building the Peking–Wuhan railway line in 1923, which was bloodily suppressed. There is a small exhibition inside. (*From the Zhongzhou Hotel, take a No. 2 bus heading west and get off at the fifth stop.*)

The HENAN PROVINCIAL MUSEUM (Renmin Lu) contains some interesting artifacts from the Shang dynasty, 3000 years and more ago. (*From the February 7 Pagoda, take a No. 2 bus heading northeast and get off at the fourth stop.*)

There is also a YELLOW RIVER EXHIBITION HALL about a 15 minutes' walk from the Zhongzhou Hotel, which explains the efforts being made to control 'China's Sorrow'.

The closest excursion is to the YELLOW RIVER, 15 miles (24 kilometres) to the north. The road leads to the point, near the village of Huayuankou, where Chinese soldiers dynamited the dykes one night in April 1938 to stop the advancing Japanese army. The result: floods which killed nearly one million people and left up to 11 million more homeless and starving. The dykes were dynamited on the orders of Generalissimo Chiang Kaishek, leader of the Nationalist Chinese government. The floods delayed the Japanese for a few weeks, but it is difficult to imagine the sort of man who could issue such an order, condemning so many of his countrymen to death at one stroke.

An American journalist, Jack Belden, was there when the dykes were breached and wrote of how the waters of the river flowed along their old channel for a moment after the explosion ripped a hole in the earthworks, then suddenly, with 'a terrible roar', surged through the breach and churned away across the low-lying countryside to the south. The floods re-occurred every year until the dykes were finally re-built in 1947 with American assistance.

Today, the Yellow River looks more peaceful. The point where the soldiers breached the dykes has been transformed into an irrigation sluice gate with a huge slogan-command from Chairman Mao etched into the embankment: 'Control the Yellow River.' But the river still has the potential to cause death and destruction. Its fast-running waters carry more silt than any other waterway in the world – 37 kilograms per cubic metre – and as the river bed has risen over the centuries, the peasants living along its banks have continually had to build the dykes higher to prevent it from overflowing. The result of this long process is the stupendous sight of the river flowing along an elevated channel one mile (1.6 kilometre) wide and up to 24 feet (7.3 metres) above the surrounding plain.

The best excursions from Zhengzhou are to Kaifeng, Luoyang and the Shaolin Monastery (all dealt with in separate sections). There are local buses to each from the bus terminus near the station.

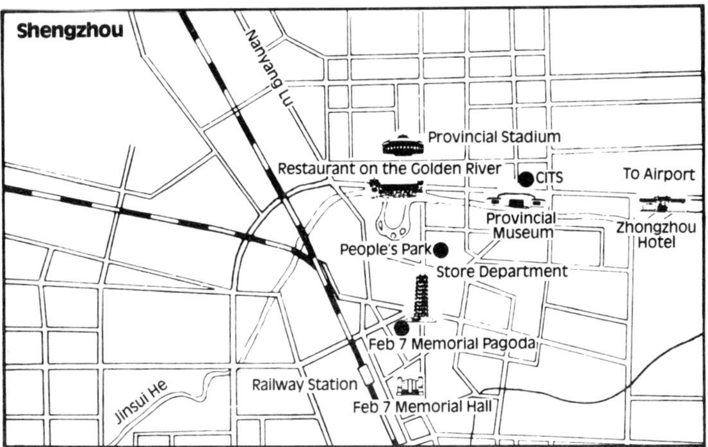

How to get there and where to stay

Being a major rail junction, transport to and from Zhengzhou is no problem. There are direct trains every day to Peking, Shanghai, Canton and Xi'an. There are also flights to Shanghai and Peking, and buses to Luoyang and Kaifeng (the bus terminus is just outside the railway station).

Most foreigners stay at the *Zhongzhou Hotel*, a large place far away from the centre of town (take a No. 2 bus from the railway station, and get off at the sixth stop). Better located but usually closed to foreigners is the *February 7* (Erqi) *Hotel* (Jiefang Xi Lu; take a No. 2 bus from the railway station, and get off at the first stop).

Kaifeng

This bustling market town, about 50 miles (80 kilometres) east of Zhengzhou, was once the capital of Henan Province and is a much more interesting city than the present one. It has retained much of its pre-1949 flavour, and walking round the streets past the old shops and houses is a pleasure. The city has a number of temples, almost all of them in an appalling state of repair. One has disappeared completely. Another, the XIANGGUO MONASTERY in the centre of town, was obviously once a magnificent structure, with an extremely unusual octagonal altar hall featuring a multi-armed Buddha. Some repair and restoration work is underway but, even now, part of the main altar hall is used as a sort of amusement parlour with oddly shaped mirrors, hardly a laughing matter considering the circumstances.

The other historical site on the official tourist route is the so-called 'IRON PAGODA', which is, in fact, made of normal bricks and faced with specially coloured tiles to make the structure look like iron. Built in the eleventh century when Kaifeng was the capital of the southern Song dynasty, it also shows some scars dating from the Cultural Revolution – many of the Buddhist images on its surface have been mutilated. The 177-foot (54 metre) high pagoda was once open for visitors to walk up the winding stairs inside, but the doorway is now barred. One local resident told me that it had been closed after some visiting schoolchildren inside panicked and charged back down the stairs, killing and injuring some of their number. A guide claimed that the top of the pagoda is lower than the bed of the Yellow River only a few miles away, which seems impossible, but may be true given the height of the dykes along the river in Henan.

The two most interesting things about Kaifeng are rarely men-

A doorway and pavilion in the Zhongyue Temple, Henan Province

The tomb of Qinshihuang in Xian

Above Checking out the latest hairstyles in Peking *Below* Portable peasant and orange grove in the market at Qufu, Shandong Province – the birthplace of Confucius

Traffic on Suzhou (Soochow) Creek, Shanghai

Bronze warriors practise their Kung Fu in the Zhongyue Temple, Henan Province

A peasant wood market in North China

An ordinary heap of earth in Qufu, Shandong Province, under which may lie the remains of Confucius, China's mortal answer to Jesus Christ

A winter's supply of cabbage stacked outside the Mosque in Huhehot, Inner Mongolia

Above The tombs of ancient monks – the Forest of Stupas outside the Shaolin Monastery, Henan Province *Below* The horrors of capitalism past – an archaeological relic from the 1940s preserved at Pumpkin Lane, Shanghai

tioned in guidebooks, and one of them has almost become a state secret: Kaifeng was the home of China's largest community of Jews, and was also the place where the country's President, Liu Shaoqi, died in horrifying circumstances in prison in 1969, the most prominent victim of the Cultural Revolution.

The story of how a wandering band of Jews came to settle in this city is one of the mysteries of Chinese history. No one knows for sure when they came or by what route, but their ancestors are still here and regard themselves as Jewish, even though the religion and almost all the social practices associated with it – such as the ban on eating pork – have disappeared.

The last synagogue in Kaifeng reportedly collapsed in the 1860s and has never been replaced. 'There is no one left here who believes in the Jewish religion,' one old Chinese Jew, Mr Shi Zhoingyu, told me during my visit to the city. 'My own parents were Buddhists, but my mother used to tell me stories about Abraham and other Jewish things. In every way, we are just like the Chinese around us. We look the same, we eat and dress the same, but I still consider myself to be Jewish. When I fill out forms on which I have to state my race, I put "Jew".'

The best historical research can do is to suggest that perhaps the ancestors of the Kaifeng Jews came to China by sea from Jewish communities in India. Another theory is that they made their way from Palestine overland via the Silk Road. Perhaps the fact that they gathered in Kaifeng indicates that they arrived in the tenth or eleventh centuries when Kaifeng was the imperial capital. No one will probably ever know.

The synagogue was located on Beitu Jie, on a site now used as a hospital. Not far away is a narrow street called NAN JIAO JING, which was the main Jewish area in town. In one of the courtyards along the street are a number of steles (inscribed stone tablets) telling the history of Kaifeng's Jewish community.

The story of the death of Liu Shaoqi, President of China, in a secret prison in Kaifeng, was revealed in 1980 for use as ammunition by Deng Xiaoping, the present leader, in his campaign to oust the former Communist Party chairman Hua Guofeng. Having served its purpose, Chinese officialdom now apparently wants to pretend that his death never happened, or at least not in Kaifeng.

The *People's Daily*, in an article on Liu in 1980, said that he died in the vault of the former Kaifeng branch of the Golden City Bank. I asked city officials to show me the building, but they said it was impossible. 'There is a directive,' they replied. 'We cannot help you.'

Liu had been the second-most powerful man in China after Chairman Mao, but by the mid-1960s, Mao began to see Liu as an opponent and worked to engineer his downfall. The removal of Liu appears to have been one of the reasons why Mao started the disastrous Cultural Revolution. In 1967, Liu was confined to his living quarters in Peking and was 'struggled' by Mao's fanatical Red Guards ('struggling' was a form of psychological and sometimes physical torture used to break a victim). He wrote to Mao protesting that the charges against him – that he opposed the Communist Party and wanted to restore capitalism – were entirely false, but there was no reply from the Great Helmsman. In mid-1968, having been deposed from power, Liu fell ill and spent the rest of his life bed-ridden. Mao had him expelled from the Communist Party in October 1968, but Liu was not informed of the decision until his birthday on 24 November.

A year later, in October 1969, Liu was close to death from pneumonia, and according to the official story, Mao's 'comrade-in-arms', Defence Minister Lin Piao, ordered Liu to be transferred in extreme secrecy to Kaifeng where it was apparently thought that there was a better chance of keeping his death a secret than in Peking with its well-oiled rumour mill. He was flown to Kaifeng in a special plane at the dead of night and, according to the *People's Daily* report, placed in a 'special prison' in the former Golden City Bank building where he died on the morning of 12 November 1969 which, by coincidence, is also the birthday of the father of modern China, Sun Yatsen.

With local officials unwilling to guide me towards the Golden City Bank, I went out on the streets and asked a few old men, and quickly found one who remembered its location, on Nantu Jie opposite the Kaifeng Opera House. Outside the old, deserted bank building, its windows still covered with bars, were some men playing dominoes and I asked if this was the former Golden City Bank.

'Yes,' they replied.

'And is this where Liu Shaoqi died?'

'No, he died down the road on the left,' they said.

Following their directions, I came to the entrance of a courtyard now used by the Kaifeng City People's Government. The doorman confirmed that Liu had died inside and said the building was now used as an office.

But there is no plaque to Liu, no sign of the role that the courtyard has played in the history of modern China.

How to get there and where to stay
Kaifeng is on the main east–west railway line from Zhengzhou to Shanghai, but to travel north–south you have to return to Zhengzhou. The train services are good, and there are also buses between Kaifeng and Zhengzhou about every 30 minutes from outside the railway station.

The main hotel in Kaifeng is called, logically enough, the *Kaifeng Hotel* (take a No. 3 bus from the station, get off at the third stop). A double room costs 18 yuan.

Luoyang
This ancient town has, at one time or another, served as the capital of the Chinese empire under nine different dynasties, and was for centuries an important centre of culture and of Buddhism. Today, it is another large, grey, industrialised Chinese city, but there are still a number of places in and around the town which hint at the glory of Luoyang's past. The first Buddhist temple to be built in China after the religion's introduction from India was the Baima Si (white horse temple) near Luoyang, and it was here that the first Chinese translations of the Buddhist sutras were done. When Luoyang was capital of the Northern Wei dynasty (386–534), there were supposed to be more than 1300 Buddhist temples operating in the area, and at the same time, work was begun on the magnificent Longmen (dragon gate) Caves, one of the best examples of Buddhist rock carving in the country. Luoyang ceased to be a place of political importance almost 1000 years ago, but it remained the capital of Henan Province until after 1949 when the provincial administration moved east to Zhengzhou and industrialisation began.

The one tourist 'must' is the LONGMEN CAVES complex, about ten miles (16 kilometres) south of the city. Construction of the caves began in about A.D. 500 and continued for four centuries, filling the cliffs on either side of the Yi River. Even now, there are still more than 1300 caves and grottoes still in existence as well as 40 pagodas and more than 100,000 images of the Buddha in one form or another, the biggest of which is more than 55 feet (17 metres) tall.

As with other similar sites in China, the Longmen Caves have suffered from the chaos and lawlessness which has cursed China for the past century, from the acquisitive European adventurers who hacked heads off statues to take home, to the iconoclastic Red Guards hoping to gain political points through some wanton vandalism. One of the best of the Longmen murals is now displayed in the New York Metropolitan Museum of Art.

Further vandalism has occurred during the past few years. The *People's Daily* reported in an outraged article that vandals had chopped the heads and arms off more than 60 Buddhist statues in 1981 alone.

The oldest and largest of the caves is the Guyang Cave begun in the Northern Wei dynasty about 1500 years ago. Other caves worth visiting are the Yuefang (medical prescription) Cave, the Lianhua Cave and the Wanfuo (ten thousand buddhas) Cave, which lives up to its name. Outside the Medical Prescription Cave are a number of stone blocks on which are carved the remedies for more than 100 diseases. (*CTS will be pleased to arrange a taxi to take you to the caves, but there are cheaper ways of getting there. A local tourist bus reportedly leaves from the train station at 7.00 a.m., 9.00 a.m. and 1.00 p.m., but check first. An even cheaper method is to take a No. 8 bus from near the Friendship Hotel to the bus terminus outside the west gate of the Old City and then take a No. 3 bus from there all the way to the end of the line. Alternatively, take a No. 10 bus heading east on Dongfanghong Lu, one block south of the Friendship Hotel, which also terminates at the caves.*)

The BAIMA SI (white horse temple) is about eight miles (13 kilometres) northeast of Luoyang, and although the original temple was built almost 2000 years ago, the present buildings date from the Ming and Ching dynasties. In front of the temple are two Song dynasty stone horses, while to the east there is a 13-storey pagoda built in A.D. 1175. (*For those on their own, take a No. 8 bus from near the Friendship Hotel to the bus terminus outside the west gate of the Old City, then take a No. 6 bus to the end of the line.*)

In the city itself, the WANGCHENG PARK on Zhongzhou Lu contains two subterranean tombs dating from the Han dynasty, which can be visited. The OLD CITY area with its old buildings and the remains of its wall, is well worth walking round.

A sensible way to take in all the sights of Luoyang in one day would be to take a No. 10 bus out to the Longmen Caves in the morning; then take a No. 3 bus back to the west gate of the Old City; have lunch at a local restaurant there and walk round the streets; then take a No. 6 bus out to the Baima Si in the afternoon.

How to get there and where to stay
Luoyang is accessible by train from Yichang in the south, Xi'an in the west and Zhengzhou in the east.

The hotel most people stay at is the *Youyi Binguan* (Friendship Hotel) on Anhui Lu. If you're on your own, take the No. 2 bus from the railway station and get off at the seventh stop. Walk back to the first intersection, turn right, and right again into Anhui Lu, and the hotel is on your right. A normal room costs 30 yuan a night, and there are dormitory beds for four yuan.

It is also possible to get a bus from Luoyang to the Shaolin Monastery, about a four-hour ride to the southeast. The round trip from the railway station takes in the Shaolin and the Zhongyue Temples (*see* next entry for details).

Shaolin Monastery

This monastery, about 50 miles (80 kilometres) west of Zhengzhou, is one of the most famous in China due to its connections with Chinese kung fu. Replicas of the monastery have featured in literally hundreds of second-rate kung-fu flicks produced in Hong Kong and Taiwan over the past decade or more, and a Communist-made film produced recently which actually used the real Shaolin Monastery as a film set became, as a result, an instant box-office hit in Japan and Hong Kong. Unfortunately the film was little better than the standard run of 'fake' Shaolin movies.

A wealth of legend and myth surround the Shaolin Monastery, which became famous more than 1000 years ago for the martial arts fighting talents of its monks. A special style of kung fu was developed there which has since gained a huge following among martial arts devotees in Japan. Stories are told of how the monks fought against invaders and led rebellions against non-Chinese dynasties. Partly as a result of this tradition, the monastery has been burned down three times in its long history, the latest occasion being 1928 when a local warlord decided to leave his mark there.

Restoration work has begun recently, and in a couple of years time, the Shaolin Monastery will be a sparkling, freshly painted tourist attraction. But in many ways it will still be little more than a shell of its former self.

The heart of the Shaolin legend is its great martial, religious and medical traditions, but little is being done to restore them in the way that the buildings are being restored. Only a few of the original monks are left, including the venerable old abbot, De Chen ('moral meditation'), who was born in 1907 and doesn't look a day over 150. The monks who used to be kung-fu experts are mostly too old and decrepit to perform the complex moves any more, let alone teach anyone. For more than two decades, they have been forbidden from accepting any young apprentice monks, and so when they die, most of the Shaolin traditions will die with them. Under new regulations governing religious affairs, all Buddhist monks must be trained under the centralised authority of the Chinese Buddhist Association and the Communist Party.

A revival of interest in Chinese kung fu has been underway in China itself during the past three years or so, and dozens of young men from all over the country have made their way to the Shaolin Monastery in the hope of being taken in and trained in the secret art, but they have all been turned away.

The temple was first founded in 495 by an Indian monk who allegedly spent several years sitting in a cave staring at the wall while meditating. The 1928 fire destroyed most of the monastery's buildings, and the Maoist Red Guards of the Cultural Revolution vandalised the place further. But there is still plenty to see, particularly the martial arts practice hall, which has regular depressions in the stone-flagged floor, allegedly caused by the monks as they drove their heels downwards during training. Also impressive is the 'forest of pagodas' (or stupas) just outside the monastery walls, each one built in remembrance of a monk and inscribed with the names of all his disciples. Some of the pagodas date back to the seventh century A.D.

Close by the Shaolin Monastery is one of only a handful of Taoist temples open in China, even though Taoism is China's only indigenous religion. The ZHONGYUE TEMPLE is a massive, sprawling place which shows the marks of the serious vandalism that occurred during the Cultural Revolution. It features a number of huge cast-iron statues which are very impressive.

How to get there

Individual tourists can rent a car from either Zhengzhou or Luoyang through CTS. The charge is expensive (perhaps 100 yuan for the round-trip), but is not so bad if divided two or three ways. For budget travellers, local bus tours leave from outside the railway stations in both Luoyang and Zhengzhou.

HUBEI PROVINCE

Wuhan

Wuhan, the largest city in central China, is in fact an amalgamation of three cities – Wuchang, Hankou and Hanyang – on the middle reaches of the Yangtse River. The oldest of the three is Wuchang on the eastern bank, which has been a provincial capital for a number of centuries, but Wuhan only developed into a major commercial and industrial centre after the foreign powers, led by Britain, forced the imperial government to open up the Yangtse to foreign trade in 1861, following the second Opium War. The foreigners built their enclaves across the river in Hankou (then spelled Hankow), and the arrival of the railway in the 1920s further speeded development. World-wide economic depression and the Japanese war in the 1930s and 1940s, however, forced many factories to close, although Wuhan was once more built up as an important industrial base after 1949.

Today, it is a city of three million people with several important industries, including the Wuhan Iron and Steel Works, one of the country's biggest. The heavy industry has given the city a bad air pollution problem, but it is still an interesting place to visit, and Hankou especially is worth walking round. But be warned: in midsummer it lives up to its reputation as one of the 'ovens' of China.

Wuhan has been the scene of two important incidents in China's recent history: the first uprising in the 1911 Revolution which overthrew the last imperial dynasty and established the Republic of China under Sun Yatsen took place here, as did one of the most serious political crises of the Cultural Revolution in the 1960s.

The revolution of 1911 started early by accident when two revolutionaries were arrested by the imperial authorities after a bomb exploded in their house in Wuchang. The leaders of the planned uprising decided to bring their plans forward and rose on 10 October, the date still considered by the Nationalists on Taiwan to be China's national day. During the street battles between imperial troops and local revolutionaries, virtually the whole of Hankou was burned to

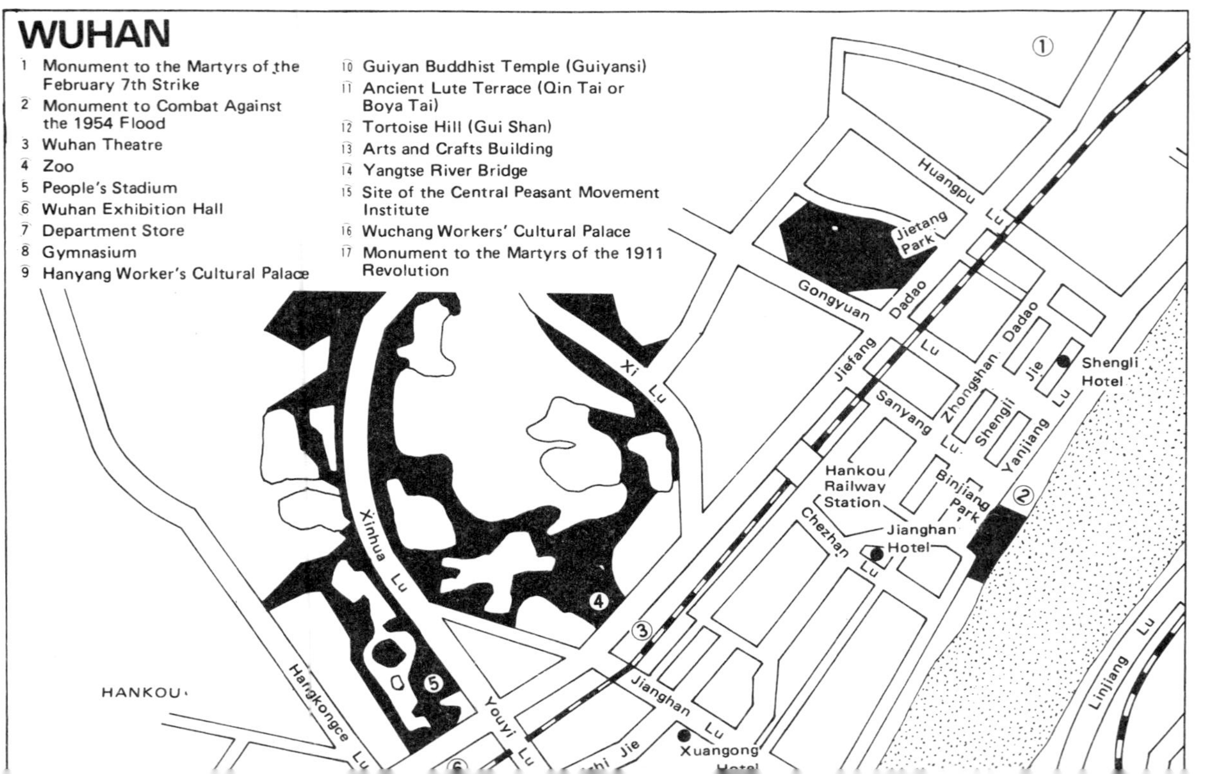
WUHAN
1 Monument to the Martyrs of the February 7th Strike
2 Monument to Combat Against the 1954 Flood
3 Wuhan Theatre
4 Zoo
5 People's Stadium
6 Wuhan Exhibition Hall
7 Department Store
8 Gymnasium
9 Hanyang Worker's Cultural Palace
10 Guiyan Buddhist Temple (Guiyansi)
11 Ancient Lute Terrace (Qin Tai or Boya Tai)
12 Tortoise Hill (Gui Shan)
13 Arts and Crafts Building
14 Yangtse River Bridge
15 Site of the Central Peasant Movement Institute
16 Wuchang Workers' Cultural Palace
17 Monument to the Martyrs of the 1911 Revolution
Huangpu Lu
Jietang Park
Gongyuan
Dadao
Jiefang
Lu
Dadao
Zhongshan
Jie
Shengli Hotel
Lu
Sanyang
Lu
Shengli
Yanjiang
Hankou Railway Station
Binjiang Park
Jianghan Hotel
Chezhan Lu
Xi Lu
Xinhua Lu
Linjiang Lu
Jianghan Lu
Xuangong
Jie
Youyi Lu
Hangkongce Lu
HANKOU

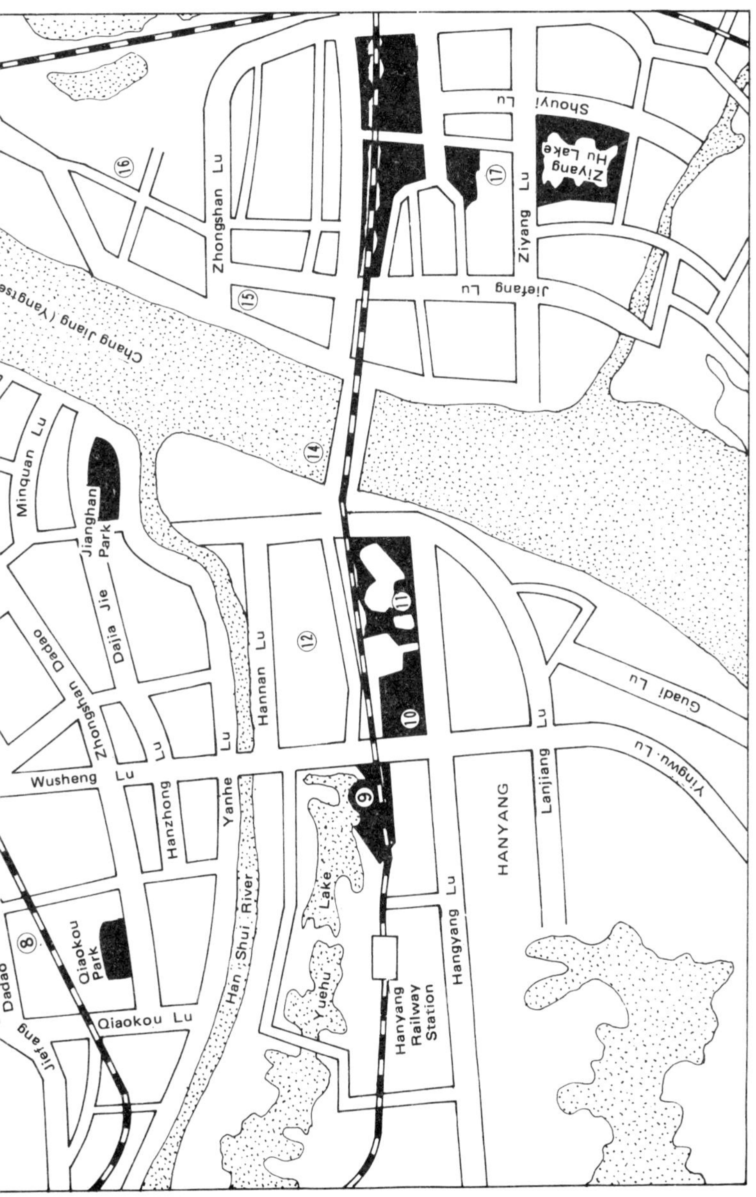
Shouyi Lu
Ziyang Hu Lake
Ziyang Lu
17
16
Zhongshan Lu
Jiefang Lu
15
Chang Jiang (Yangtse
14
Minquan Lu
Jianghan Park
Dajia Jie
Zhongshan Dadao
Hannan Lu
12
11
10
Guadi Lu
Yingwu Lu
Lanjiang Lu
Wusheng Lu
Hanzhong Lu
Yanhe Lu
9
HANYANG
Lake
Yuehu
Han Shui River
Hangyang Lu
Hanyang Railway Station
8
Qiaokou Park
Qiaokou Lu
Jiefang Dadao

the ground, but the rebels won and the uprising sparked a series of incidents in other parts of the country, the governors of many provinces seizing the opportunity to declare their independence from the central government.

In February 1923, there were bloody riots in Hankou after a strike by workers building the north–south railway was crushed by the government. In late 1937, Wuhan briefly became the capital of China as the Nationalist government fled westwards from Nanking before the advancing Japanese armies.

The Cultural Revolution was another eventful time for Wuhan. On 16 July 1966, Chairman Mao, then 73 years old, is supposed to have swum across the Yangtse at Wuhan. At the time, few people had an inkling of the Cultural Revolution that he was about to unleash on the country, but with hindsight it is clear that Mao used the swim as a way of telling his opponents that he was still a force to be reckoned with.

The climax of the early part of the Cultural Revolution was the so-called 'Wuhan Incident' of July 1967, a confrontation between two political factions in the city which reportedly resulted in thousands of deaths.

In the summer of 1967, the whole of China was seething with revolutionary fervour as young people, and many older people too, banded together in organisations pledged to defend Chairman Mao's correct revolutionary line. There were, of course, differences of opinion about what that line constituted. In Wuhan, a group called the Million Heroes sprang up, which was opposed to many of the extremist policies being propagated in Peking. Lined up against them were the radical Wuhan Workers General Headquarters. The local military commander decided to support the Million Heroes, which by mid-July had more than 1.2 million members. Information on what exactly happened in the incident is sketchy, but according to one report, the first serious clash occurred on 19 June when members of the two groups fought each other on the bridge spanning the Yangtse, leaving several people dead.

During the following month, the situation in Wuhan became so sensitive that the central government sent a delegation to the city, consisting of Premier Chou Enlai, Wang Li (another Party leader) and Xie Fuzhi, the Minister of Public Security. Mao also happened to be in town at the time, planning to swim the Yangtse again, as he had done to great propaganda effect the year before.

Meanwhile, the Million Heroes had been branded a 'reactionary organisation'. Chou and Mao kept out of sight, but the other two members of the delegation were surrounded by irate representatives of the Million Heroes, demanding to be told why they had been labelled reactionary. On 20 July, the Heroes seized Wang Li and paraded him through the city as crowds taunted and beat him, shouting 'Down with Wang Li!' Commando squads of the Million Heroes organisation decided the time had come to wipe out the radicals, who were holding the Wuhan University campus and the Iron and Steel Works. With at least the tacit approval of the local army units, the Heroes, armed with machine guns, stormed the radical barricades and captured both places after a bloody fight.

At 2.00 the next morning, Mao flew out of Wuhan in extreme secrecy, and once back in Peking, issued a directive praising the Wuhan Workers General Headquarters as being 'revolutionary', and said the Million Heroes had been misled by 'some military leaders in Wuhan'.

The upshot of the incident was that the Wuhan military commander was arrested and taken to Peking, while the Million Heroes were suppressed in a terrible campaign which, according to official figures released in 1980, left 184 000 people either dead, wounded or crippled.

The madness of the Cultural Revolution now seems a long way away, and there are naturally no monuments in the city commemorating the political and military battles of the late 1960s.

There is, however, a tomb honouring those who died in the 1911 revolution in Hankou, but at last report, the tomb compound was being used as a wood storage yard, which hardly seems in keeping with its historical significance. (*From the Xuangong Hotel, take the No. 7 bus heading northeast along Zhongshan Dadao, get off at Qiuchang Lu and the tomb is on the right.*)

MAO TSE-TUNG lived in Wuhan briefly in 1926, and his residence (41 Dufuti) and the CENTRAL PEASANT MOVEMENT INSTITUTE (13 Hongxiang) where he taught are both maintained as tourist sites. (*From the Xuangong Hotel, walk down Jianghan Jie to the river, and take a No. 1 ferry to Wuchang. Turn left, walk along the river and turn right at the first intersection.*)

The PROVINCIAL MUSEUM on the shores of the Dong Hu (east lake) is worth a visit. (*Take a No. 1 ferry to Wuchang, then a No. 14 bus from the nearby terminus to the end of the line. Walk back along the road and the museum is on the left.*) The EAST LAKE is as picturesque as a lake can be in the middle of a polluted industrial city. It is one of the largest in east China and has a number of pavilions around it. (*The No. 14 bus terminus is close to the park entrance.*)

The only temple in Wuhan is the GUIYUAN TEMPLE in Hanyang, a 300-year-old structure, which contains a white jade Buddha and a complete set of the Buddhist sutras, one of the few in China. Near the main entrance, you will see people trying to get small coins to stick to the smooth, vertical sides of an old bronze incense burner. It looks impossible, but it can be done, and those who succeed are supposed to be granted good fortune.

Food

Wuhan's most famous dish is Wuchang fish (Wuchang yu), which Chairman Mao liked enough to mention in one of his poems. Apart from the hotels, there are a number of good restaurants on Zhongshan Dadao, the main street through the centre of Hankou.

How to get there and where to stay

Wuhan is linked to all major Chinese cities by air, and is on the main north–south railway line from Peking to Canton. Ferries also ply up and down the Yangtse from Chongqing in the west down to Nanking and Shanghai in the east.

The most popular hotel is the *Xuangong* (45 Jianghan Lu in Hankou; take the No. 7 bus from the railway station, and get off at the second stop). Other hotels, all in Hankou, include the *Shengli* (Victory; 11 Siwei Lu) and the *Jianghan Hotel* (211 Shengli Lu), both of which have good restaurants and are within walking distance of the railway station. The local Friendship Store is next to the Jianghan Hotel.

If you arrive in Wuhan by ferry – from Chongqing, for example – you will land at the main Hankou terminal. Walk along Jianghan Lu at right angles to the river past five intersections and the Xuangong Hotel will be on the left.

Shennongjia

In this inaccessible mountainous area in northwest Hubei Province, there may live a tribe of wild apemen, relatives of the Himalayan Yeti and of Big Foot on the west coast of North America. There have been endless sightings of these Chinese 'Wild Men' and scientists combing the densely forested area during the past couple of years have found some interesting evidence to suggest that they do exist. But as with other monsters and apemen the world over, the Wild Men of Hubei always seem to be able to evade capture.

The official Chinese magazine, *China Reconstructs*, published a long article on the Wild Men of Shennongjia in 1979 which contained the following eye-witness account from a peasant who had encountered one of them in a gully two years earlier:

> He was about seven feet tall with shoulders wider than a man's, a sloping forehead, deep-set eyes and a bulbous nose with slightly upturned nostrils. He had sunken cheeks and ears like a man's but bigger, and round eyes also bigger than a man's.
>
> His arms hung down below his knees. He had big hands with fingers about six inches long and with thumbs only slightly separated from the fingers. He didn't have a tail and the hair on his body was short. He had thick thighs and walked upright with his legs apart.
>
> He was a male. That much I saw clearly.

Whoever he was, he certainly sounds like a Neanderthal caveman.

One of the Wild Men's strange habits, according to one report, is that when they come upon a human, they grab him by the arm and refuse to let go. Some peasants reportedly counter this by carrying bamboo arm sheaths so that, when a Wild Man catches them, they can slip their arms out of the sheaths and escape.

And if that sounds ridiculous, what about this: a Shanghai newspaper reported in 1980 that one of the scientists tracking the Wild Men had brought an ape suit with him so he could get close to the creatures, and 20 pounds (9 kilograms) of dates to give them as an 'introductory present'. 'If there really are creatures that are half-man, half-ape I want to go among them and become one of them,' he said.

A major hunt for the creatures was mounted in 1980, and the scientists involved found 1000 huge footprints and other tell-tale signs including bits of hair and excrement. In March 1981, one Shanghai newspaper reported that two scientists had actually caught sight of a Wild Man sitting on a rock about 250 yards (225 metres) from them.

'It had long hair hanging over its shoulders and particularly long thighs,' the paper said. One of the scientists raised his rifle to shoot the apeman, but the other restrained him, and as they made their way towards him, the apeman disappeared while out of view for a moment.

Another piece of evidence reported by the Chinese press was the discovery of a woman in the Shennongjia area who was allegedly captured by the creatures and later gave birth to a 'monkey child'. The *Guangming Daily* published in Peking reported that the woman disappeared for 27 days in 1939. 'She admitted that she had been seized by the apemen but denied having any relations with them,' it said.

The monkey child that she bore died in 1960 aged 21, but its bones were recently dug up and examined. 'From photographs and an analysis of the skeleton, the child had both the characteristics of an ape and a human. But it is impossible for a human and an ape to procreate as they are of different species, so an ape could not have been the father of the monkey child. Based on the fact that the Wild Men appear to be active in that area, it is probable that the child was a cross-breed between a civilised human being and a "Wild Man",' the newspaper said.

Evidence of their existence there may be, but the Wild Men lumbering around the forests of Shennongjia have shown themselves to be extraordinarily adept at avoiding scientists. The mystery will probably be solved around the same time as the Loch Ness monster is trapped. That is, most likely, never.

How to get there

You can't. Foreigners are not allowed anywhere near Shennongjia, a rugged, and probably very poor region. The nearest you can get to it is by floating down the Yangtse River from Chongqing to Wuhan. As you pass through the Yangtse Gorges, Shennongjia is on your left, about 100 miles (160 kilometres) into the hills.

Yichang

This industrial town just below the Gezhouba dam project on the Yangtse River is a convenient place to get off the ferry from Chongqing if you don't want to float down to Wuhan and beyond.

There is a railway line from Yichang heading north to Xiangfan and Luoyang. To get to the railway station from the ferry wharf, turn left and walk to the bus terminus nearby. A bus leaves from there for the station.

HUNAN PROVINCE

Hunan Province has the honour of being the birthplace of more Communist revolutionaries than any other province in China. The late Chairman Mao was born here in the village of Shaoshan 50 miles (80 kilometres) to the southwest of Changsha, the provincial capital, and the former president of China, Liu Shaochi, whom Mao had purged in 1967, was also born nearby. (*See* Kaifeng, p. 144, for details of Liu's death.) Three of the members of the present ruling Politburo come from one county – Liuyang County, 30 miles (48 kilometres) east of Changsha – including the present Communist party chief, Hu Yaobang.

Just why Hunan should have spawned so many future Communists is something of a mystery. Chairman Mao himself put it down to the hot peppers which the Hunanese like to mix in liberally with their food. More likely, it had something to do with the political situation in Hunan in the first decades of this century when the province was generally ruled by incompetent, greedy, opium-smoking warlords whose behaviour actively encouraged peasant uprisings and the quest by intellectuals for some alternative political system.

Changsha

Changsha, the capital of Hunan Province, is now noted basically for two things: places where Chairman Mao studied, ate and swam as a young man, and the best-preserved 2000-year-old corpse in the world. The corpse is that of a woman who died one summer afternoon around 160 B.C., after eating a melon. She was found in 1974 in an elaborate tomb so heavily insulated with wood and cloth that oxygen and bacteria could not get in to perform their usual functions of decay, and when modern doctors performed an autopsy on her, they found that her body was in good shape for its age. A film of the operation was a box-office hit in China in 1975, an indication of how entertainment-starved the country was in the days when Mao's wife, Jiang Qing, was still dictating the nation's cultural fare.

What the doctors found indicated that the woman's time had definitely been up: she had heart disease, tuberculosis, gallstones, a slipped disc and worms. Inside her stomach was found a large quantity of melon seeds, and melons being a summer fruit, it was deduced that she died on a summer's day.

The body of this 2000-year-old woman now lies stretched out on a tiled slab in the CHANGSHA MUSEUM. An expression of what appears to be absolute terror sits on her face, and with specimen bottles containing her various internal organs arranged nearby, perhaps this is not surprising. (*To get to the museum, turn left out of the Xiangjiang Hotel and, at the next intersection, take a No. 3 bus heading north, getting off at the third stop.*)

As for Mao, whose own body lies preserved in a mausoleum in the centre of Peking, Changsha contains many memories. The city was his first stop on the road from Shaoshan village to supreme power over his countrymen, and at least three buildings are maintained as

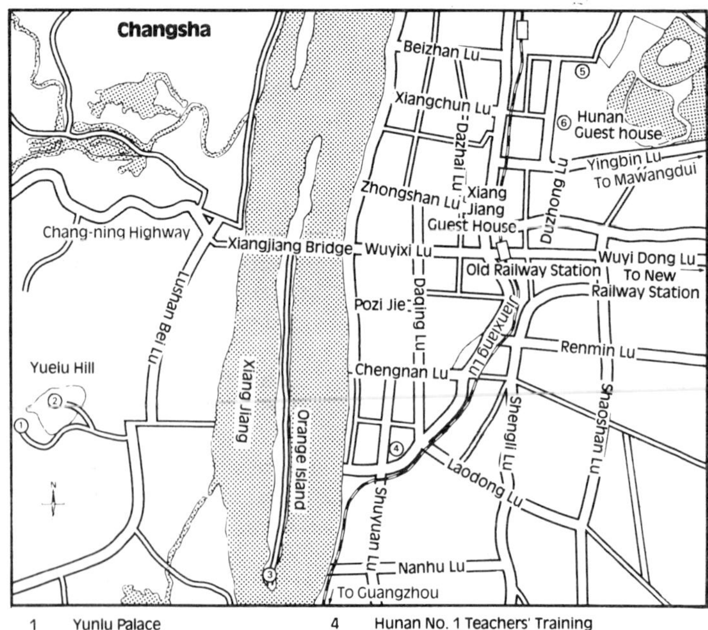

1 Yunlu Palace
2 Loving Dusk Pavilion (Aiwanting)
3 Orange Island Pavilion (Juzizhoutou)
4 Hunan No. 1 Teachers' Training School (Diyi Shifan)
5 Monument to Martyrs
6 Hunan Provincial Museum

memorials to schools which he attended during his formative years. Visitors to the CHANGSHA NORMAL COLLEGE (Shuyuan Lu) are reverently shown a classroom and a dormitory, but in fact the whole place burned down in 1938 and was only rebuilt in the 1950s, although to a similar design. Behind the school is a well where Mao used to douse himself with cold water every morning. The well would still be usable, the guide said, except that children keep throwing rubbish down it. (*For the Normal School – Diyi Shifan – take a No. 1 bus from the main square, heading south, and get off after it turns left.*)

The best restaurant in town, the HUO GONG DIAN (fire palace altar), was built in the early part of the century and much of its now-tatty decoration is reminiscent of the 1920s. If you concentrate, it's not hard to imagine an earnest young man in a long Chinese gown sitting in the corner, poring over some book, a plate of hot Hunan food in front of him, dreaming of a Marxist revolution. The tea in this restaurant, by the way, comes in big mugs and is among the best I have tasted in China. Outside the restaurant when I visited it was a large poster commemorating the twenty-third anniversary of that historic day in 1958 when Mao had a meal there.

Changsha has a huge MAO MUSEUM, but in line with the policy to tone down the Mao cult, half of it has been turned over to an exhibition of archaeological exhibits. Further changes can be expected, although the 60-foot (18-metre) tall statue of Mao outside, one of the biggest in China, will hopefully stay put for a while.

Changhsa itself is a very Chinese city, and the narrow, rambling streets in the old part of the city with their distinctive architecture are a real joy. The hundreds of licensed hawkers plying their various trades on the streets are a welcome and colourful result of the new liberalised economic policies.

For a walking tour of the city, turn right out of the Xiangjiang Hotel and walk along Zhongshan Lu, and then left along Dazhai Lu or Daqing Lu, both busy shopping streets.

The city was only opened up to foreigners for the first time in 1904, but its strategic position as the capital of Hunan quickly attracted a number of foreign consulates as well as numerous religious and education missions. Most of the property owned by Westerners in the city was destroyed during anti-foreign riots in 1910, which may account for the rather peculiar location of the former consulates – on an island in the middle of the Xiang River, which runs through Changsha. ORANGE ISLAND must have been the perfect haven for times when the natives got restless. Many of the consulates were housed in magnificently robust buildings, although the former British mission with its tall chimneys and Victorian red-brick façade looks as if it would be more at home in a Charles Dickens novel than in one of the hottest cities in China. In the old days, the representatives of His Britannic Majesty must have sweltered inside, as nowadays do representatives of the Changsha River Engineering Company. (*The No. 16 bus, starting just to the east of the main square, goes to the tip of Orange Island.*)

One pleasant place to visit just outside the city is the YUELU SHAN PARK on the opposite bank of the river. The large wooded reserve, dotted with temples and pavilions, makes a pleasant afternoon's walk and there's a good view of Changsha from the top. (*Take a No. 3 bus, heading south, to its terminus, then a No. 5 bus; get off at the fourth stop and walk up the hill.*)

How to get there and where to stay

Changsha is connected by air services to Peking, Canton and Shanghai, and is also on the main Peking–Canton trunk railway line, about 20 hours from the former and 15 hours from the latter. The best hotel to stay at is the *Xiangjiang Hotel* on Zhongshan Lu, which has double rooms for 22 yuan and dorm beds in three-bed rooms for six yuan each (take a No. 1 bus from the station, and get off at the fourth stop.)

Shaoshan

Shaoshan is a tiny village 50 miles (80 kilometres) south of Changsha, which is famed as the birthplace of the late Chairman Mao Tse-tung. Ten years ago, more than a million people a year used to make the pilgrimage to this Mecca of Maoism, but it has now virtually reverted to being the sleepy village in a sea of rice paddies that it was before Mao came to the world's attention.

The old Chairman is now no longer considered to be the infallible Helmsman that he once was and the whole Mao cult has been sharply cut down to size, thanks to the more sensible approach of China's present leader, Deng Xiaoping. Most of the outrageous political slogans praising Mao and his invincible Thoughts have been removed, and the village factory, which used to churn out millions of Mao badges to sell to visitors, now makes tea canisters and other consumer products instead.

The Mao cult may be a thing of the past, but Shaoshan will not be able to forget its famous son so quickly – the place is littered with memorials to him and his doings as a young boy. The FORMER HOME OF THE MAO FAMILY, once a shrine of mystical significance to the millions of Maoist Red Guards who tramped through it during and after the Cultural Revolution, is open to tourists now, following a period of renovation. The house is almost palatial by peasant standards, and gives the lie to the Cultural Revolution propaganda line about Mao being born into a poor peasant family, an attempt to establish his proletarian credentials.

Nearby is the MAO EXHIBITION HALL filled with Mao memorabilia. Each room in the exhibition deals with a different period in his life, but the last room, dealing with the years after the Communist victory in 1949 when he made most of his serious mistakes, has been closed for several years for 're-adjustment', and looks likely to stay that way for a while yet. The exhibition used to have two complete sets of rooms with identical exhibits to handle the massive flow of visitors, but now one set has been closed.

The man credited with making Shaoshan such a revered, almost holy spot, is Hua Guofeng, who succeeded Mao as Chairman of the Chinese Communist Party in 1976, only to be toppled from the post by Deng Xiaoping in 1981 after a long political battle. Hua was Party boss of the Shaoshan area in the early 1960s, and obviously did all he could to ingratiate himself with Mao. But in the end, his efforts worked to undo him. His close association with the discredited Mao cult proved to be a powerful weapon which his enemies did not hesitate to use against him.

Shaoshan is best seen as a day-trip from Changsha. There is a daily train which pulls in at a huge, almost-deserted station built in 1968 to handle the hoards of Red Guard pilgrims.

However, for those wanting to stay the night, there is the *Shaoshan Guesthouse*, in which Mao and the then-President Liu Shaoqi stayed during a visit in the early 1960s. Visitors can ask to sleep in Mao's or in Liu's bed, and can marvel at the huge bathrooms these men had at their disposal. I, for one, can proudly claim that I Have Slept on Mao's Bed.

INNER MONGOLIA

Seven hundred years ago, the Mongols controlled the largest empire the world has ever seen, stretching from western Europe to Korea, from Siberia to Burma. Now they are divided in their own homeland, some living in Outer Mongolia, a country firmly under the thumb of the Soviet Union, and the rest in China where officially organised emigration has made them a minority in their own so-called 'autonomous region'.

The Mongol empire was established by that larger-than-life figure, Genghis Khan (1167–1227) and his fearless warriors. In the centuries that followed his death, the empire gradually contracted until, by the early nineteenth century, Mongolia was considered, by the Chinese at least, to be a part of China. The Russians, expanding eastwards, gradually established control over the region and in 1911 supported the Outer Mongolians when they took advantage of the political chaos in China to declare their independence. The autonomy of Outer Mongolia under Chinese suzerainty was recognised by Russia and China in 1913, but in 1945 China agreed to its independence and its control by the Soviet Union. Since then, Outer Mongolia has come increasingly under the sway of the Soviets.

In the 1950s, the Peking government began moving Chinese from the central areas to settle in Inner Mongolia, and the 3.5 million Mongols in the region are now out-numbered four-to-one. Living standards in Outer Mongolia (which has a population of 1.5 million) are higher than those in Chinese-controlled Inner Mongolia, but officials say that there is no desire among the Mongols to become part of the Mongolian state next door. 'There is not one Mongol here who would want to join up with Mongolia,' said an official, a Mongol named Siqinbeilige who had spent 40 years in the Communist Chinese army and could hardly speak Mongolian any more. Nevertheless, there have been cases in the past of Mongols being sent to labour camps for the crime of 'Mongolian nationalist chauvinism'.

The Mongolian Steppe is one of the largest grassland regions on earth, and the Mongols have long lived as nomadic herders, moving several times a year with their herds to fresher pastures. In Inner Mongolia, most of the herdsmen have been persuaded to give up their nomadic life and settle down in one place. The Sino-Soviet split in the early 1960s and the sealing of the Mongolian border caused great problems for these people, dividing many families and making correspondence impossible for nearly two decades. It was not until 1982 that the first letters passed over the border once more. The border area, is still a sensitive military zone, and tourists are not supposed to take photographs of the open steppe, presumably for fear of them being passed on to the Soviet tank officers just over the border.

Inner Mongolia suffered badly during the Cultural Revolution, and more than 10000 people are said to have died during fighting in the region. Another result of the years of radicalism has been the advance of the Gobi desert and a rapid deterioration in the extent and quality of farmland in the region. Stupid cadres took Mao's exhortation to 'grasp grain as the key link' and applied it to Inner Mongolia's grasslands, ordering peasants to abandon their herds, plough up the ground and plant wheat. 'It was like the dustbowl conditions in the United States and Canada in the 1930s,' said one grasslands official. 'The land was ploughed and the soil blew away.' As a result, the desert on the western fringes of Inner Mongolia has been expanding. In 1960, it occupied 55 million acres of the region, but by the early 1980s, it controlled 74 million acres. The government has approved the transformation of some ploughed land back into grassland and is trying to build a 'Green Great Wall' of trees and shrubs to halt the desert's advance.

Huhehot (Hohhot)

Huhehot – 'green city' in the Mongol language – is the capital of Inner Mongolia, and it is relatively well laid-out compared to many other Chinese cities, for a Chinese city it is. Very little remains of the old city, established by the Mongols in the sixteenth century; it now appears as if most buildings were erected in the 1950s.

The Mongols traditionally worship Lama Buddhism, and Huhehot supported dozens of temples and monasteries before the Communists closed them all down, mostly during the Cultural Revolution. The most impressive of the handful which still survive in any form at all is the DAZHAO TEMPLE, most of which has been turned into a clothing factory. If you can get someone to open the doors, inside you will find a Tibetan-style temple hall impressively decked out in all its flags and finery. A couple of old monks have been allowed to return to it, but one said that local worshippers needed a special letter of permission from their work units before being allowed to enter. There is also a 'Living Buddha' in residence, a Tibetan from Qinghai Province who was born on about the same day in 1943 when the former Huhehot Living Buddha died. He says that there were 650 temples in Inner Mongolia in 1965, the year before the Cultural Revolution started, but only five remain that can be restored to any degree. The other temple of note in Huhehot is the WUTASI (five pagoda temple), built in a classical Indian style, although it is no longer used for religious purposes. In the old section of town near Zhongshan Lu is an eighteenth-century MOSQUE built in the Chinese-Islamic style. In early 1983, it had not yet been opened to the public.

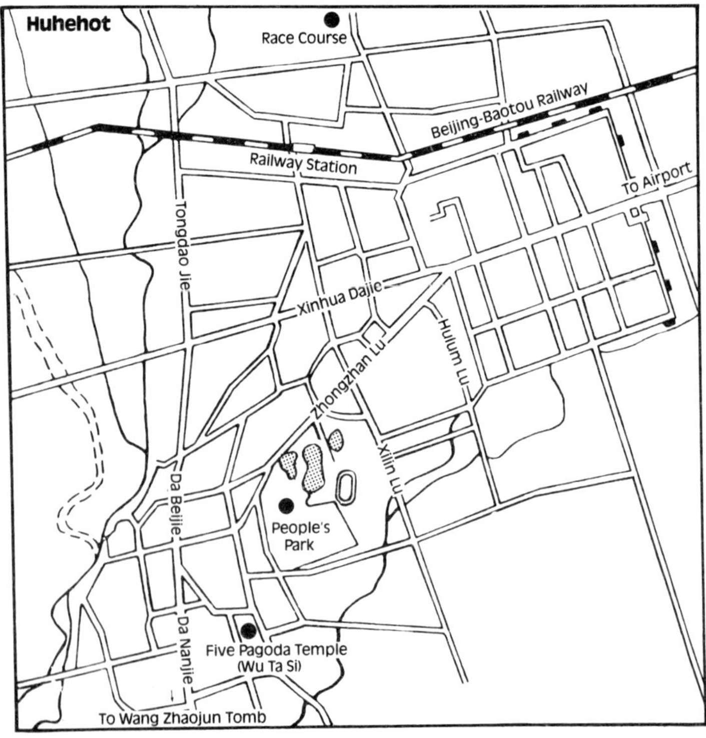

Beneath Huhehot is one of the most extensive systems of air-raid tunnels in China, in parts big enough to handle light tanks and mini-buses, but unlike many other cities, these have rarely been shown to visitors. With the border only a couple of hundred miles away, security is tighter here. The tunnel network links up with the Daqing mountains to the north of Huhehot, and is planned to provide a defence system which would allow the Chinese to fight a prolonged guerrilla war against an invader.

The main excursion from Huhehot is up to the GRASSLANDS to the north. The trips are arranged by the China Travel Service, and can be expensive unless you have some friends with you, but for many people it will be a once-in-a-lifetime opportunity to see the central Asian steppe. Most people go to the ULAN TUGE (red flag) COMMUNE about 80 miles (130 kilometres) north of Huhehot where special versions of the traditional Mongol yurts – portable tent houses – have been set up in a compound for tourists. In the afternoon, horses and a bored camel are led out for the visitors to ride and, for large groups, a rodeo of sorts is sometimes staged. Ulan Tuge commune is, in fact, on what is known as the 'little grassland'; the real thing is further out, and is rarely visited by foreigners. The commune, which has been making a fortune out of tourism since it opened in 1980, is about the least typical farming community in Inner Mongolia. Renting a taxi for the return trip to the commune costs about 200 yuan, although it's cheaper if you go in a group in a mini-bus. (Trips can be arranged through the CTS office in the Huhehot Friendship Hotel.)

The best part of the trip is the scenery as the car climbs up the Daqing mountains outside Huhehot on to the Mongolian plateau, a tree-less, windswept expanse of undulations which bears some resemblance to the English moors. You also pass by one of the biggest open-cut coal-mining projects in China which, by the late 1980s, will make Inner Mongolia the second largest coal-producing province after Shanxi.

Other places in Inner Mongolia worthy of consideration include BAOTOU, the region's biggest city which lies to the west of Huhehot. Baotou is a very industrialised place with a number of military factories, including one which turns out tanks. It is situated on the upper reaches of the Yellow River, and is on the main railway from Huhehot to Yinchuan (in Ningxia Province) and all points northwest. The main tourist attraction is the large, beautiful WUDANG ZHAO Lama monastery about two hours away by bus. (Take a No. 7 bus from the

East River bus station, which leaves about 7.00 a.m. CTS also operates regular tours.) It is possible to stay overnight at the monastery, which was built in the eighteenth century and features flat, Tibetan-style roofs. In Baotou, stay at the *Baotou Guesthouse* (Baotou Binguan; take a No. 1 bus from the railway station; dormitory beds are four yuan).

Also in southwestern Inner Mongolia, in the Ih Ju League, is GENGHIS KHAN'S MAUSOLEUM, ransacked by Red Guards in the late 1960s, and re-opened in late 1982.

Another possible excursion is to the town of XILINHOT in northeast Inner Mongolia, which looks and feels like the Wild West, with (Mongolian-style) cowboys and tumbleweed on the main street. Foreign tourists are supposed to travel to Xilinhot by air.

How to get there and where to stay

Huhehot is a couple of hours by plane and 12 hours by train from Peking. The main hotel is the *Friendship Hotel* (walk out of the station, turn left at top of the square and then right), which has nice rooms, and dormitory beds for the budget traveller. The hotel restaurant is terrible.

JIANGSU PROVINCE

Nanking (Nanjing)

Nanking, on the southern bank of the Yangtse River about 200 miles (320 kilometres) west of Shanghai, has served as the capital of China a number of times during the past 2000 years, and the Nationalists on Taiwan still consider it to be the theoretical capital of their Republic of China. Today, it is just the capital of Jiangsu Province and a pleasant city with many tree-lined streets and a number of interesting tourist sites.

In A.D. 221, at the beginning of the Three Kingdoms period, Nanking became the first city in central China to play host to the 'Son of Heaven', and it remained the imperial capital until 589 when the last Zhen emperor was dragged off to the Sui capital at Xi'an after being found hiding in a well with two of his concubines. Nanking continued to prosper nevertheless, and became an important centre for iron-making and textiles. In the mid-fourteenth century, as the Mongol dynasty crumbled, a Buddhist-novice-turned-bandit-chief named Zhu Yuanzhang seized the opportunity and established his own dynasty, the Ming, in Nanking, and finally drove the Mongols out of China altogether. He had a magnificent imperial palace built, which later served as the model for the present Imperial Palace in Peking, and had a 22-mile (35-kilometre) wall constructed round the city, most of which is still standing, reputedly the longest city wall in the world. About 20000 wealthy families from all over the country were 'invited' to set up house in Nanking to add to its splendour, but the third Ming emperor abandoned the city and moved the capital back to Peking.

In 1851, the Taiping rebels, led by the self-proclaimed younger brother of Jesus Christ, Hong Xiuquan, captured Nanking and made it the capital of their 'Kingdom of Heavenly Peace' which, for 13 years, controlled most of southern China. The Manchu dynasty, already declining into corruption and feebleness, was barely able to stand up to the Taiping rebels, but the decision of the foreign powers to support the Manchus rather than the Taipings eventually helped to turn the tide. The Taiping Rebellion is a fascinating period, as it in some ways foreshadowed the Communist revolution nearly a century later. Inspired by a foreign ideology, the Taipings carried out policies which would have been called socialist if there had been such a word in China in those days. They instituted land reform in the areas under their control, and treated women much more equally than traditional Chinese society. They also believed fiercely in the Christian God. But the Western powers, after flirting briefly with them, decided to support the more pliable Manchus, and sent in an army led by 'Chinese' Gordon (of Khartoum fame) to help put down the rebels.

In the final assault on Nanking in 1864, the city was almost completely destroyed. Hong Xiuquan died shortly before the Manchus took the city (there is no record of him having risen from the dead three days later). As many as 100 000 Taipings are reported to have been slaughtered in the first days after Nanking was taken.

The city slowly recovered from the devastation of the Taiping Rebellion, and in 1911, representatives from all over China met there and nominated Sun Yatsen as the first president of the Republic of China. He was forced to step aside in favour of the old Manchu general, Yuan Shikai, who insisted on making Peking his capital, but the Nationalist Party, which Sun Yatsen had founded, moved the capital back to Nanking in 1927. Many of the government offices in the city, Western-style buildings with Chinese-style roofs date from this era.

The invading Japanese armies took Nanking in 1937, and during their occupation killed a huge number of its residents in what appears to have been almost a calculated attempt to depopulate the city. The exact number that died will never be known. The *People's Daily*, in June 1981, said that the Japanese killed 300 000 people in Nanking in 1937 alone. One Japanese professor replied that the Japanese army could never have managed to dispose of such a huge number of bodies and put the number of dead at between 2000 and 3000. The Chinese figure is probably closer to the truth. The Japanese outraged east Asia in 1982 by altering the accounts of the Second World War in their school textbooks, watering down the image of the Japanese conquerors as barbaric imperialists. One change made was the insertion of the claim that the Nanking massacre was largely the fault of the people of Nanking who had provoked the reprisal killings.

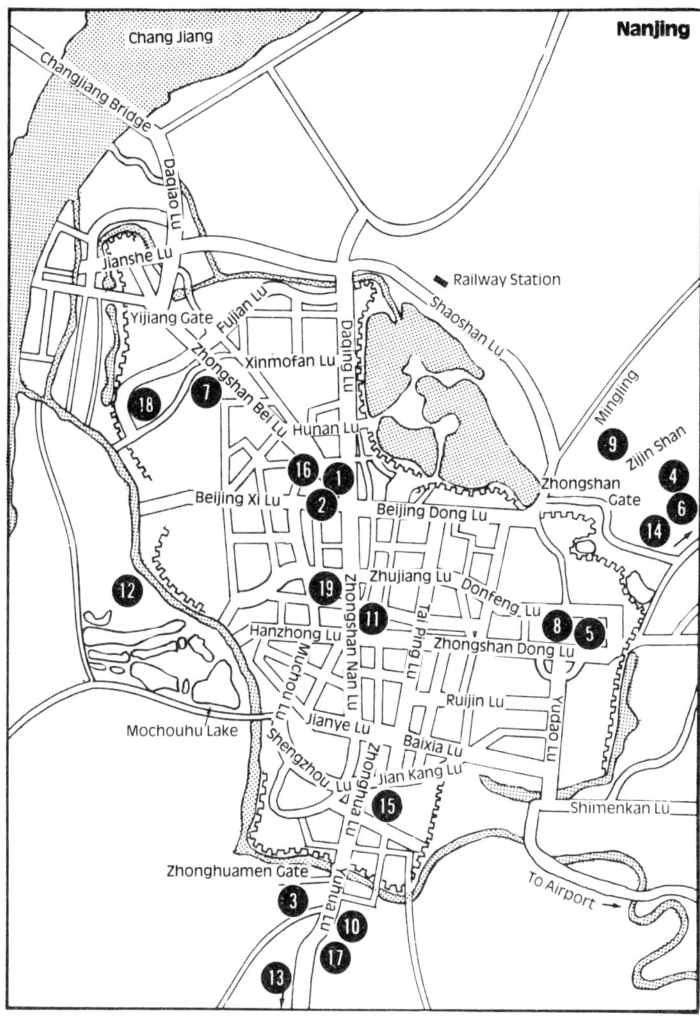

1) Bell Tower (Zhong Lou)
2) Drum Tower (Gu Lou)
3) King of Borneo's Tomb
4) Linggu Temple
5) Remains of Ming Palace
6) Mingxiaoling (Ming Tomb)
7) Nanjing Fandian (Hotel)
8) Nanjing & Jiangsu Museum
9) Observatory
10) Rain of Flower Terrace (Yu huatai)
11) Renmin Bazaar
12) Shitoucheng (Stone City)
13) Southern Tang Tombs and Bull's Head Hill
14) Dr. Sun Yat-sen's Mausoleum (Ling)
15) Taiping Museum
16) University of Nanjing
17) Yuhuatai Martyr's Memorial Park
18) Dingshan Binguan (Hotel)
19) Shengli Hotel

Nanking today has a population of over three million people and a varied industrial sector. The Nanking bridge across the Yangtse River, four miles (6.4 kilometres) in length and one of only three along the river's length, was finished in 1969.

In early 1976, as the radicals and moderates in the Chinese leadership geared up for the big struggle that would inevitably follow Mao's death, Nanking once more played an important role in national politics. In March, the radicals published a veiled attack on the late Premier Chou Enlai in a Shanghai newspaper. (Chou, who had died in January, was the leader of the moderate faction in the leadership and very popular with the ordinary people of China.) Absolutely incensed by this attack, students and workers in Nanking pasted up posters censuring 'conspirators' they said were attempting to 'usurp power', i.e., the radicals led by Madame Mao and Zhang Chunqiao. There were mass meetings and some people daubed slogans on the sides of trains heading for Peking to make sure people in the capital knew about the uproar in Nanking. The seeds of dissent spread and resulted in the mass demonstrations in the centre of Peking in early April, known as the Tiananmen Riots.

Just inside the eastern city gate is the PROVINCIAL MUSEUM, south of which are the remains of the Ming dynasty's Imperial Palace, which once covered a huge area. The DRUM TOWER in the centre of town also dates from the Ming period, and is probably the best-preserved building from that era in Nanking. Stretching west from the Drum Tower is Beijing Xilu, lined with buildings which were once the embassies and consulates of the foreign powers.

At the southern end of the city walls is the magnificent ZHONGHUA GATE, built at the same time as the city wall in the late fourteenth century. Just outside the gate once stood the Porcelain Pagoda, considered by many European travellers of the early nineteenth century to be one of the wonders of the world. It was destroyed during the Taiping Rebellion.

Little remains of the 11 years that Nanking served as capital of the Taiping empire. Hong Xiuquan's former PALACE was almost completely destroyed by the Manchu troops, and the Nationalists built government offices on the site (east of Taiping Lu on Changjiang Lu); just about all that remains of it is a stone boat sitting in a pond. The TAIPING MUSEUM (Zhonghua Lu, just north of the Zhonghua Gate) was once the palace of one of Hong Xiuquan's lieutenants.

On Muchou Lu in the western part of the city is the CHAOTIAN

GONG, a beautiful former Confucian temple dating from the 1860s. The area in front of the temple is now a local recreation area and is a pleasant place to go and people-watch.

Northeast of the city centre is XUANWU LAKE PARK, which includes a zoo with a few pandas. Part of the city wall also lies within the park for you to clamber along.

The most important tourist sites are found to the east of the city (take a No. 9 bus), including the TOMB OF THE FIRST MING DYNASTY EMPEROR, built in 1381. Nothing much remains of the tomb except 12 pairs of stone animals and statues of officials lining the path to the entrance. Further to the east, at the No. 9 bus terminus, is the SUN YATSEN MAUSOLEUM, built by the Nationalists in the 1920s. The mausoleum is set in a large wooded park, and Dr Sun's coffin stands in a domed vault at the top of a hill. There was a debate a few years ago about whether his body was really in the coffin or whether the Nationalists had taken it to Taiwan with them, but the authorities insist that it is still there.

Further east again from the Sun Yatsen Mausoleum is the LINGGU TEMPLE, of which only one building remains – the Wuliang (beamless) Hall, first built in 1381, which is distinguished by its lack of wooden beams.

South of the city centre in another park is the YUHUATAI (rain flower terrace), which serves as a memorial to the 100 000 people that the Communists say the Nationalists executed in Nanking during their years of rule there. Further south still is the TOMB OF A KING OF BORNEO who died in Nanking in 1408 while on a visit to pay homage to the Emperor of the Central Kingdom.

Food and shopping

Most of the best restaurants in town are strung out along Zhongshan Road. Try the *Peking Mutton Restaurant* at 94 Zhongshan Dong Lu, or the *Old Canton Restaurant* at 45 Zhongshan Lu, north of Xinjiekou, the main intersection. The local Friendship Store is on Daqing Lu.

How to get there and where to stay

Nanking is connected to most major centres by plane, and is a major stop on the Peking–Shanghai railway. There are also daily ferries on the Yangtse River to and from both Shanghai and Wuhan upstream.

The main tourist hotels are the *Nanjing Hotel* (259 Zhongshan Bei Lu; take a No. 32 bus from the railway station), and the *Dingshan Hotel*

(90 Chahaer Lu) which is less conveniently located. Budget travellers usually like to stay at the *Shengli* (victory) *Hotel* (75 Zhongshan Lu; take a No. 1 or No. 33 bus from the railway station).

Suzhou

As the saying goes: 'Above there is Heaven, below there is Suzhou and Hangzhou.' Maybe it's the build-up that spoils it, but I find Suzhou to be disappointingly similar to most other cities in central China. Nevertheless, its tree-lined streets and white-washed buildings are a pleasant change after the grey of Peking. And according to tradition, Suzhou girls are supposed to be the most beautiful in China, which helps.

The Grand Canal, first built in the seventh century as an inland transport route for grain, is close by the city, and like many other places along the canal's path, Suzhou prospered from its presence. Marco Polo, in his *Travels*, refers briefly to Suzhou, noting that rhubarb grew in great abundance in the surrounding hills.

Suzhou became a major centre of the silk industry and the home of many rich merchants who spent part of their profits building classically designed gardens, some of which are considered to be the best Chinese gardens in existence. Unfortunately, the town became a battleground during the Taiping Rebellion in the mid-nineteenth century and was badly damaged. Since 1949, it has grown and become partially industrialised, and the ubiquitous factory chimneys have gone a long way to destroying the atmosphere of this ancient town. That's progress. The good news is that there are still plenty of old things to see, including about a dozen gardens.

The gardens were built as secluded retreats for the rich, and probably looked better in the old days when they were virtually deserted except for the odd concubine or two draped over a distant rock. Today, the gardens are a major tourist attraction and on most days are packed with visitors, which tends to destroy the atmosphere. Some are also looking a bit tatty. The HUMBLE ADMINISTRATOR'S GARDEN, in the north of the city on Beisita Lu, is the best known. It was built in 1513 and completely restored in the 1950s. Another famous one is the LIUYUAN – 'garden to linger in' – constructed a couple of centuries later, which includes a famous 20-foot (6-metre) tall rock named Guanyun Feng (cloud-capped peak), taken from nearby Taihu (Tai Lake), a piece of naturalistic art.

The smallest of the Suzhou gardens is WANGSHI YUAN (fisherman

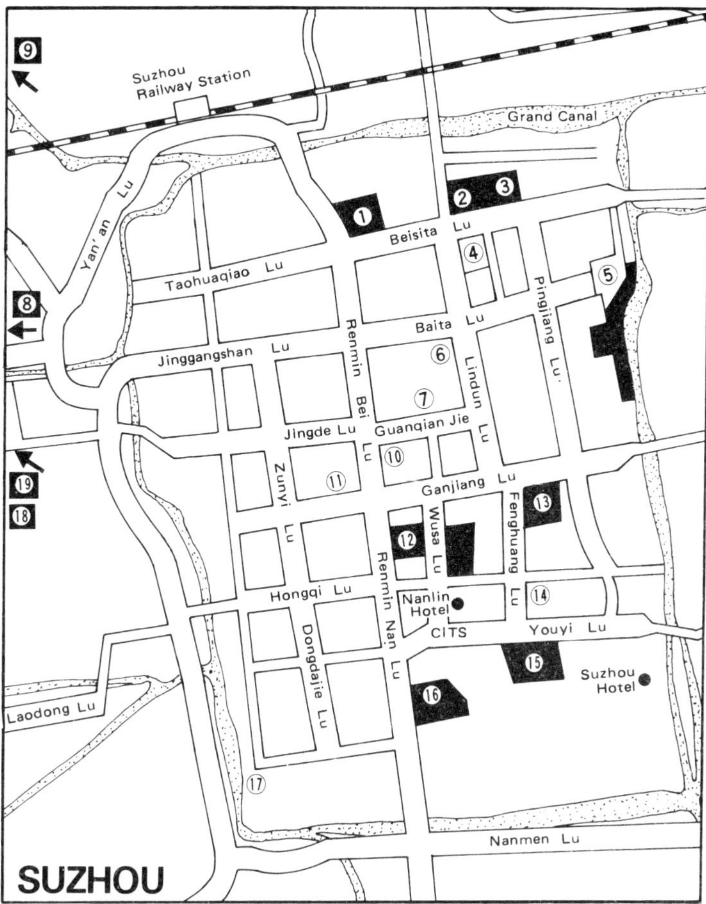

1 North Temple Pagoda (Beisita)
2 Suzhou Historical Museum
3 The Humble Administrator's Garden (Zhuozhengyuan)
4 Lion Grove (Shizilin)
5 Zoo
6 Daoist Temple of Mystery (Xuanmiaoguan)
7 Friendship Store
8 Liuyuan (Garden to Lingerin)
9 Tiger Hill (Hu Qiu)
10 People's Bazaar
11 Garden of Harmony (Yiyuan)
12 Stadium
13 Twin Pagodas (Shuangta)
14 No. 1 People's Hospital
15 Garden of the Master of the Nets (Wangshiyuan)
16 Surging Wave Pavilion (Canglang)
17 Pagoda of the Temple of the Good Omen Light (Ruiguangsita)
18 Han Shan Temple (Hanshansi)
19 West Garden (Xiyuan)

garden). It comprised three courtyards, one of which has been reproduced in the New York Metropolitan Museum as an exquisite example of the art of Chinese gardens. My guide, however, said that as far as she was concerned, the museum had got the wrong courtyard. They should have chosen the one next door, which is, she reckoned, much more beautiful.

Just outside Suzhou is TIGER HILL (Huqiu) topped by a 1000-year-old pagoda which is China's answer to the Leaning Tower of Pisa. The hill itself is said to have been constructed as a funeral mound for a local king, 2500 years ago. The 150-foot (137-metre) tall pagoda on top began to tilt several centuries ago, and has now reached such a precarious angle that it has had to be propped up with concrete supports.

The ancient king buried under the hill is said to have a huge treasure trove with him, including 3000 swords and a hoard of gold and jade, but the entrance to the tomb has never been found. At one point, just below the pagoda, is a large slab of red-stained stone, which is said to have gained its pigment from the blood spilled by the workmen killed after constructing the tomb, so that the secret would be safe.

A number of factories in Suzhou are open to tourists, including silk and sandalwood workshops. One place that is not open, but is nevertheless worth a mention, is the SUZHOU ARTS AND CRAFTS RESEARCH INSTITUTE where several young men spend all day carving Chinese poems and pictures on to miniscule objects such as slivers of ivory or even strands of hair. One of the workers has even carved the words 'Panda, the envoy of friendship' on a panda hair. In 1981, another worker produced an ivory carving of a Buddha only three millimetres tall, the robes and face of which can only be distinguished through a microscope. It is said to be the world's smallest carving.

Suzhou is known for its various handicrafts, including silks, sandalwood fans and embroidery which are available at the local Friendship Store (92 Guanqian Jie) or the Arts and Crafts Sales Department (274 Jingde Lu).

Suzhou cuisine is distinctive and noted particularly for various kinds of seafood, including crab and eel dishes. Noted restaurants include the *Songhelou Caiguan* (141 Guanqian Jie), and the *Xinjiufeng Caiguan* (657 Renmin Lu). Also, buy some Chinese nibbles at the *Daoxiangcun Sweet and Cake Shop* (35 Guanqian Jie), a famous Suzhou landmark.

How to get there and where to stay
Suzhou is only a couple of hours' train ride from Shanghai and makes a good day-trip from that city. If you want to stay overnight, foreigners usually stay at the *Suzhou Hotel* (115 Youyi Lu) which, apart from having nice regular rooms, also has a dormitory for budget travellers. The *Gusu Hotel*, next door to the Suzhou, is relatively new. Another hotel is the *Nanlin Hotel* (19 Gunxiu Fang).

Wuxi
Wuxi (pronounced wu-see), situated on the shores of Tai Lake (Taihu) not far from Suzhou, is considered to be one of the most picturesque towns in China and is therefore included on many official tourist itineraries. Unfortunately, much of the 'olde worlde' charm has been lost in the past 30 years as Wuxi has been developed into a major light industrial centre, but there are still streets which have retained their character. According to legend, the area once had a number of tin mines and was thus called Youxi – literally 'have tin' – but about 2000 years ago, the tin ran out, and the name was changed to Wuxi, 'no tin'.

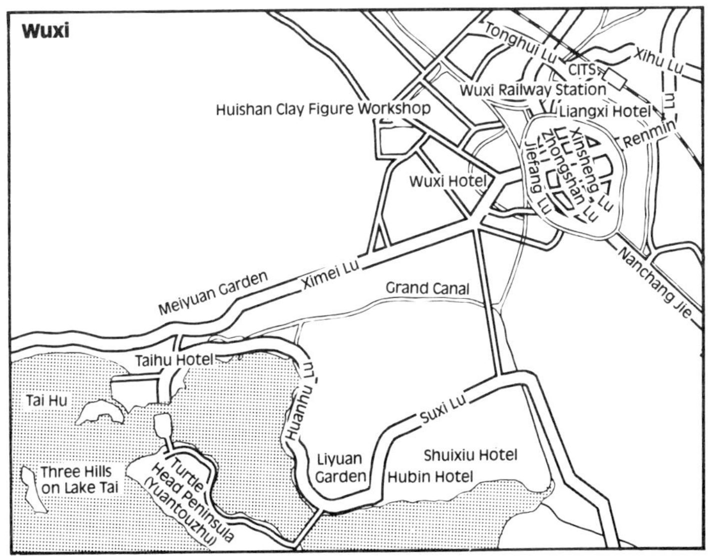

Wuxi has been a silk-producing centre for centuries (the NUMBER 1 SILK REELING MILL is open to visitors), but the GRAND CANAL, built in the seventh century, has been the town's economic lifeline for most of its history. Standing on one of the little bridges and watching life float by on a motley collection of junks and sampans is an educational way to spend an hour.

The town's biggest tourist attraction, however, is TAI LAKE, the fourth largest freshwater lake in China although it only has a depth of ten feet (3 metres) at its deepest point. The China Travel Service (local office: 42 Yucainong, Shixin Lane) operates boat trips on the lake. There are a number of classically designed gardens nearby, including the Liyuan, but they are not as interesting as the gardens of Suzhou.

How to get there and where to stay
Wuxi is on the main Shanghai–Peking railway line, a short ride northwest of Suzhou. Most foreigners stay at the *Shuixiu Hotel* or the *Hubin Hotel* (next to each other on Liyuan Lu). Some budget travellers have managed to get into the dormitory at the *Taihu Hotel* (Meiyuan Lu).

Yangzhou (Yangchow)

This town has more history than most places in China, and thankfully still looks like it. The beauty of Yangzhou and its surroundings has been the subject of poets for centuries, and the town has been spared the sort of indiscriminate industrialisation which has ruined so many other beautiful cities.

Yangzhou lies on the Grand Canal just to the north of the Yangtse River, and the construction of the canal in the seventh century, for the transportation of grain from Hangzhou to Peking, was what made Yangzhou a thriving commercial centre.

According to Marco Polo's account of his travels, he was governor of Yangzhou for three years in the 1290s while an official in the Mongol administration of Kublai Khan. None of the Chinese records mentions him, so he could not have been the official governor of the city, but one version of the *Travels* perhaps explains the mystery, by adding that he held office 'by the Great Khan's commission in place of one of the . . . barons'.

During the Qing dynasty, Yangzhou grew in importance again as a centre of the salt trade, and the rich merchants who lived here at that time built gardens and pavilions and supported an artists' colony which gave rise to a distinctive and well-known school of Chinese painting.

Of the many gardens and temples to be visited in Yangzhou, the most famous is the FAJING SI (Fajing temple) in the northwest of the town, which is dedicated to the monk Jian Zhen, credited with introducing Buddhism to Japan 1500 years ago. Most of the temple buildings, however, were destroyed during the Taiping Rebellion in the mid-nineteenth century and were only rebuilt in the 1930s. (Take a No. 5 bus to the terminus.)

There are a number of classical-style gardens to be seen, the best-known of which is the GE YUAN (Ge garden) in the northeast. In the east of the town is the SHITA (stone pagoda), built in the Tang dynasty.

How to get there and where to stay

Yangzhou is a couple of hours away by road from Nanking, and is probably best treated as a day-trip from that city. Foreigners who spend the night in Yangzhou stay at the *Xiyuan Hotel* (Fenglousheng Lu).

JIANGXI PROVINCE

Nanchang

The city of Nanchang, the capital of Jiangxi Province in southeast China, has a population approaching one million. In modern history, it is most famous as the first place that the embryonic Communist army attacked after forming up in the nearby mountains. The troops under the command of Chou Enlai stormed Nanchang on 1 August 1927 and held the city for seven days before the Nationalists pushed them out again. There are various 'revolutionary sites' in the city, including the HEADQUARTERS OF THE NANCHANG RISING on Shengli Lu (victory road), and Nanchang has long been a destination for pilgrims visiting the various spawning grounds of Chinese Communism.

Like many other places in China, Nanchang was severely disrupted by the Cultural Revolution and the campaigns which followed it up to and beyond the death of Mao in 1976. The city's tractor factory, for instance, was forced to close for almost two years between 1974 and 1976 while groups of workers belonging to different political factions engaged in occasional running battles with wooden clubs, stones and bottles of acid. According to one report, the directors of the factory were besieged in their offices on more than 50 occasions, and the radicals took over local militia groups to form their own army. When foreign journalists visited the factory in 1977, one worker told them that he had spent half of 1976 just sitting at home because the radicals had told him not to follow 'the theory of productive forces' by continuing to work. But, he added, he did go to the factory once a month to collect his pay.

There are a number of possible excursions from Nanchang – to the summer resort of Lushan (*see* p. 184), to the pottery-making town of Jingdezhen (*see below*), and to the sacred birthplace of the Chinese People's Liberation Army, the Jinggangshan mountains (*see* p. 182).

How to get there and where to stay

Nanchang is connected by plane to Shanghai, Canton and Peking,

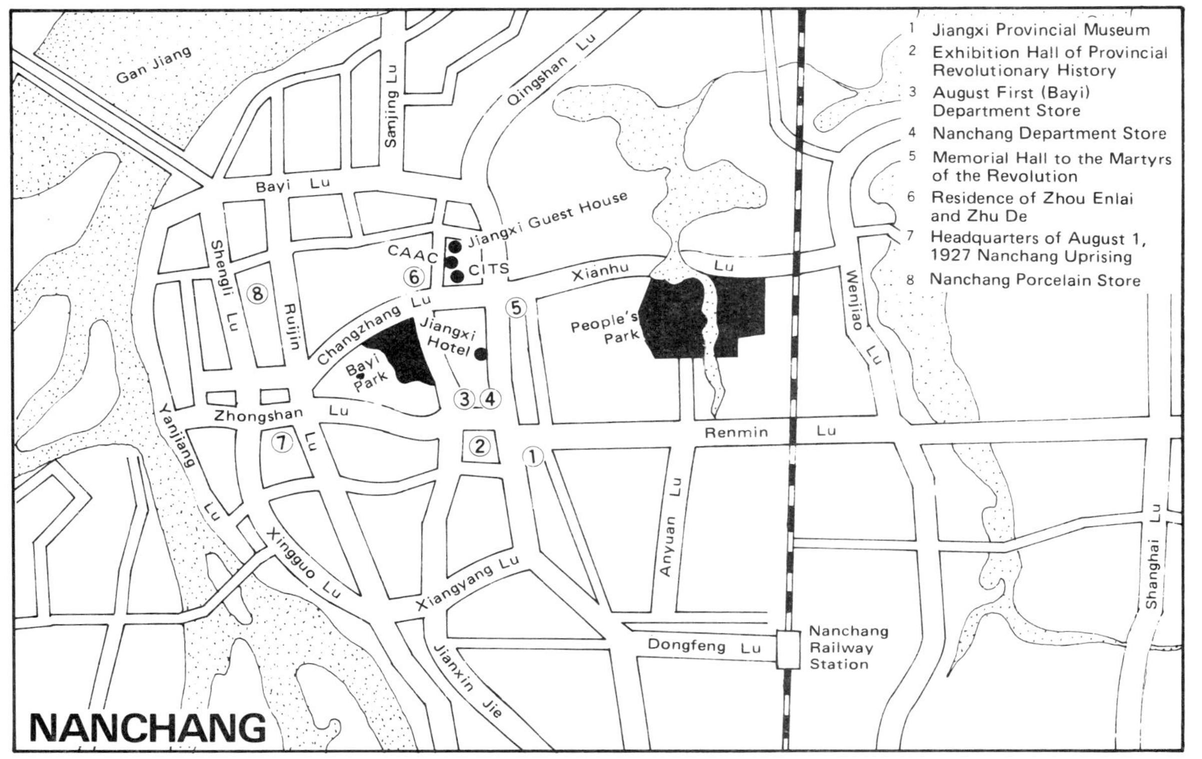
NANCHANG
1 Jiangxi Provincial Museum
2 Exhibition Hall of Provincial Revolutionary History
3 August First (Bayi) Department Store
4 Nanchang Department Store
5 Memorial Hall to the Martyrs of the Revolution
6 Residence of Zhou Enlai and Zhu De
7 Headquarters of August 1, 1927 Nanchang Uprising
8 Nanchang Porcelain Store
Gan Jiang
Sanjing Lu
Qingshan Lu
Bayi Lu
Jiangxi Guest House
CAAC
CITS
Xianhu Lu
Shengli Lu
Ruijin
Changzhang Lu
Jiangxi Hotel
Bayi Park
People's Park
Wenjiao Lu
Zhongshan Lu
Yanjiang Lu
Renmin Lu
Anyuan Lu
Xingguo Lu
Xiangyang Lu
Jianxin Jie
Dongfeng Lu
Nanchang Railway Station
Shanghai Lu

and is also on the main Shanghai–Canton railway line. There is a large number of hotels and guesthouses in the city, presumably because of the great many visitors who have come over the years to inspect the relics of the youth of Chinese Communism.

The three main hotels are all close together, not far from the centre of town. The *Jiangxi Hotel* (Changzheng Lu) is the one most frequently used by foreigners, but there are also the *Nanchang Hotel* (Zhanqian Lu) and the *Jiangxi Provincial Guesthouse* (Bayi Lu) for especially honoured guests.

Jingdezhen

Jingdezhen in northeast Jiangxi was once famous for producing fine Chinese porcelain coveted throughout China and much of the rest of the world, especially Europe. However, in the words of one writer: 'China's ceramics industry never fully recovered from the ravages of the Taiping Rebellion over a century ago. Today, the tradition of fine quality chinaware formerly associated with Jingdezhen is kept alive in Derby, Limoges and other ceramic centres in Western countries.'

Ceramics are still produced in Jingdezhen, but of a very inferior quality compared to the old days. Nevertheless, it is a major industry, and Jingdezhen's 30000 ceramics workers produce about 250 million pieces a year, about half of them for export. (*To get to Jingdezhen, take a train. There is a branch railway line from Nanchang.*)

Jinggangshan

In this isolated mountain area on the border between Jiangxi and Hunan provinces, is a sacred place for Chinese Communists, and a place of great interest for students of modern Chinese history. The National Party under Generalissimo Chiang Kaishek tried to destroy the Communist Party in 1927 and was nearly successful. Abortive raids by the fledgling Communist army against Nanchang and Changsha in the same year left the Party even weaker, but some key Party members, most notably Mao Tse-tung, made their way into the isolated Jinggangshan mountains and spent the next four years there, building the Chinese brand of Communism – revolution based not on the urban proletariat but on the rural peasantry. The first Chinese Communist government, called a soviet, was established here with its headquarters at Chaling across the provincial border in Hunan, and Mao's men worked at expanding the territory under their control and experimenting with land reform. It was here that Mao met up with Zhu De (Che Teh), known as the 'Father of the Red Army', an experienced soldier who was instrumental in making Mao's political ambitions militarily possible.

The Communist Party Central Committee, still loyal to the Russian idea of urban revolution, was disdainful of Mao's attempts to organise the peasants and gave him and his band of mountain guerrillas little support. In 1929, the Party leadership ordered Mao to dissolve the Red Army and return to Shanghai, but Mao refused in spite of increasing pressure from Nationalist troops.

In 1930, Chiang Kaishek began the first campaign of 'encirclement and annihilation' against the Communists, which failed – just as the other five subsequent 'annihilation' campaigns did – when the Communists captured the Nationalist general in charge of the campaign. The fifth campaign in 1934 was much more successful, however, and the Nationalists forced the Communist forces to abandon their strongholds in the mountains of southeast China and embark on the epic Long March, eventually ending in Yan'an in Shaanxi Province.

Visitors to the Jinggangshan mountains go by road from Nanchang to the village of CIPING, a journey of more than 200 miles (320 kilometres) to the southeast. Jiangxi is a poor province although the countryside is interesting, but the journey is recommended only for specialists and those with a specific interest in the history of the Chinese Communist Party.

In Ciping, visitors are shown a house which Mao used as his headquarters and a museum which contains various relics relating to the formation of the Red Army. One item is a wooden pole General Zhu De is supposed to have used to carry buckets of water in spite of protests from his underlings, thereby showing he had a good proletarian outlook. During the Cultural Revolution, when Zhu De came under criticism, the pole was redesignated as having belonged to Lin Piao, then in the political ascendant. The name was changed back to Zhu De when Lin Piao was killed after allegedly attempting to assassinate Mao in 1971.

Some Chinese tourists still visit Ciping, although far fewer than during the Cultural Revolution, which means that there is probably a bus from Nanchang (I have, unfortunately, not been able to discover any information).

Lushan

Situated in the very north of Jiangxi Province in southeast China, this mountain resort has been the site of a number of important events in modern Chinese history which makes it more than just a pretty scenic spot.

Generalissimo Chiang Kaishek had a great liking for Lushan and had a residence on the mountain which can still be visited, and even rented, today. The Nationalist Party (Kuomingtang) under Chiang's leadership held a number of important meetings here in the 1930s, but the meeting which really put Lushan on the historical map took place in 1959, exactly ten years after the Communist victory.

It was a gathering of the Politburo of the Communist Party, and the main topic on the agenda was Mao's disastrous Great Leap Forward and his decision to push ahead with the grouping of China's peasantry into 'people's communes', which together threw China into almost unprecedented economic chaos. Mao, the incorrigible dreamer, could not see past his vision of a massive collective effort dragging China into the modern world. The Politburo was a little bit more down-to-earth.

The man who stood up and took it upon himself to criticise Mao was General Peng Dehuai, a peasant soldier from Mao's home province of Hunan, who had followed the Chairman since 1928. He read out a long submission to Mao which attacked the Great Leap Forward policy for attempting too much too quickly and throwing the economy out of balance. The other military leaders at the conference apparently supported Peng, and when a vote was taken, Mao reportedly lost. Mao, however, was not one to allow himself to be beaten by the democratic process. He called for an enlarged Politburo meeting, and the vote was reversed.

Although Mao had to admit some of his errors, he continued to promote the Great Leap Forward and insisted that China's economy would surpass the economy of Great Britain within 15 years. Peng Dehuai was forced to resign his post as Defence Minister and was replaced by Lin Piao, the man who was accused in 1971 of attempting to assassinate Mao. It was a victory won at a huge cost. Mao lost the post of State President to Liu Shaoqi, and after the Lushan conference and the 'Three Terrible Years' which followed, when the harvests failed and probably millions of people starved to death, he was virtually pushed aside and only regained supreme power by starting the Cultural Revolution. Peng Dehuai, meanwhile, was eventually jailed and died in 1974 in extreme secrecy. His death was only officially reported in 1981.

In 1970, the Politburo held another meeting in Lushan. This time, Lin Piao, now officially named as Mao's chosen successor, allegedly attempted to have himself made President. He reportedly suggested that Mao become President, in the belief that Mao would decline, leaving the way open for himself. The plot, if that is what it was, did not work, but as with most struggles in Chinese history, we only know the winner's side of the story.

The conference hall where these battles took place still exists but visitors are not allowed inside. It is marked by a plaque which simply says 'Conference site'.

There are a number of other scenic attractions in Lushan, including a cave where a monk is supposed to have discovered the secret to immortality, and a botanical garden which swaps cuttings with Kew Gardens.

How to get there and where to stay

Lushan is not far from the town of Jiujiang (nine rivers) which is connected by rail to the city of Nanchang, with train services several times a day. If you are travelling under the care of the CTS, you will be met at Jiujiang station and whisked away by car. If you are on your own, there is a hotel in Jiujiang called *Nanhu Binguan* (South Lake Guesthouse). There are no buses, so you have to walk from the station, or rent one of the small three-wheeler mini-vans which abound throughout China. Rooms in the guesthouse cost 20 yuan each. From Jiujiang to Lushan, there are public buses which leave at around 6.30 each morning and at one o'clock each afternoon. The bus station is about 15 minutes' walk from the Nanhu Binguan. Once in Lushan town, there are three guesthouses to choose from: the *Lushan Binguan* on Hexi Lu, about ten minutes' walk from the bus station, the *Yunzhong Binguan* on Xiangshan Lu, about 20 minutes' walk, and the *Lulin Fandian* (hotel) at Lulinhu, about 30 minutes' walk. The Lushan Binguan, closest to the centre of town, is probably the best.

For those with a sense of history and a sufficient amount of money, cabin No. 180 at the Lushan Binguan was used by the late Generalissimo Chiang Kaishek on several occasions. The paltry sum of 180 yuan will buy you a night in the Generalissimo's bed.

JILIN PROVINCE

Changchun

Another major industrial city in the northeast of China, Changchun was once the capital of Manchukuo, the Japanese puppet-state set up in 1932 with the former Manchu emperor, Henry Pu Yi, as its figurehead leader. The main government and university buildings of the city mostly date from that era. Manchukuo folded in 1945 when the Japanese surrendered.

Changchun, now the capital of Jilin Province, has a population of nearly two million and contains a number of important factories, including a vehicle plant that turns out the ubiquitous Liberation truck, the main workhorse of Chinese industry and agriculture alike. The plant also used to produce the Red Flag luxury limousine in which China's top leaders and honoured foreign guests ride, but the cars, which are built like tanks, gulp fuel faster than an alcoholic downs whisky and rust like crazy, were deemed too wasteful and production was halted in 1982.

How to get there and where to stay

Changchun is well served by both air services and trains – the main railway line from Peking to Harbin in the far northeast passes through the city. The main hotel is the *Chunyi Hotel* (2 Stalin Dajie; just opposite the railway station), which also contains the city's CITS office.

LIAONING PROVINCE

Shenyang (Mukden)

Formerly known to foreigners as Mukden, Shenyang is heavily industrialised and one of the largest cities in northeast China. It is now the capital of Liaoning Province, but was once the capital of the Manchurian kingdom which, in the seventeenth century, invaded and conquered China. In the late nineteenth century, with foreign powers vying for 'spheres of influence' in many parts of the country, Russia acquired the rights to build the Trans-Siberian Railway through Manchuria, and both Japan and the Russians began a tussle for supremacy in the region which lasted right through to 1945.

In 1931, Japan engineered the so-called 'Mukden Incident' (when a bomb exploded on the track of the South Manchurian Railway) as a pretext to seize the whole of northeast China, and then established the puppet-state of Manchukuo with the former Chinese emperor, Henry Pu Yi, as its nominal ruler. After the civil war in the late 1940s which resulted in the Communist victory, the Soviets returned in force as advisers and helped rebuild Shenyang's industrial base, which is now one of the most important in the country. Factories include a military aircraft plant which produces China's fighter aircraft, based on Soviet designs. The city's population is now over three million.

During the latter part of the Maoist era, Shenyang became an important 'base' for the radical faction in Chinese politics. Mao Yuanxin, Mao's nephew, was nominally Deputy Secretary of the Liaoning Province Party Committee, but in reality appears to have been the effective overlord of the northeast region during the early 1970s. He was seized by the moderate faction soon after the so-called 'Gang of Four' radicals were taken into custody in Peking in October 1976, and he has been languishing in jail ever since. At the time of the 'Gang of Four' show-trial in late 1980, the official press said Mao's nephew would soon be put on trial in Shenyang, but by early 1983, the trial had still not been held, for some obscure political reason. The commander of the Shenyang military units – that is, of northeast China – is General Li Desheng, a powerful, shadowy figure who is the only regional military commander from the Maoist era to have retained his post.

Shenyang is probably most famous, however, for its heavy air pollution, its greyness and its grim forbidding character, particularly in the winter which is Siberian. A number of British students used to be sent to Shenyang University each year but, in 1980, a group quickly dubbed the 'Shenyang Fifteen' refused to go.

The majority of Western visitors to the city are now probably businessmen, most of whom spend as little time there as they possibly can. However, there are some interesting sites to be viewed, mostly relics of the former Manchu kingdom in the days before the successful raid south.

The MANCHU IMPERIAL PALACE, built soon after the Manchus made Shenyang their capital in 1625, is to the east of the present city centre, on Zhongyang Lu. The palace was built as a copy of the Forbidden City in Peking, although it is on a much more modest scale. It is now a museum. (*Take a No. 13 trolley from the railway station, get off at the ninth stop, and the palace is on the left.*)

The last two Manchu leaders, who built up their state to the point where it could threaten the entire Chinese empire, are buried in separate tombs to the north and east of the city. Abukai, who proclaimed the Qing (Manchu) dynasty, but died in 1643, one year before Peking was taken, is buried at BEILING (north tomb), now surrounded by a park of the same name (take a No. 10 bus from the station). His father, Nurhachi, is buried in DONGLING (east tomb), which is also a park (take a No. 18 bus from near the palace museum).

The main downtown area of Shenyang is just to the east of the railway station. Restaurants include the *Shaoyuan* on Zhonghua Lu, and the main local dish is so-called 'Mongolian' hot-pot, which is, in fact, eaten all over northeast Asia in one form or another. A small burner is placed on the table with boiling water on top into which you put slivers of meat, vegetables and other edibles to cook. Shuangyangrou – mutton hot-pot – is the most common. The local Friendship Store is in the People's Department Store (12 Zhongshan Yi Lu).

How to get there and where to stay

Shenyang is connected to Peking by air, and is a 12-hour train journey from the capital. The main hotel used to be a beautiful old place called the *Liaoning Guesthouse* near the station, but foreigners now have to stay at the *Liaoning Mansions* (Huanghe da Jie) in the north of the city (Liaoning Daxia; take a No. 6 trolley from the railway station).

Dalian (Luda, Dairen)

This town in northeast China is an important seaport, and a pleasant place to visit. In the old days, it was known in the West as Dairen, and today is often referred to in China as Luda. It is a large industrial city, but has somehow managed to remain neat, tidy and pleasant. There is nothing much to see there except for the harbour and a number of beaches.

To the southwest of Dalian city, further down towards the tip of the peninsula, is Lushun, formerly called Port Arthur, but now the base of the North China Fleet and closed to foreigners. In 1898, Russia forced the Chinese government to hand over the area on a 25-year lease, and began building the harbour. As a result of the Russo–Japanese War of 1904–1905, the Russians were forced to cede the territory to the Japanese who ruled it until they were defeated in their turn in 1945. Construction of the harbour was completed in 1930.

The main tourist activity, apart from visiting factories, is walking around the hilly city, admiring the harbour views. There are some good restaurants in which seafood of all kinds is the speciality.

How to get there and where to stay

There are regular flights to Dalian from Peking, and also train services. The nearest hotel to the railway station is the *Dalian Binguan* (Zhongshan Guangchang). The *Nanshan Binguan* (56 Fenglin Jie) is a little further away near the harbour, and contains a CITS office. Right on the coastline is the *Pangcui Dao Binguan* (Pangcui Island Hotel).

NINGXIA PROVINCE

This area of northwest China is very poor and backward and is closed to foreigners. Most of the region is desert. About a third of the four million people in Ningxia are local Muslims, the rest are Han Chinese, most of whom have been moved in by the government during the past 30 years. The main city is Yinchuan, which is also closed to foreigners and likely to remain so, although people travelling by train between Lanzhou and Baotou in Inner Mongolia pass through it.

There are occasional hints in the official press of friction between the local Muslims and the Chinese. One such was a report in 1981 that Muslims in the region were being required to make a 'pledge of patriotism'. 'A few people have said things which do not benefit unity and we must re-educate them,' said the local daily newspaper.

QINGHAI PROVINCE

Qinghai Province, in the northwest of China, north of Tibet, is one of the least hospitable places on earth. Most of it is desert or rugged mountain, bitterly cold in winter and blindingly hot in summer. In mid-1982 when the national census was taken, the population of this huge area was only 3.9 million people.

The province is closed to foreigners, although Xining, the provincial capital, and Qinghai Lake are fairly close to Lanzhou and have been visited by some foreign delegations, suggesting that the authorities may soon be willing to open the door just a crack. One problem with developing tourism in Qinghai is that it has the reputation of being the labour camp province (it is not known if the population figure includes prisoners). Because of its isolated position and barrenness, the Communist government has apparently made use of prison labour to help develop the province. Many of the original inhabitants of Qinghai are Tibetans, and the exiled Tibetan god-king, the Dalai Lama (who was born in Qinghai), considers a large slice of the province to be rightfully part of his kingdom.

Visitors to XINING stay in a large Soviet-style guesthouse surrounded by high walls. The drive to QINGHAI LAKE to the west is spectacular: wide open spaces with occasional Tibetan herdsmen, while to the south are majestic mountains guarding the approaches to Tibet. The lake is a large inland saltwater sea which supports a fishing industry. At the western end is BIRD ISLAND, a famous rookery where thousands of birds nest in summer. When they migrate south, they are replaced by Siberian swans flying in from further north.

But best of all, the Qinghai Lake has its own monster, a cousin of the Loch Ness monster. On 23 May 1982, men fishing near an island in the centre of the lake reported seeing a huge animal rising out of the water nearby. It was black and yellow in colour, about 13 or 14 metres long and had the shape of an over-turned boat. Tibetan herdsmen living near the lake reported having seen the animal many times, and said it usually surfaced on very hot days.

SHAANXI PROVINCE

Xi'an (Sian)

Xi'an has been the capital of China for a longer period of time throughout history than Peking. A total of 11 dynasties have used it as their capital for more than 1100 years, beginning with the Zhou dynasty 3000 years ago. As a result, Xi'an and the surrounding country are an archaeological treasure trove, with more finds being made all the time.

The earliest of the sites is the remains of the Neolithic village at BANPO which have been covered with a large dome-like building and opened to tourists, who can see the remains of living quarters, some graves and a pottery kiln. It is the best-preserved example of New Stone Age life ever found in China. (*Take a No. 11 bus from outside the Liberation Hotel and get off at the seventh stop. Walk to the next intersection, turn right and you're there. From the People's Hotel, take a No. 3 bus to the end of the line near the Liberation Hotel, then a No. 11 bus.*)

The main reason most people go to Xi'an is to see the TOMB OF QIN SHI HUANG, the first emperor of China, who decreed that he be guarded in death by a huge army of life-size terracotta soldiers estimated to number over 6000 in all. Qin Shi Huang (259–210 B.C.) was the king of one part of north China, and he conquered six other kingdoms to form the first Chinese empire. Even today, more than 2000 years after his death, he remains a controversial figure, revered as the man who first unified China and masterminded the construction of the Great Wall to keep out the barbarians to the north, and hated for burning books and burying scholars alive.

He built his capital just to the east of present-day Xi'an, and reportedly had 700000 workers conscripted to build his tomb, a job which took 36 years. According to historical records, the tomb contains a magnificent throne room full of jewels and precious objects and a river of mercury with gold ducks floating on it, but it has yet to be excavated. The hill under which the tomb is supposed to be situated is on the slopes of Mount Li. Tourists can view this rather ordinary mound of earth by the roadside, and wonder if any grave plunderers managed to find their way into the tomb during the past 2000 years, or even if the tomb is there at all.

But it probably is. Three vaults have been found around the mound, which contained the army supposed to protect Qin Shi Huang in the after-life. The first vault was discovered in 1974 when peasants were sinking a well. The other vaults were found in 1976.

Vault No. 1, the biggest of the three, has been covered by a huge hangar-like structure to protect it. More than 6000 pottery foot-soldiers, cavalrymen and chariot riders are believed to be in the vault, although only a few hundred have so far been unearthed and restored. The slow, careful work will continue for many years to come. The figures are all life-size, and each one has a different facial expression. They are arranged in battle formation, and carry real swords, spears and crossbows. In the vanguard are three rows of 70 soldiers behind which is the main body of the army, 38 rows of troops.

Vault No. 2 contains about 1000 more soldiers, while the third vault, the smallest of the three, was apparently built as the 'command headquarters' for the other two troop formations.

The main vault was opened as a museum in 1979, and visitors are allowed to walk over the excavations on a wooden walkway. The taking of photographs is usually strictly forbidden unless a large fee is paid first, a ruling which naturally enrages tourists. People who are caught taking a couple of snaps on the sly are often forced to hand over their film.

Another regular item on tourist itineraries in Xi'an are the HUAQING HOT SPRINGS, a few miles northeast of the city. Various emperors through the ages have had palaces built on the site, the first in A.D. 747. The hot springs and its attendant buildings nestling into a hillside are best known for being the scene of the so-called 'Xi'an Incident' in 1936 when Generalissimo Chiang Kaishek was kidnapped by a local warlord and forced to halt his war against the Communists and form a united front with them to fight the Japanese. The story is extremely bizarre: it began when Chiang flew into Xi'an to direct the sixth anti-Communist 'extermination' campaign, then in progress under the command of a local warlord. But the warlord was secretly in contact with the Communists, and sent troops to the Huaqing Hot Springs to kidnap Chiang at dawn on 12 December 1936. Hearing gunshots outside, Chiang fled from his bedroom and up the mountain slope behind, and was found there cowering among some rocks in his nightshirt. (A pavilion has been built on the spot which bears the inscription: 'Chiang was caught here.')

Having got their arch-enemy in their grasp, the Communists wanted to kill him, but Stalin, dreading the chaos which Chiang's death could unleash in China, warned against it, saying that Chiang was the only possible leader of a united front against Japan. After several days of intensive negotiations between the Communists, the warlord and his prisoner, Chiang was released on Christmas Day, but only after agreeing to a united front and the payment of a huge ransom to the warlord.

Captain Harald Herzog, a German pilot, was the man chosen to fly the ransom money from Shanghai to Xi'an. 'The Nationalists gave me a call and sent me over to a military base near Shanghai where a Junkers JU-52 had been filled up with banknotes to pay the ransom,' he said. 'The plane was so full of banknotes that the co-pilot and I could not get in by the normal door – the glass had to be taken off the cockpit, and we got in that way. When we arrived at Xi'an, we circled above the airfield until we saw Chiang's plane take off, and we handed the money over as soon as we landed.'

(There are local buses going to Qin Shi Huang's tomb and other places of interest, from the bus station just outside the south gate of the city wall. However, it is probably more convenient to get on one of the cheap local tours, and take in all the sights at once. Tickets for the tours can be bought at the Liberation Hotel, among other places. A tour of the tomb, the Huaqing Hot Springs and the Neolithic village costs six yuan, but you're supposed to be a resident of the Liberation Hotel in order to buy a ticket. The bus leaves at 7.00 a.m., with a boring three-hour stop at the hot springs to give tourists a chance to have lunch and a soak in the supposedly medicinal waters.)

In Xi'an itself, there are a number of important historical sites to see. The SHAANXI PROVINCIAL MUSEUM, just inside the south gate of the old city wall, is one of the best museums in China, although a couple of galleries are only open to foreigners on payment of an exorbitant fee. The museum is a former Confucian temple, and has China's best collection of stone-engraved calligraphy (steles). To foreigners who can't read Chinese, stone tablets are of little interest, but just inside the second pavilion, on the left, is a tablet which tells the story of how a branch of Christianity came to China over 1000 years ago.

The tablet, topped by a cross supported by two dragons, tells the story of how Jing Jiao – apparently Nestorian Christianity – was introduced to the Chinese empire and flourished for several hundred years. The Nestorians believed that Jesus Christ was two distinct persons, one divine and one human, and the sect's disciples spread out from Syria, and established colonies in all the cities along the Silk Road through central Asia. Marco Polo mentions finding communities of Nestorians in several cities in China, including Fuzhou.

The tablet in the Xi'an museum is signed by 'Adam, County-Bishop and Pope of China' and was engraved in 781 to mark the opening of a church. It tells of how a Syrian named Raban appeared at the Chinese imperial court in Xi'an (then called Chang'an) in 635 and presented holy scriptures to the court which were translated and read by the emperor. The emperor, the stone says, was impressed and ordered that a monastery dedicated to the new religion be established. In the end, the Nestorian religion is believed to have died out in China in the fifteenth century, just two centuries before the Jesuit priest Matteo Ricci arrived in Peking to propagate the Roman form of Christianity. Ricci searched for some sign that Christianity had existed in China in the past, but found none. However, only 15 years after his death in 1610, workmen digging foundations for a building near Xi'an came upon the great stone now in the Shaanxi Provincial Museum, which proved what Ricci had been unable to discover.

The BIG GOOSE PAGODA, built in 652 to house Buddhist scriptures brought from India by the monk Xuan Zhuang, is well worth visiting. The monk, also called Tripitaka, is said to have brought back 657 volumes of scriptures with him and to have sat in the pagoda, with a Sanskrit expert on one side and a Chinese expert on the other, and translated the whole lot over a period of 14 years. The pagoda was rebuilt in 1580. (*The pagoda is outside the city wall. Take a No. 5 bus from the railway station and get off at the eighth stop, just before the bus turns right. The pagoda should be in front of you.*)

There is also a small WILD GOOSE PAGODA, built in 709 (take a No. 3 bus from the railway station and get off one stop after passing the south gate of the city wall. The pagoda is on the right, down Youyi Xi Lu), and the local mosque, a fascinating structure called the QINGZHEN SI. The mosque, built in 1742, is on Xiyang Shi Jie, just northwest of the Drum Tower in the centre of town. The DRUM TOWER and BELL TOWER, dating from the Ming dynasty, are also both worth a visit.

There are many restaurants in Xi'an, but Shaanxi Province is not noted for any special dishes. One thing worth trying, however, is the local wine, called Xifeng Jiu, which is milky in appearance and, unlike most Chinese wines, very pleasant to drink. Some of the local restaurants are the *Xianfang Fanzhuang* on Dongda Jie, east of the Bell Tower, and the *Baiyunzhang Dumpling Restaurant* nearby; another dumpling restaurant is the *Defazhang* near the Bell Tower.

How to get there and where to stay

Xi'an is accessible by plane from Peking, Shanghai and most other major cities, and is also on the national railway network.

The main hotel used by foreigners is the *Renmin Daxia* (people's mansion) on Dongxin Jie, generally considered to be an appalling place. (From the railway station, take a No. 3 bus, get off at the third stop on the square and walk another few minutes. The hotel is on your left.) One traveller has stated that the new *Xi'an Hotel* was preferable to the Renmin Daxia – 'A better class of cockroach,' he said.

Budget travellers usually stay at the *Liberation Hotel* opposite the railway station where a room costs 12 yuan and a bed-space six yuan.

Yan'an (Yenan)

This town on the barren plains of northern Shaanxi Province was once a regular stopover for foreigners doing the full China tour. But that, as they say, was in the days of the 'Gang of Four'. The town was the endpoint of the epic Long March undertaken by the Communist groups in southeast China to escape from the 'annihilation campaigns' launched by the Nationalists. The main column of 90 000 soldiers and dependants left their bases in Jiangxi Province in late 1934, but only 5000 of the original number reached Yan'an in early 1936, the rest having dropped out or died in battle or of hunger, cold and exhaustion. Mao himself described the 6000-mile (9600-kilometre) march as the worst period in the struggle of the Communist Party to gain victory.

Those who took part underwent great hardships, and many displayed great heroism against often overwhelming odds. But at the end of it, the Communist Party had been completely re-shaped: Mao had taken control, and the trials of the march had welded the Party into a formidable force, ripe for expansion. 'For 12 months, we were under daily reconnaissance and bombing from the skies by scores of planes, while on the land we were encircled and pursued, obstructed and intercepted by a huge force of several hundred thousand men and we encountered untold difficulties and dangers on the way,' Mao said later. 'Yet by using our two legs, we swept across a distance of more than 6000 miles through the length and breadth of 11 provinces. Let us ask, has history ever known a long march to equal ours' No, never.'

From 1936 to 1947, Yan'an served as the headquarters of the Communist forces, who lived for the most part in the caves used by the local peasants. The area became a symbol of the Communist Party's resilience and will to win and, almost immediately, people began to make the pilgrimage up to this primitive, poverty-stricken part of China to honour the future rulers of China. One of the first was the American journalist Edgar Snow, who wrote the classic *Red Star Over China*, based on extensive interviews with Mao and the other Communist leaders in the Yan'an caves.

Snow described Mao as being a 'gaunt, Lincolnesque figure' with an intellectual face of great shrewdness. 'Mao seemed to me to be a very interesting and complex man. He had the simplicity and naturalness of the Chinese peasant, with a lively sense of humour and a love of rustic laughter . . . He was plain-speaking and plain-living, and some people might have considered him rather coarse and vulgar. Yet he combined curious qualities of naïveté with incisive wit and worldly sophistication.'

In 1947, Generalissimo Chiang Kaishek attacked Yan'an and captured it. But it was an empty gesture. By then, the Communists had become a national force and no longer needed the town. Within two years, the Nationalists were on the run from the mainland and the Red Army took Yan'an once more.

There is little to see in and around the town except for various sites of revolutionary significance. There is a museum, and at least four places where Mao lived at one time or another. At WANGJIAPING, to the south of Yan'an, there is a replica of the hall in which the Party held its Seventh Congress. The original was destroyed by the Nationalists.

The town is strung out along the valley of the Yan River, which has cut itself a deep channel in the plain. Dominating the whole area is the BAOTA (precious pagoda), built in the Song dynasty, which became a potent revolutionary symbol, particularly during the Cultural Revolution.

How to get there and where to stay

Visitors to Yan'an usually fly there from Xi'an, the provincial capital, 300 miles (480 kilometres) to the south, although there are also local buses. There is a guesthouse which is suitably spartan for pilgrims.

SHANDONG PROVINCE

Jinan

Jinan is the capital of Shandong Province, and has been known for centuries as the 'city of springs'. Unfortunately, most of the 100 springs have dried up in recent years, due to increasing industrial use of underground water and prolonged droughts, but a water project designed to restore the springs, and Jinan's reputation, has been started. Time will tell.

Jinan's most interesting buildings are of German design and were built during the 15 years or so from 1898 that Shandong was a German 'sphere of influence'. The railway station is pure Bavaria, and so are a couple of streets in the centre of town. The Germans built the railway through to Qingdao (Chingtao) on the southern coast of Shandong, connecting a large part of the province up with the outside world for the first time. There is little else to see in Jinan, although some of the older parts of the city are pleasant to walk around.

To the south of Jinan city is the THOUSAND BUDDHA MOUNTAIN (Qianfuoshan), but it is a depressing place to visit because so few Buddhas are left. The Red Guards were let loose on the place during the Cultural Revolution and destroyed hundreds of ancient statues and carvings in a frenzy of vandalism inspired by Mao's directive to destroy everything old. Apologists for the Chairman would say that he had not meant it so literally.

The other thing worth seeing in Jinan is the YELLOW RIVER DYKES, huge earthworks built up over the centuries to prevent 'China's Sorrow' from spilling over and inundating the surrounding countryside, as it has done from time to time (*see* Zhengzhou, p. 142, for a further description of the Yellow River).

How to get there and where to stay

There are flights from Peking to Jinan, and the city is also on the main Peking–Shanghai railway line, about nine hours' journey from Peking.

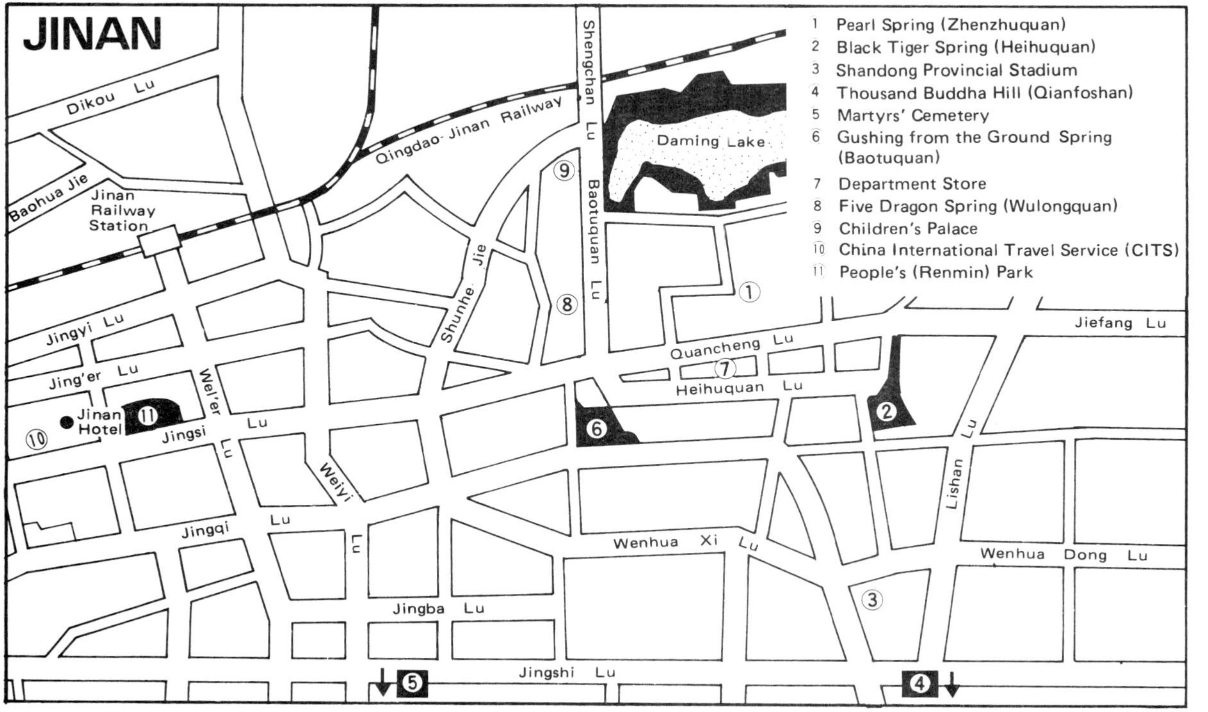
JINAN
1 Pearl Spring (Zhenzhuquan)
2 Black Tiger Spring (Heihuquan)
3 Shandong Provincial Stadium
4 Thousand Buddha Hill (Qianfoshan)
5 Martyrs' Cemetery
6 Gushing from the Ground Spring (Baotuquan)
7 Department Store
8 Five Dragon Spring (Wulongquan)
9 Children's Palace
10 China International Travel Service (CITS)
11 People's (Renmin) Park
Dikou Lu
Baohua Jie
Jinan Railway Station
Qingdao-Jinan Railway
Shengchan Lu
Baotuquan Lu
Daming Lake
Shunhe Jie
Jingyi Lu
Jing'er Lu
Wei'er Lu
Jinan Hotel
Jingsi Lu
Weiyi Lu
Jingqi Lu
Jingba Lu
Jingshi Lu
Quancheng Lu
Heihuquan Lu
Jiefang Lu
Lishan Lu
Wenhua Xi Lu
Wenhua Dong Lu

The main hotel is the *Jinan Hotel* (372 Jingsan Road), which also houses the local CITS office. The hotel served as headquarters for the Japanese during their occupation of Shandong in the 1930s and 1940s and, ironically, many of the tourists who now stay there are old Japanese soldiers on trips down a rather blood-stained memory lane. Another hotel is the *Nanjiao* (2 Ma An Shan Road) on the southern fringes of the city in quieter and more scenic surroundings. However, the Jinan Hotel is probably the better of the two simply because it is more centrally located.

Taishan

For centuries, Taishan has been regarded by the Chinese people as the holiest of their holy mountains, a sort of Chinese Mount Olympus inhabited by the gods. Every day, come rain or shine, old women clamber up the 7000-odd steps on the 'Stairway to Heaven' to make their offerings, fulfilling a tradition which probably goes back more than 2000 years. Many of the women have deformed feet only a few inches long, a sign that, when they were young, their feet were bound to make them more desirable in the eyes of Chinese men, and they sometimes have to crawl up the slope as they go. They do so without complaint. It is a moving sight, and one which proves that China's traditions die hard.

A thousand years ago, emperors of China used to come on pilgrimages to Taishan. In 1980, the present Communist Party chief, 67-year-old Hu Yaobang, made the same pilgrimage just before officially taking up his new post, and he climbed to the top of the mountain in less than five hours. One hopes he was aware of the irony of his visit.

The steep steps start just outside the town of Tai'an at the foot of the slope and wind upwards through a Chinese painting-like landscape of rocky outcrops and fir trees with occasional resting places for travellers who find the path heavy-going. Halfway up, you pass the Middle Gate to Heaven, then continue up to Heaven's Southern Gate. After that, there are a few more hundred steps up to the TEMPLE OF THE AZURE CLOUD, probably one of the most spectacular buildings in China – for those who get to see it.

But a new era is approaching for Taishan, the summit of which has until now been accessible only to the fit and the fervent. A newly opened road allows visitors to ride up to the Middle Gate, and a cable car is being built (with Japanese assistance) from there to the summit, which is expected to open in 1983.

Until now, everything at the top of the mountain from bread to building materials has had to be carried up the steps from the plain 5000 feet (1525 metres) below, by workers who earn the equivalent of about one British penny for each pound in weight they take up. Watching the coolies, many of them old men and girls, jogging stoically up the mountain with up to 100 pounds (45 kilograms) slung over their shoulders is a sobering experience. The fittest of these workers make two trips a day, providing them with reasonable wages and huge leg muscles.

Taishan is becoming a major tourist attraction, but it is never likely to regain its former glorious position as a religious centre, in spite of the peasant women who still come to perform openly the 'superstitious rites' which the Communists have worked so hard to suppress. Most of the temples and shrines have either been vandalised and left to crumble or have been renovated as tourist sites and kiosks. Taishan used to be particularly sacred for disciples of Taoism, China's only indigenous religion which was suppressed with especial vigour by the Communists. However, there is one Taoist priest left on Taishan – a toothless 76-year-old man named Sun who has been allowed to move back into the Temple of the Heavenly Dowager (also known as the Pool of the Queen Mother) near the base of the mountain after many years of hard labour. Or at least he was still there when I visited Taishan in 1981. He looked very frail.

Beneath Taishan is the town of TAI'AN, which owes its existence to the mountain and the pilgrims who passed that way on their way to the summit. The main attraction in the town is the DAIMIAO TEMPLE, a large, rambling place which has been in existence since the Han dynasty 2000 years ago.

How to get there and where to stay

Taishan is on the main railway line from Peking through Jinan to Shanghai, and is a couple of hours south of Jinan, the provincial capital of Shandong.

The guesthouse for foreigners in Tai'an is on Wenhua Yi Lu (Wenhua first road), about ten minutes' drive from the Bavarian-style railway station, a relic of the days when the area was a German 'sphere of influence'. There is also a hotel at the summit of Taishan where visitors can stay overnight. Food and drinks are available at various points on the way up the mountain.

Qufu (Chufu)

Qufu, a delightful little town to the south of Taishan, is famous for being the birthplace of the sage Confucius, who probably bears more responsibility than anyone else for shaping the Chinese personality and Chinese society as we know it. Confucius was born in Qufu in 551 B.C. at a time when China was divided into a number of states, all constantly at war with one another. His philosophy, in a nutshell, envisioned a system of human relationships in which people occupy different ranks within society and within the family. Those above have a duty to look after those below, while those below have a duty to respect and obey those above. For much of the past 2000 years, Confucianism was, in effect, the state religion of China, although it makes no claim to explain the higher mysteries of life.

In Chinese, Confucius is called Kong Fuzi (Master Kong), and about one-fifth of the 30000 people in Qufu today still have that surname. People will tell you that they are the seventy-fourth or seventy-third generation in a direct line from their great ancestor. The present head of the family, the seventy-seventh direct descendant of Confucius, Professor Kung Deh-cheng, fled to Taiwan with the Nationalists in 1949. (Kong is the Pinyin spelling of the name, which Professor Kung, as a resident of Taiwan, would certainly object to.) Now aged 62, Professor Kung has four children, including two sons, as well as one grandson, so the family line would appear to be secure at least up to the seventy-ninth generation. Meanwhile, back in Qufu, Professor Kung is viewed as a traitor to the socialist motherland, but the places where he grew up are being renovated and opened up as tourist attractions.

There are three major places of interest connected with Qufu's most famous son: the KONG FAMILY MANSION, the KONG TEMPLE next door and the 'KONG FOREST', or family graveyard, a mile or so outside the town. All were damaged during the Cultural Revolution of the late 1960s when the Red Guards obediently followed Chairman Mao's order to 'smash the four olds'. Mao issued his call in July 1966, and in October a special group of Red Guard radicals was dispatched from Peking to purge Qufu of its feudal relics. Officials of the local cultural heritage office were given some notice, and wrote the character *liu* (preserve) on as many ancient objects as they could in the hope that the radicals would leave them alone. The Red Guards marched into town shouting their slogans, and the local officials tried to reason with them. 'Most understood, but others just smashed whatever they found,' said one official. The crowd pulled down a large statue of Confucius, paraded it through the town and then ceremoniously burned it. The leader of that Red Guard band, a female fire-brand named Tan Houlan, was jailed in 1978 for her excesses, and was put on trial in late 1982.

More damage was done during the 'criticise Lin Piao and Confucius' campaign in 1974. The campaign, ostensibly aimed at exorcising the influences of the late Defence Minister (killed in 1971) and the Great Sage, turned out in the end to be a veiled attack by the radicals on Premier Chou Enlai, possibly orchestrated by Mao himself. But it had its repercussions in Qufu, where just about everyone is open to the charge of being Confucianist, by descent if not by inclination. The Red Guards attacked and sometimes beat people accused of harbouring Confucianist ideas and went out of their way to leave their mark on the age-old monuments of this ancient town.

One person who remembers those days is Liu Chenghou, who became an acolyte in the Confucius temple at the age of seven and later an attendant in the Kong household. When the Communists came in 1949, they asked him to stay on at the residence as historical guardian, but at the height of the anti-Confucius campaign, he was 'struggled' by mobs of Red Guards who denounced him as a 'watchdog for the royalists'.

'All I could think of was the master's words: Do unto others what you wish done to you,' he said.

Luckily, the huge Kong family archives survived both the Communist and Cultural Revolutions intact, and are now being sorted and examined by scholars.

The mansion is a huge, rambling collection of buildings which, nowadays, is partly used as a hotel for foreign tourists. The temple is also large, but the main feature is the curious emptiness of most of its halls – a sure sign that the Red Guards passed that way. The Kong Forest, beyond what remains of the city walls, is reached by walking along a road lined with some of the most ancient, gnarled cypress trees in the world. They create the right atmosphere for a visit to one of the most peaceful and beautiful spots in China. Walking through the 'forest' among the trees and mounds of earth marking the graves is a wonderful way to spend an afternoon. Some of the graves are marked with tall steles giving details of the Kong family members buried beneath, although many of the steles were toppled and smashed during the Cultural Revolution. In the centre is the largest mound of all under which are supposed to lie the remains of the man who started it all, Kong Fuzi.

Having been denounced and pilloried in the most outrageous fashion only ten years ago, Confucius has today been rehabilitated. His ideas are now cautiously praised by the Communist ideologists who explain his feudalistic errors away by saying that at least he was ideologically 'advanced' for his era.

His temple has been opened to the public again purely as a tourist attraction, although one official (surnamed Kong) told me that occasionally people come wanting to pray or offer incense to the memory of the Master. They are discouraged. There may be so-called 'freedom of religion' in China, but only with religions not classified by the Communist Party as superstitions. Confucianism is considered a superstition and is therefore outlawed, except as a subject of debate by philosophers.

Twice a year, in the spring and autumn, Qufu is the scene of a huge market fair which attracts more than 150 000 peasants as well as artisans, shopkeepers, acrobats, magicians, snake charmers and itinerant medicine men. During the market, which has a history of more than 2000 years, the streets of the small town are absolutely jam-packed with people buying and selling all manner of goods. Most of them are poor peasants, and they look like what they are: many wear ragged clothes; some of the children have eye sores obviously caused by vitamin deficiencies. It is a China that foreigners are rarely allowed to see, something close to that elusive creature, the 'real' China.

How to get there and where to stay

Qufu is about 12 miles (19 kilometres) east of Yanzhou, a stop on the main railway line from Jinan to Shanghai. There is a bus from the station, and taxis can be arranged through the China Travel Service. There is only one place to stay in Qufu, the Kong family mansion, but who would want to stay anywhere else? I shared my room with a couple of rats, but don't let that put you off. It's a fascinating town and a hotel to remember.

Qingdao (Chingtao)

Qingdao, on the south coast of the Shandong peninsula, is rightfully famous for two things: its beer and its beaches. The Germans forced China to cede the town to them in 1898 using good old-fashioned gunboat diplomacy. The pretext was the murder of two German missionaries, but in fact the Kaiser simply wanted a port for his navy in the Far East. To their credit, the Germans developed the place quickly, building a thriving German-style community in less than a decade. They built a railway from Jinan, constructed a port and put picturesque Germanic mansions along the beautiful coastline, which is lined with some of the best beaches in China. When the First World War started, the Japanese snatched Qingdao away, and only handed it back to the Chinese government in 1922.

The town has grown substantially in the past three decades, and Qingdao is now Shangdong's biggest industrial centre. But it still has the beaches (which attract huge numbers of Chinese in the summer months) and the old-world feel of the German architecture, most of which is still in good shape. They obviously expected to stay.

The QINGDAO BREWERY, however, is the town's main claim to fame. Started by the Germans, it produces what is considered to be the best beer in China, and possibly the best in Asia. The quality is attributed to the fact that the water used in its production comes from the Laoshan mountain mineral water spring not far from town. Most of the beer is exported to Hong Kong and elsewhere, or else drunk by foreign tourists in China. It is an important foreign exchange earner, so very little is wasted on the locals. Visits to the brewery (which naturally include samples) can be arranged.

How to get there and where to stay

There are now a couple of scheduled flights a week from Peking. Otherwise, Qingdao is a 15-hour train ride from the capital. The two main hotels in town are both situated on the sea in picturesque settings. The *Huiquan Guesthouse* (Nanhai Road) is near Beach No. 1, while the *Zhanqiao Guesthouse* (Taiping Road), the better of the two, is near Beach No. 6.

Yantai

This little port on the north coast of the Shandong peninsula used to be a favourite seaside retreat for foreigners in the old days. As a result, many of the older and sturdier buildings are of European design. Around the old city, formerly known as Chefoo, Yantai has grown considerably during this century, and now has a number of important industries, the most famous being a wine factory which produces a brandy considered to be one of China's best (not a great recommendation). The port continues to be important, and there is a large fishing fleet.

There are beaches close to the town which are good for walks, although the large amount of seaweed in the water makes them not so attractive for swimming.

There is one interesting excursion from Yantai, west along the coast to PENGLAI, a strange castle perched on a cliff. A part of the fort was built as long ago as 1042 as a naval base to guard against a Japanese invasion, but most of the structure dates from the Ming and Qing dynasties.

How to get there and where to stay

Yantai is connected to Jinan, the provincial capital, by a railway line. The main hotel for foreigners is on the coast to the east of town.

SHANXI PROVINCE

Taiyuan

Taiyuan is the capital of Shanxi Province, a city with a long history which is now an important industrial centre of more than one million people. In the vicinity of Taiyuan are a number of ancient Buddhist temples, including the XUANZHONG MONASTERY, birthplace of one of the largest Buddhist sects in Japan. In modern history, Taiyuan is most interesting for having been the headquarters of Yan Xishan, a warlord who supported the republicans in the revolt against the imperial Manchu dynasty in 1911, and then promptly made the province his own personal empire, ruling it until the Communists swept through in 1949 on their way to complete victory on the Chinese mainland. His former residence on Victory Street (Shengli Jie) is now used by his successors, the Shanxi Provincial Communist Party Committee, and the Provincial People's Government.

The PROVINCIAL MUSEUM is housed in a huge Taoist temple in the centre of town, and has a superb collection of antiquities on display, including a statue of the founder and patron saint of the Taoist religion himself, Laọzi. During my visit, I asked the guide if the temple would be opened again for Taoist worship in the same way as many of the Buddhist temples around China have been. She seemed stunned for a second before replying: 'But there aren't any Taoists left.'

Also on show is a large block of stone intricately carved with dozens of tiny Buddhas, dating back 1600 years. Having made it safely through 16 centuries, the heads of each and every Buddha were knocked off during the Cultural Revolution by some Red Guard who deserves a similar fate.

Another interesting site in the city is the ZHONGSHAN TEMPLE. The main hall was built during the Ming dynasty and houses a huge collection of Buddhist scriptures, including some items dating back to the Yuan and Song dynasties, which are on view.

In late 1980, there was some serious labour trouble at the Taiyuan

Iron and Steel Works, apparently including calls by some workers for the establishment of a trade union independent of the Communist Party. The local paper gave only sparse details, but indicated that whatever had happened had been crushed pretty quickly. The incident, perhaps inspired by the rise of the Solidarity Union in Poland a few months before, included demands by some workers 'that they be allowed to solve their own destinies', the local *Taiyuan Daily* said. Leaders of the workers' protest used slogans such as 'down with bureaucracy, down with privilege, down with dictatorship'. It was never revealed how many workers were involved in the protest or what happened to the ring-leaders. Needless to say, foreign tourists get no hint of whatever labour problems may still be bubbling away in the factories of Taiyuan. The most interesting excursion from Taiyuan is to the JINCI TEMPLE, about 15 miles (24 kilometres) to the southwest. Taiyuan was the capital of the Jin state about 1500 years ago, and the temple was first built to commemorate the founder of that little kingdom. Many of the buildings in the complex were built 900 years

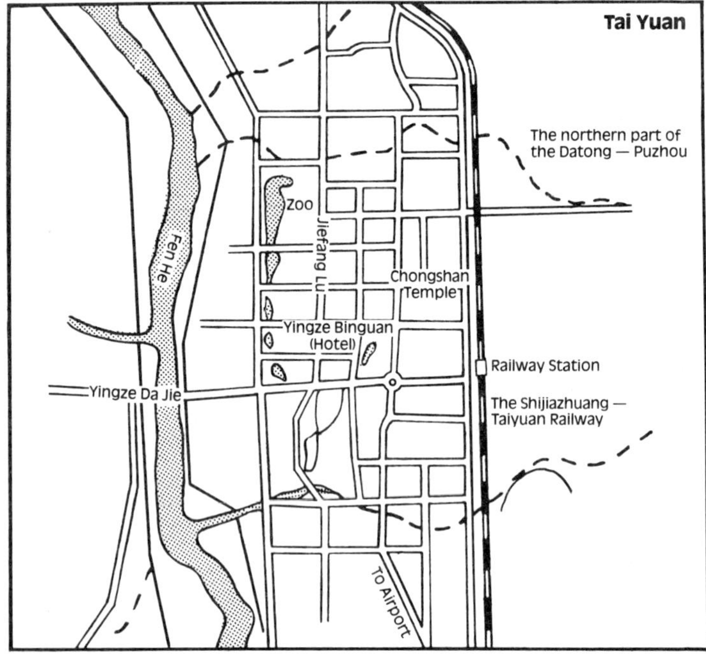

ago during the Song dynasty. The largest is the SHENMUDIAN (Hall of the Holy Mother), along the walls of which are some interesting statues of officials, maids and eunuchs waiting on the Holy Mother in the centre. One of the cypress trees nearby is said to be over 3000 years old. (*Local tourist buses leave regularly from the square to the east of Yingze Lu where the main hotels are. The No. 8 bus from the railway station also passes by Jinci Temple. Get someone to tell you where to alight.*)

How to get there and where to stay

Taiyuan is a 13-hour train ride from Peking. The city is on the main line to Xi'an, and could be treated as a one-day stopover on a trip from one to the other. There are also regular flights to Peking and Xi'an.

The two main hotels are the *Yingze Binguan* (17 Yingze Street) and the *Bingzhou Fandian* almost next door (2 Yingze Street). The Yingze is the one usually used by foreigners.

Datong

The main reason for Datong's existence these days is the huge coal reserves lying just under the surface of the surrounding countryside. It is not a beautiful city by any stretch of the imagination, but for railway buffs at least, it is worth visiting. The DATONG LOCOMOTIVE FACTORY is the only place in the world still commercially producing steam engines. The factory was opened in 1959 and produces 22 or 23 engines a month, to a design based on a Soviet model from the 1950s. After viewing the factory, visitors are given what train freaks presumably consider to be the ultimate experience – *you get to have a ride in the engine driver's cabin.*

If you go to Datong specifically to see the steam engine factory, make sure you go on the right day – the factory only receives visitors on Tuesdays and Saturdays.

There are few interesting buildings in Datong city itself, but like anywhere in China, it is well worth just taking a walk round the back streets. Old Datong is laid out according to the traditional pattern of Chinese towns, with a picturesque DRUM TOWER in the centre of the rectangular network of roads. There are two old Buddhist monasteries, the upper and lower HUAYAN MONASTERIES which are now used as museums. A former temple dedicated to the sage Confucius in the southeast quarter of the old city is now used as a middle (secondary) school. Another site shown to visitors is the 'NINE DRAGON SCREEN', a huge wall decorated with multi-coloured tiles which was built in the

Ming dynasty as part of a nobleman's residence, long since destroyed. It is the finest example left in China of a form of decoration popular with the imperial Chinese aristocracy.

The best local restaurant in Datong is the *Fenglinge*, in an alley-way just to the west of the Dragon Screen. It's best to book in advance. The restaurant in the Datong Guesthouse is terrible: the attendants are surly, the table-cloths filthy, and the food drab and often cold. The jiao-zis (meat dumplings) are not bad, however.

Ten miles (16 kilometres) or so to the west of Datong are the YUNGANG CAVES, considered by some to be the finest Buddhist rock carvings in China. The shrine consists of hundreds of Buddhas gazing out of niches dug into a long sandstone cliff. Most of the Buddhas were carved in the late fifth century and the largest and most impressive one at the western end of the cliff is 55 feet (17 metres) tall. The shrine bears the scars of vandalism, both human and natural; there are some empty niches from which Chinese iconoclasts (including Red Guards) or European treasure hunters have removed statues. Wind erosion has also taken its toll over the centuries, and from the look of the smooth, swirling grooves along the base of some of the statues, flood waters must have also engulfed the shrine on at least one occasion. Halfway along this row of archaeological marvels is a temple built in the seventeenth century which climbs almost vertically up the cliff face. The temple buildings have been left pretty much alone and look delightful in their shades of fading red and blue. Unfortunately, it is probably only a matter of time before the local antiquities preservation committee decides to 'restore' the temple and paint it up in the gaudy colours that in the past few years have made so many antique buildings around China look slightly ridiculous, like old ladies with too much make-up. (*To get to the caves, take a No. 1 bus from close by the hotel to its terminus at the West Gate bus station. Then take a No. 3 bus to the caves. The journey takes about 45 minutes.*)

How to get there and where to stay

Datong is about eight hours by train west of Peking, and is best treated as a one-day stop on the way to or from somewhere else, most likely Inner Mongolia. The only hotel in town which takes foreigners is the *Datong Guesthouse*, a grim 1950s structure which is one of the worst tourist hotels in the country. A standard room with bath costs an exorbitant 32 yuan a day. For the budget traveller, the hotel has dormitory rooms on each floor with bed-spaces for six yuan a day.

Dazhai (Tachai)

All over China, on walls and buildings, are the fading remains of millions of slogans reading: 'In Agriculture, Learn from Dazhai.' This tiny village of about 80 families in eastern Shanxi province, was selected by Chairman Mao in 1964 as being a good example of self-sufficiency and revolutionary spirit, and a propaganda campaign was cranked up to elevate it into a national model. Tourists, both local and foreign, were taken in droves to view this wonder, where the happy, simple peasants, using only Mao Tse-tung Thought as their guide, had managed to build huge irrigation channels and aqueducts, and raised grain production every year. At least that was the Gospel According to Chen Yonggui, the peasant leader of the Dazhai Production Brigade, who rose to national political prominence on the back of the 'Learn from Dazhai' campaign. He became both a vice-premier and a member of the Communist Party Politburo, and always appeared at meetings in Peking with a peasant towel wrapped theatrically around his head as if he'd just walked in from the fields.

In fact, the whole Dazhai 'miracle' was a fake. The irrigation works, supposedly built by the Dazhai peasants themselves, were actually financed by the central government and built largely by army units. Grain production, far from rising steadily, fell every single year from 1973 to 1977. Nevertheless, Mao's successor, Hua Guofeng, personally took control of the Dazhai campaign and built it up to even crazier heights, insisting that every part of the country should apply the lessons of Dazhai whether they were relevant or not. The aim of every village and county was to be named 'Dazhai-style'.

According to press reports in 1980 and 1981, Chen Yonggui, the simple peasant with the towel round his head, was in fact corrupt, autocratic, given to personal vendettas against anyone who even slightly crossed him, and a liar when it came to production figures. His son, Chen Mingzhu, was denounced at the same time for being promiscuous and for allegedly raping at least one girl.

Of course, neither father nor son are now in a position to give their side of the story.

In the late 1970s, the 'Learn from Dazhai' campaign was dropped. Chen was removed from his post as head of the Dazhai brigade in late 1979, and from his post of vice-premier in September 1980. He remained a member of the Politburo, at least nominally, up until the Twelfth Party Congress in mid-1982, although he had certainly ceased to play any role in politics at least two years before that.

One perplexing aspect of the Chen Yonggui affair is that, in all of the dozens of articles published in 1980 and 1981 criticising him, he was never once mentioned by name. The articles only ever referred to 'the former responsible person in Dazhai' or some similar construction, and he has never been publicly criticised by name in the official press. The only explanation can be that he had some influential friends.

Not surprisingly, the official media carried stories in 1981 saying how excellent the situation in Dazhai was, following the departure of 'the former responsible person', and how the peasants were beginning to recover from the years when 'ultra-leftism' ran amok in their little village.

How to get there and where to stay

Dazhai used to be on the regular tourist route for foreigners in China, but for obvious reasons, it is no longer featured. However, some visitors have received permission to go there and, compared to similar villages around China, Dazhai is well equipped to handle them.

To get there, take a train to Yangquan, a stop on the railway line between Taiyuan and Shijiazhuang to the east. Dazhai is about 40 miles (64 kilometres) south of Yangquan by road. Visitors stay in the *Dazhai Guesthouse*. One of the guesthouse rooms used to be reserved for Chen Yonggui, and his son is alleged to have used it when he wished to have his way with young ladies.

SICHUAN PROVINCE

Sichuan, with over 100 million people, is the most populous of all the Chinese provinces. It was once an independent kingdom known as Shu, but became a permanent part of the Chinese empire about 1000 years ago. It is a very fertile basin, and the mountains that separate it from central China once prompted a poet to remark that 'the road to the Kingdom of Shu is harder than climbing to Heaven.' Much of the western part of the province is inhabited by Tibetan people.

During the Cultural Revolution, Sichuan was a centre of factional fighting and saw pitched battles between Red Guards and workers, and Red Guards and army units. The combination of political chaos and Maoist agricultural policies resulted in Sichuan becoming, by the mid-1970s, a net importer of rice and one of the poorest parts of China. The poverty was so bad that there were reports of families selling off their daughters in exchange for rice ration coupons just to stay alive.

The man credited with dragging Sichuan back on to the road to prosperity is Zhao Ziyang, the present Premier of China. He was purged during the Cultural Revolution, but re-appeared in the early 1970s, and became the Community Communist Party chief of Sichuan in 1975, apparently chosen for the job by China's present leader, Deng Xiaoping.

In 1978, with Mao dead, and Deng making his bid for supreme power, Zhao abandoned the radical agricultural policies which had led to such a drastic drop in production, and pioneered the more flexible 'capitalist' agricultural ones now enforced throughout China. Private plots, free markets and the popular contract production system were all first introduced in Sichuan.

In 1981, the province was hit by severe flooding, the worst in a century, during which more than 750 people died and 1.5 million people were made homeless. Railway lines and roads were cut and looting occurred in some areas. In order to ensure that production was kept as high as possible in the wake of the floods, the land in many areas was handed back to the peasants who were told that they could keep whatever they grew on it.

Chengdu

The capital of Sichuan Province, Chengdu is a delightful city with a lot of history, although there is less evidence of it now than there used to be – the city walls were pulled down in the 1960s, and in the early 1970s, a Ming dynasty palace once used by a relative of the emperor was pulled down to make way for a Soviet-style 'Cultural Palace'. One hopes that the man who gave the demolition order is now washing out toilets.

The centre of town is a good place to walk round. Many of the buildings are made of wood and the architecture is very distinctive.

Visitors to Chengdu generally pay a visit to the DUJIANG YAN IRRIGATION PROJECT, northwest of the city, an amazing engineering feat dating back to 250 B.C. The irrigation system, greatly improved and expanded in the past 30 years, controls the waters of the Min River and provides irrigation water for a huge area of farmland. Half an hour's walk away is the Taoist ERWANG (two kings) TEMPLE, credited with containing some of the most ancient buildings in the country. The kings referred to are Li Bing, chosen to rule Sichuan more than 2000 years ago by the first emperor of China, and his son. (*Take a No. 25 bus to the West Gate bus terminus in Chengdu, then take a mini-bus to the irrigation system. Buses leave every half hour, and the journey takes about 90 minutes; tickets cost 1.50 yuan.*)

Another excursion is to the county seat of XINDU about an hour's bus drive north of Chengdu. The main attractions are the BAOGUANG (precious light) TEMPLE, a huge palace dating back over 1000 years, and a small lake nearby called GUIHU. The temple, largely rebuilt in the Manchu dynasty following a fire, includes 500 Buddhas, each one different. (*Take a No. 16 bus heading north from outside the Jingjiang Hotel to its terminus at the northern railway station. Buses for Xindu leave from there every half an hour or so.*)

Of the more centrally located sights, there is the PEOPLE'S PARK about 20 minutes' walk from the Jinjiang Hotel (head north and then west along Shengli Xi Lu), the WU HOU TEMPLE, a shrine to a military strategist named Zhuge Liang who lived in the third century A.D. (about 20 minutes' walk west of the Jinjiang Hotel on Jiefang Nan Lu) and a SHRINE TO DU FU, one of China's most famous poets who lived in the Tang dynasty. He lived in Chengdu for a while after having been forced to leave the Chinese capital at Xi'an due to poverty. (*From the Jinjiang Hotel, walk south two or three intersections to Yihuan Lu, then take a No. 27 bus heading west to its terminus. Walk west for ten minutes and the shrine will be on your left.*)

Chengdu, being the capital of Sichuan, has some of the best Sichuanese food restaurants in the world. The food is usually hot and spicy, and one famous dish is Maopuo Doufu (pockmarked grandma beancurd) which consists of beancurd, mince and red peppers. The dish was invented, it is said, by an old woman surnamed Chen in

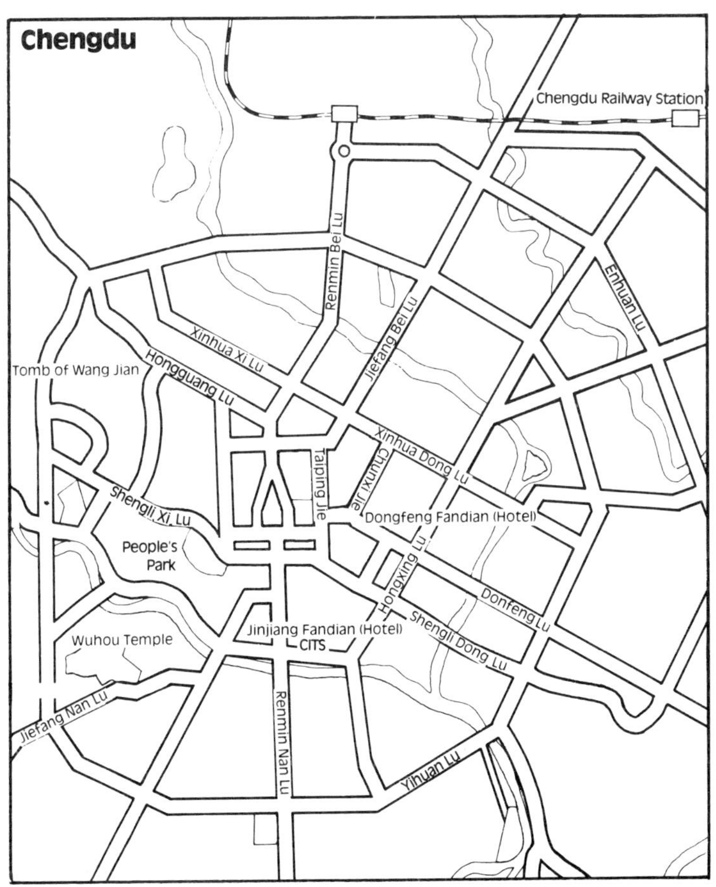

about 1860, and a restaurant, until recently run by her descendants, called *Chen Maopuo Doufu Dian* is in the centre of Chengdu at 113 Xiyulong Jie. Another famous Sichuan dish is a type of noodles called *Dandan Mian*. Try them at a restaurant of the same name at 53–55 Dongfeng Lu Yi Duan (Dongfeng Road Section One). Other well-known restaurants include the *Chengdu* (Shengli Zhong Lu) and the *Furong* (27 Renmin Nan Lu).

For those who appreciate the unusual, may I also suggest a recently opened eatery called the *Tongrentang Restaurant* set up by the Chengdu Crude Drugs Company in 1980 to serve medically beneficial dishes. The menu features such items as Pheasant Dumpling Soup (good for diabetes), Carp with Red Beans (good for oedema) and Ginseng Soup (good for neurasthenia, cardiac senility and splenic-gastric weakness). Customers may choose their own dishes from the menu or consult the deputy manager about their complaints and get his recommendations about what they should eat.

How to get there and where to stay

Chengdu is connected by air services to all major cities in China, and is on the main southwest railway line, accessible from Xi'an, Kunming, Changqing or, ultimately, anywhere else on the railway network.

Almost everyone stays at the *Jinjiang Guesthouse* (sometimes spelt Jingjiang: 180 Renmin Nan Lu). (Take the No. 16 bus from the station, get off at the seventh stop, and it's on the right-hand side of the road.) It's a Stalinist piece of architecture, but not bad as such hotels go in China. There's a dormitory on the seventh floor, and beds cost four yuan each; there is more expensive accommodation if you want it. Opposite the entrance is what is probably the largest Mao statue in China.

Another hotel is the *Dongfeng Hotel* (2 Dongfeng Lu).

Chongqing (Chungking)

When you arrive in Chongqing, you realise instantly that there is something different about this city – there are almost no bicycles. The heart of the city is built on a steep promontory at the confluence of the Yangtse River and another important river, the Jialing, and the roads are too steep for cyclists to stand much of a chance. As a result, the public buses are even more crowded than they are in other Chinese cities.

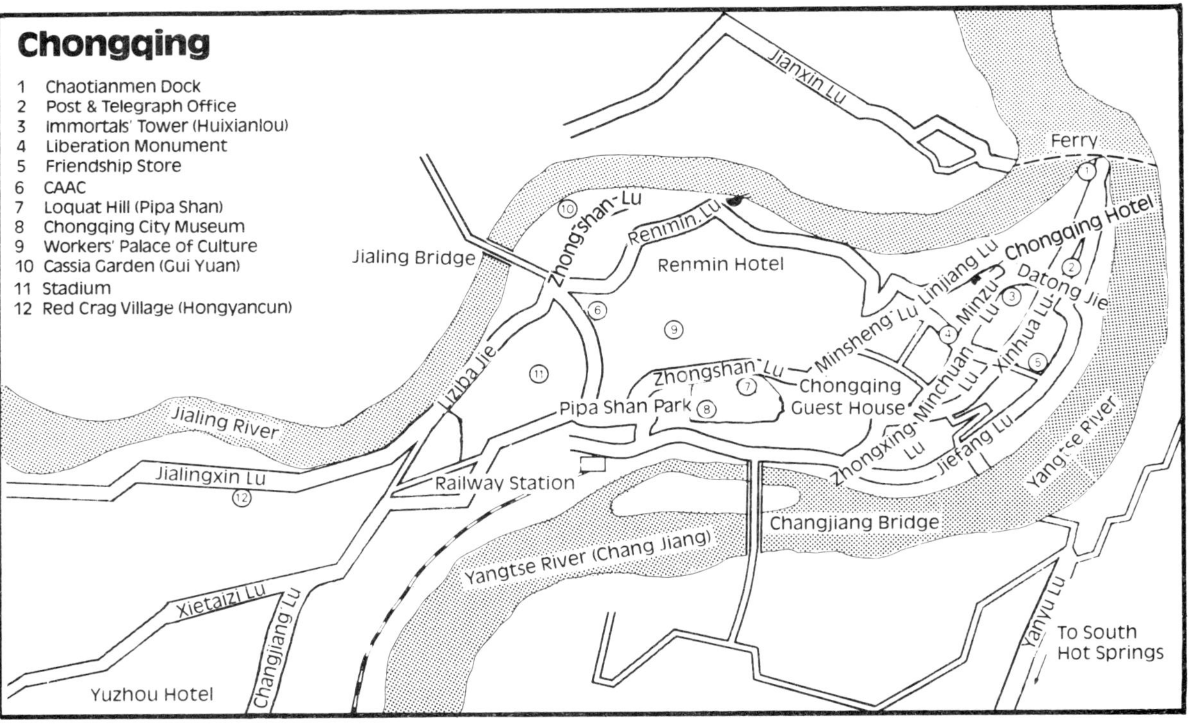

Chongqing
1 Chaotianmen Dock
2 Post & Telegraph Office
3 Immortals' Tower (Huixianlou)
4 Liberation Monument
5 Friendship Store
6 CAAC
7 Loquat Hill (Pipa Shan)
8 Chongqing City Museum
9 Workers' Palace of Culture
10 Cassia Garden (Gui Yuan)
11 Stadium
12 Red Crag Village (Hongyancun)
Jianxin Lu
Ferry
Chongqing Hotel
Datong Jie
Linjiang Lu
Minzu Lu
Xinhua Lu
Minsheng Lu
Minchuan Lu
Zhongxing Lu
Jiefang Lu
Yangtse River
Zhongshan Lu
Renmin Lu
Renmin Hotel
Jialing Bridge
Zhongshan Lu
Chongqing Guest House
Pipa Shan Park
Lizipa Jie
Jialing River
Jialingxin Lu
Railway Station
Changjiang Bridge
Yangtse River (Chang Jiang)
Xietaizi Lu
Changjiang Lu
Yuzhou Hotel
Yanyu Lu
To South Hot Springs

Chongqing leapt on to the pages of history in 1938 when Generalissimo Chiang Kaishek made it the wartime Chinese capital following the capture of Nanking by the Japanese. Refugees flooded into the city from all over China, and it quickly swelled into a metropolis of over two million people.

Barbara Tuchman, in her superb book *Stilwell and the American Experience in China*, described the state of the city and the corruption which sapped the Nationalist government's strength:

> With its extra wartime population stuffed into meagre, overstrained facilities, Chongqing was more uncomfortable, unsanitary and ill-provisioned than ever – and the climate was still the same: humid heat in summer, rain and mud the rest of the time. Bomb-shattered houses were leaky and shaky, filth and smells were increased by the crowding, rats came out at night, clerks and workers were underpaid, giving rise to the article of belief among American correspondents that 'no one ever saw a fat Chinese under the rank of Minister of Finance.'

The Japanese bombed the city repeatedly although they never captured it, and many older buildings still bear the marks of that time. Since 1949, Chongqing has grown, and the city and surrounding countryside now have a population of more than six million. A large number of factories were relocated here from other parts of the country during the Second World War, and Chongqing has remained an important industrial city. Since the war, bridges have been built over the two rivers which once isolated the old city, and a large amount of building has been done. 'Old China hands' from pre-1949 days say that they hardly recognise the place.

The alleys and staircase-streets in the old part of the city are fascinating to walk round. Stroll down to the end of the promontory where the two rivers meet – CHAOTIANMEN DOCK – and watch the ferries and barges fighting the strong current. Walk west along Zhongshan Road to PIPA SHAN PARK, the highest point on the peninsula, which provides a splendid view of the whole city. There is a tea garden there which is open in the evenings.

The most interesting off-beat tourist attraction is the 'US–CHIANG KAISHEK CRIMINAL ACTS EXHIBITION HALL', a display of instruments of torture used by the Nationalists on captured Communist prisoners at the 'Sino–American Special Technical Co-operation Organisation' headquarters west of the city. Further up the hill, there are two prisons, the BAIGONGGUAN, about 20 minutes' walk west of the exhibition hall, and the ZHAZHIDONG, another 20 minutes' walk north of that. (*Take a No. 13 bus west to the end of the line, then get on a No. 17 bus at the nearby terminus and say you want to get off at the Lieshi Mu – Martyr's Tomb. The exhibition hall is on the left-hand side of the road.*)

Other tourist sights include the former Communist representative office in war-time Chongqing at HONGYANCUN (Red Crag Village; on the No. 17 bus route closer to town).

There are lots of restaurants in the old part of Chongqing. Try the *Renmin Fandian* (110 Zourong Jie; take a No. 1 trolley bus east to the end of the line) or the *Lao Sichuan* (200 Minsheng Lu).

For most of the year, the weather in Chongqing is unappealing. It is famed as one of the three 'furnaces' of China due to the intense heat of summer, and is cold, clammy and misty in winter. As with many other parts of China, the best times to visit are in spring and autumn, say, April and September.

The local Friendship Store is on the top floor of the Chongqing Department Store on Minquan Lu.

How to get there and where to stay

Chongqing is connected to most major cities by air, and is on the Chengdu–Guiyang railway line.

Foreigners often stay at the *Chongqing Binguan* at 235 Minsheng Lu. Budget travellers should try the *Renmin Da Litang* (Great People's Guest Hall, Minsheng Lu; a dormitory bed costs five yuan).

Tickets for the ferries down the Yangtse River to Wuhan and Shanghai can be bought at the Chaotianmen ferry terminal at the top of the promontory, but it is best to book a few days in advance through CTS.

Dazu

This interesting town in central Sichuan is very beautiful, and feels almost as if it belongs in the Middle Ages. There are many small teahouses and restaurants, and the whole population seems to eat out at night.

Near the town are two places famous for Buddhist rock carvings. The closest is BEISHAN, a mile's walk up the hill. The other is BAODING SHAN (precious summit mountain) which is about 15 miles (24 kilometres) away by bus. The grottoes and niches contain some exquisite statuary dating from the Tang and Song dynasties, and some are also painted with murals featuring scenes from the daily life of about 1000 years ago. (*The public bus for Baoding Shan leaves from the*

Dazu bus station at about 7.30 a.m. Turn left out of the guesthouse, buy the bus ticket from a kiosk on the main street and the bus station is on the left.)

How to get there and where to stay
The Public Security Bureau in Chongqing appears to be the only place at which tourists can obtain permits for Dazu. In Chengdu, the Public Security office has refused to issue permits for the town even though it is roughly halfway between Chongqing and Chengdu. Take a bus from Chongqing. The only place to stay in Dazu is the *Dazu Guesthouse* which has ordinary rooms and dormitory beds.

Emei Shan

Emei Shan (mountain) in the central province of Sichuan is considered to be one of the most beautiful areas of unspoiled countryside in China. It is possible to climb to the top, except in deepest winter, although it can be hard going for the unfit. Some people spend two or three days doing the full trip to the peak and back, but everyone who goes up says that it was worth it. The mountain is often shrouded in clouds and mist, but when it is clear, the views are magical, each one an inspired Chinese painting. On summer days, there are hundreds of Chinese visitors and pilgrims climbing up and down the mountain. Emei Shan is one of the most sacred Buddhist mountains in China, and apparently has special significance for Lamaist Buddhists from Tibet. All the way up the steep path, there are temples, many of which were damaged during the Cultural Revolution and have since been renovated.

Climbers start the ascent at the BAOGUO TEMPLE. There are two paths, a north route which is 27 miles (43 kilometres) long and a southern route which is 40 miles (64 kilometres). In the old days, there were supposed to be 70 temples scattered about the mountain, all dedicated to the Buddha Pu Xian. A common stopping-point for climbers and pilgrims is the ELEPHANT BATHING POOL TEMPLE (Xixiangsi), named after a presumably mythical incident when a Buddha who happened to be flying by on his elephant stopped off to give the animal a quick wash.

Those who have stood at the top of the mountain and watched the sun rise from the sea of peaks and swirling mists below talk about the experience in almost religious terms. It is said that some people have been so moved that they have leapt off the mountain into oblivion.

Recently, Emei Shan has become famous for a gang of three

deformed monkeys, fugitives from justice, who have taken to waylaying and mugging honest travellers. The three, one of whom has a hare-lip, another only one eye and the third only three fingers on one hand, live in caves on the slopes of the mountain near the Elephant Bathing Pool Temple. They leap out at unsuspecting climbers in the hope of getting something to eat, and sometimes bite people who have nothing to give them. They are also known to steal bags and cameras and throw them down the steep mountain side. Security personnel have been scouring the area for the three outlaws, but at last report the apes were still at least one paw ahead of the law. When asked what would happen to the monkeys if they were caught, one official on the mountain drew his hand across his throat to indicate immediate execution.

How to get there and where to stay

Emei Shan is close to the main railway line running from Kunming in Yunnan Province to Chengdu in Sichuan. The town of Emei is a nice stopping-off point, and there are regular buses from the railway station there to the *Baoguosi* (Baoguo Monastery) at the base of the mountain. You can stay there or at the *Hongzhushan Temple* not far away. A good night's rest is recommended before starting the climb. You will also need a climbing permit, available at the hotel.

A number of temples along the way offer accommodation and meals at cheap rates, although conditions are understandably primitive. Temples with rooms available include the *Xixiangchi*, the *Wanniansi* and *Jinding* (golden summit) at the very top. It can be chilly on the mountain, so take some warm clothes.

Leshan

Close to Emei Shan is Leshan, the site of what is almost certainly the largest Buddha in China. The huge figure, carved out of a rockface beside the Min River to the east of Emei Shan, is 400 feet (120 metres) tall and dates from the twelfth century. A bus leaves from close by the Baoguo Temple at the foot of Emei Shan and goes directly to Leshan. Once there, walk from the bus station to the river, about a mile (1.6 kilometres) away, and take a small ferry across to see the Buddha.

TIBET

Tibet is more accessible to foreign visitors today than it has ever been before. So far that simply means an average of about 30 visitors a week (in 1981) but the number is rising. For centuries, the Himalayan kingdom of Tibet was a closed world, jealous of its privacy and eager to keep everybody else away from its mountain fastness. At some stages in its history, it has come under the influence of empires in India to the south; at others, it has been a vassal state to the powerful Chinese empire to the east. But through it all, the Tibetans have maintained a sense of their own racial, cultural – some would say, national – separateness. The Chinese government says that Tibet has been a rightful part of China for 'a long time'. Many Tibetans disagree. Whatever the truth of the matter, Tibet is now firmly part of the People's Republic of China and is likely to remain so.

For the tourist, Tibet is one of the most fascinating places that can be visited in China. Lhasa, with its rarified air, friendly locals and the towering Potala, is a palpably different world from the heartland of China, thousands of miles to the east. Travelling to Tibet can be cripplingly expensive if you go with the China Travel Service, but most people would agree that Tibet is worth the sum charged.

Until 1951, Tibet was ruled by a Buddhist theocracy, headed by the Dalai Lama, the Tibetan god-king who now lives in exile in India. Probably about 20 per cent of the male population in those days were Lamaist priests and the monasteries they inhabited were centres of power and wealth which controlled huge tracts of land and the peasants on them. There was slavery, and justice was often very cruel. Sanitation, modern medicine, even wheeled vehicles were unknown on the Roof of the World. Life there in 1950 was almost exactly as it had been in 1550.

The Communist Chinese view is that 'before liberation, Tibet was a hell on earth, where the labouring people suffered for centuries under the darkest and most reactionary serfdom. Tibetan serfs and slaves lived worse than animals.'

One of the present vice-chairmen of the Tibetan Communist Party Committee, a woman named Pasang, gave the following account of her own life, published in 1972:

> I was born in a slave's family in Konka County, Tibet. I was a slave for nine years and lived like a beast of burden. Chairman Mao and the Communist Party saved me from slavery and nurtured me to become a Communist and a responsible cadre. My mother gave birth to me, but it is the Party which saved me and Invincible Mao Tse-tung Thought which sustains me. I want to cheer again and again: 'Long live Chairman Mao!'

Contemporary accounts by the handful of foreigners who penetrated the old Tibet, however, do not wholly back the Communist picture of unremitting misery. Heinrich Harrer, a German who spent seven years there and became an adviser to the Dalai Lama, saw the Tibetans as a happy people, proud of their independence, although he had much to say on the low standards of hygiene, and estimated the average life expectancy at about 30 years. 'What saves Tibet is its cool climate and pure mountain air,' Harrer said in his memoirs. 'But for them, the universal dirt and the wretched sanitary conditions would surely engender catastrophic plagues.'

After the Communists secured their hold on the heartland of China in 1949, the following year the People's Liberation Army (PLA) began the long trek west to unite Tibet with the rest of the Socialist Motherland. In April 1951, with the Communist army already occupying most of the eastern part of his country, the Dalai Lama sent a delegation to Peking and reached an agreement with the Communists under which the PLA was allowed to occupy Tibet, while the Chinese authorities pledged to leave the existing political and social system intact, and to respect the religious beliefs and customs of the Tibetan people.

The first PLA units entered Lhasa in October 1951, but the agreement lasted less than eight years. Tibetan guerrilla forces began attacking Chinese army units in 1958, and in March of the next year, according to the Chinese, a large anti-Chinese force was gathered in Lhasa by the Tibetan ruling classes who proclaimed the independence of Tibet.

'At nightfall on 19 March, the traitorous clique launched an all-out attack on PLA units stationed in Lhasa,' said one Communist pamphlet. 'After two days' fighting, the rebellion in Lhasa city was crushed. Rebellions in other areas were also quickly quelled.' It was, the Chinese said, a revolt by the reactionary Tibetan aristocracy put down by the PLA in conjunction with the Tibetan peasantry.

Tibetan exiles, however, have a slightly different story. They say that a rumour swept through Lhasa one day in early March that the Dalai Lama, then 23 years old, had been invited by the Chinese to attend a cultural performance that evening and had been asked to go alone. The ordinary people, fearing the worst, converged on the Potala Palace to protect their god-king, and rebel leaders among the crowds formed a committee which announced Tibet's independence and demanded that the Chinese withdraw. Ironically, the Dalai Lama tried to calm the people in the hope of avoiding a bloody confrontation with the powerful Chinese forces. But he failed, and he and his immediate family disguised themselves and escaped overland to India. The Chinese, meanwhile, began shelling centres of Tibetan resistance in Lhasa and, the Dalai Lama says, 'thousands of bodies' were seen lying around the Potala afterwards. The Chinese, on the other hand, put the death toll at about 600. About 80 000 Tibetans fled the country as a result of the rebellion's failure, mostly to India and Nepal.

Tibet was now firmly under the control of the Chinese Communists who moved swiftly to destroy the old society which they saw as being so oppressive. During the 1960s and early 1970s, the whole of China was racked by the political campaigns instigated by Chairman Mao and his radical allies, and Tibet appears to have suffered more than other regions. Most of the monasteries were closed or demolished, and the vast majority of monks were forced to return to secular life. The peasants were also grouped into communes whether they agreed or not, and, in many cases, were ordered to grow winter wheat – a Chinese food grain – rather than the traditional Tibetan barley. Up to 1978, there was a concerted effort to stamp out the Lamaist Buddhist faith which the Tibetans believe in so powerfully but, as in the rest of China, this attempt to kill religion failed miserably.

During the years following the 1959 rebellion and Chinese takeover, very few foreigners were able to visit Tibet. Most of those who did were apologists such as Han Suyin and Felix Greene who, in the words of Derek Davies, editor of the *Far Eastern Economic Review*, 'wrote accounts designed not to describe the inaccessible but to excuse the undefensible'.

Han Suyin's inept book, *Lhasa, The Open City*, was written on the basis of a visit to that city in 1975, when Chinese Communist radicalism was at its height, but all she writes of are smiling Tibetans happy to have been saved by the Chinese Communist Party from the tyranny of the Dalai Lama. She writes of the Ganden Monastery, traditionally one of the three great monasteries of Lhasa, as if it still existed, never bothering to mention that this sacred Tibetan shrine had been completely demolished brick by brick by Red Guards during the Cultural Revolution. She talks of the pride she felt at meeting the Chinese Communist Party chief in Tibet, General Ren Rong, dismissed in disgrace in 1979 after the new Peking government of Deng Xiaoping realised what a mess the leftists had made of Tibet.

A more balanced view began to emerge in mid-1979 when the first group of foreign correspondents based in Peking were allowed to visit Tibet. Their reports were not flattering, and were perhaps a factor in the fall of General Ren Rong.

'The Chinese make their disdain for the Tibetans obvious,' wrote Nigel Wade, then the *Daily Telegraph* correspondent in Peking. 'Disgust with the Tibetan liking for milk and butter may be one reason, and secret jealousy of the Tibetan's achievements in art and architecture another. Besides occasional instances of Chinese bullying Tibetans which I witnessed, Chinese down to the level of museum guides adopted a patronising, paternalistic air about Peking's Tibetan subjects.

'It is not China's running Tibet as a colony which seems so offensive,' he added, 'but the smug refusal to admit that a colony is what it is.'

Hu Yaobang, the present Communist Party chief, made an inspection tour of Tibet in May 1980, as a prelude to a new, more enlightened policy towards this far-flung province. In a circumspect way, he admitted the colonial attitude taken by many Chinese posted to Lhasa. 'A minority of Han [Chinese] comrades have displayed incorrect tendencies,' he said, adding that as a result, it was necessary to 'strengthen ties between the Tibetan and Han nationalities.'

Since then, the Peking government has admitted many of the mistakes made in the years of leftist rule, and has taken some concrete steps to improve matters. The rural communes have been virtually dismantled in Tibet as in the rest of China, and the Tibetans have been allowed to grow their barley or graze livestock as they wish, rather than being forced to follow Chairman Mao's directive to mindlessly 'grasp grain as the key link'.

The more liberal religious policy in China which has led to the opening of hundreds of churches and mosques around the country has, likewise, been implemented in Tibet, where religion has a stronger hold on the ordinary people than anywhere else in the country.

Visitors to Tibet since it was re-opened in 1979 have been overwhelmed by the devotion of the Tibetan people to the Dalai Lama despite his long absence. They are also moved by the shows of deep faith displayed by many of the Tibetans, particularly the pilgrims to Lhasa who crawl round some religious sites including the Jokhang monastery, often hundreds of times, prostrating themselves and praying as they do so.

In 1979, secret talks began between the Chinese and the Dalai Lama. As a result, a number of delegations of Tibetan exiles, led by senior representatives of the Dalai (including his sister and elder brother), visited Tibet and were allowed to travel virtually wherever they liked. The leaders of one delegation that journeyed there in mid-1980 addressed a pro-Dalai Lama crowd that had gathered outside their Lhasa guesthouse; the delegates were immediately expelled from Tibet by the Chinese authorities. One delegation leader said, on his return to India, that he had been saddened by the poor living conditions of the Tibetan people.

The Dalai Lama has said that he would be willing to go back to Tibet if he was sure that most of his people were happy under Chinese rule. He has recently commented favourably on the positive changes in the Chinese administration of the region, adding that 'although things are improving, still there are a lot of things to be done.'

The Chinese want the Dalai Lama to come back to legitimise their rule, but he will apparently be little more than a religious figurehead if he does return. And there is no guarantee he would be allowed to live in Lhasa.

The Dalai's great rival, traditionally and today, is the Panchen Lama, two years his junior, who has taken a completely different road and become a vice-chairman of the Chinese National People's Congress. 'Our Tibet, which is part of China, can only go forward along the socialist road,' he says. There is no doubt that for many, perhaps most, people in Tibet, life is better now than it was before the rebellion. Serfdom has been ended, schools and hospitals have been built where before there were none. The average income of Tibetans in 1981 was reported to be 200 yuan (about UK£60) a year, 11 per cent higher than in 1980. The 1982 all-China census indicated that there were 1.8 million people in Tibet. This figure does not include the People's Liberation Army personnel stationed in Tibet which, according to foreign estimates, may number about 200 000. However, some Chinese personnel have begun to be recalled to the central provinces, to give Tibetan officials a greater role in the running of their land.

But there is also ample proof that many Tibetans are unhappy under Chinese rule. Two foreign students, Christina Jansen and Susette Terenent Cooke, spent more than a month in Tibet in the summer of 1980. 'As far as we knew, we were the first foreigners to enter Tibet along the new Chengdu–Lhasa highway,' they wrote in an article published in the *Far Eastern Economic Review*, adding: 'The message from workmen, monks, pilgrims and students was the same: they wanted us to go to the Dalai Lama and tell him of their wish for a separate Tibet under his leadership.'

Foreign correspondents who visited Lhasa again in mid-1980 were handed two unsigned letters, one of which said: 'We ask the United Nations to help us. The Chinese invaded Tibet and are destroying everything including the economy, the religion, the culture.'

The Chinese leadership is clearly aware of the problems that exist in Tibet and is taking set steps to try and lessen the poverty of the region while at the same time allowing the Tibetans a greater degree of 'autonomy'. Time will tell if the Tibetan people as a whole, and their leader the Dalai Lama in particular, can come to terms with the fact that Tibet is now a part of the People's Republic of China.

Lhasa

The city of Lhasa, which, at 12 087 feet (3683 metres) above sea level, is about 150 feet (46 metres) higher than the highest capital of an independent country (La Paz in Bolivia), lies in a river valley and is dominated by the magnificent POTALA PALACE, once the centre of government and the winter residence of the Dalai Lama.

Lhasa is, in fact, two cities, one Chinese and one Tibetan.the Chinese one, the larger of the two, is neatly laid out and consists of buildings much like those built after 1949 in other parts of China. The Tibetan quarter, by contrast, is old, ramshackle, dirty and full of atmosphere. The smell of stale yak butter hangs over everything. The houses are mostly two-storey structures with flat roofs and low doors through which you have to stoop to enter. Nearby is the JOKHANG TEMPLE, a huge structure which has been renovated and has roofs of gold which glint magnificently in the sun. The pilgrims finger prayer beads and mumble Buddhist sutras while turning prayer wheels (shaped like toy tops and containing pieces of paper inscribed with the words 'Hail! The Jewel in the Lotus' many thousands of times), sending blessings to the gods. Men and women alike smile and stick out their tongues at strangers in the age-old Tibetan sign of welcome.

One curious anomaly in Lhasa is the group of Nepalese traders who run about two dozen shops selling many goods unavailable in other stores, including tea, cosmetics, and other items imported from India. The Nepalese also sell some antiques and other bits of junk, but visitors should always be sure to haggle with them. Many of them speak English, and as people truly worthy of the phrase 'strangers in a strange land', they are interesting to talk to. To look after this community, there is a Napalese consul-general who drives an Australian-made, black Holden sedan.

There are apparently no restaurants serving Tibetan food in Lhasa – in her book, Han Suyin makes the extraordinary claim that 'Tibetan cooking does not exist.' It, of course, does, and consists largely of mutton and tsampa, a mixture of barley, tea and yak butter. If you are on a CTS tour which includes a visit to a commune near Lhasa, tell your guide beforehand that you would like a real Tibetan meal and it may be possible to arrange one. However, Lhasa does have a number of local teahouses in the city which are highly recommended – if you can find them.

The Chinese appear to have ceased, for the moment, their attempt to stamp out the Lamaist religion in Tibet. The Jokhang Temple, which in 1979 was open only once a week, is now open six days a week for worshippers, and some monasteries have started taking in novice monks again for the first time since the late 1950s. However, even those monasteries that are still open, a minute fraction of the number before the rebellion, are virtually deserted compared to the old days. The DREPUNG MONASTERY, for instance, which used to have over 10,000 lamas now has only 200.

Another of the great monasteries, the SERA MONASTERY is perhaps most interesting for what goes on behind rather than inside it. On a mountain top not far away, there is a flat rock on which takes place the renowned Tibetan 'sky burials', ceremonies in which dead people are chopped up and fed to the vultures.

This form of burial is very popular with Tibetans, and remains the most common form of funeral. The undertakers carry the bodies up the mountain at dawn and lay them face down and naked on the flat rock as mourners stand to one side. According to one description, the butchers dismember the corpses and strip the flesh from the bones, then chop off the heads and remove anything soft and edible from the skulls. The torsos are ripped open and everything except the bones chopped into pieces small enough to be swallowed by vultures. The bones are then collected and crushed into a powder as the circling vultures come closer in anticipation of the feast to come. Yak butter and Tibetan barley are mixed in with the bone, and the resulting mash sprinkled over the chopped flesh. The vultures, perhaps 50 in number, recognise this as their cue and move in to begin breakfast. When they have finished, the undertakers wash the blood off the rock, ready for the other funerals, which reportedly occur several times a week at Sera, the only 'sky burial' ground near Lhasa.

The bone is crushed and mixed with more appetising condiments because Tibetans consider it to be a bad omen if any of the body is left uneaten. In an article on the subject written from Lhasa, Reuter correspondent Richard Pascoe reported that the normal charge for a sky burial was about 60 yuan (UK £20), while the undertaker gets the clothes of the deceased as part of the fee.

The antecedents of the sky burial ceremony are not known, although it is similar to the funeral ceremony of the Zoroastrians in India who leave bodies on the top of high pillars to be eaten by vultures. One possible reason for it may be that, in much of Tibet, the ground is so hard and the earth so shallow that digging graves for the dead would be difficult.

Getting to see a sky burial is not impossible, but it's not easy either. The Sera Monastery is several miles outside Lhasa and the Chinese are unhelpful. But although the funerals take place soon after dawn, it would be worth the effort. The monastery is perhaps two hours' walk from Lhasa, or else you could try hitchhiking. At that time of the morning, you may even get a lift with the funeral cortège.

Tibet is still technically closed to foreigners, but a couple of tour companies have managed to acquire the rights to send in tour groups, and some Hong Kong and foreign travellers have made it overland from Sichuan to the east, a long, slow journey, taking two weeks or more. About 1500 tourists visited Tibet in 1982 and further increases are expected because of the area's great potential as a foreign exchange earner – foreigners appear to be willing to pay almost anything for the privilege of seeing the Potala with their own eyes. However, it is important to remember that it is not Tibet which has been opened to tourists but only the city of Lhasa and its environs, and sometimes SHIGATSE (Xigaze), a city on the road between Lhasa and Katmandu. Most of the wild and woolly territory is still very much closed, a fact which should be kept in mind when trying to judge Tibetan standards of living – Lhasa is the Mayfair and Knightsbridge of Tibet.

A large amount of Tibetan antiques were available when the first foreigners arrived in 1979 – carpets, silver items, prayer wheels, daggers and other things – but there is increasingly less to be found now and black-market prices have rocketed. One risk in buying Tibetan antiques is that the Chinese customs may decide that they cannot be taken out of the country.

The high altitude in Tibet sometimes affects visitors. People who go overland have time to get accustomed to the rarefied air as they climb slowly up on to the plateau, but those who arrive by aircraft frequently feel strangely lightheaded, a symptom sometimes followed often by nausea, headaches and fatigue. It is said to take up to two weeks for the effects of altitude sickness to wear off, and the Chinese provide pillows filled with oxygen for those who feel breathless. The cardinal rule is – don't drink too much alcohol.

How to get there and where to stay

Most foreigners visiting Tibet do so on package tours, and stay only two or three days. The vast majority arrive by air from Chengdu, although there are also scheduled flights from Lanzhou. Flight plans, however, are often cancelled or delayed due to bad weather. Once there, there is a bumpy three-hour drive from the airport into Lhasa. Some intrepid students and back-packers have managed to get travel permits for Lhasa and have made their way overland from the Chinese heartland, mostly travelling from Chengdu. However, all police stations around China now seem to be under strict orders not to issue permits for Tibet, and police reportedly check all buses heading west out of Chengdu and pull foreigners off. But for those who do manage to get through, things are a lot easier once in Tibet.

The main hotel, the *Lhasa No. 1 Guesthouse* near the Potala, has two wings, one for the regular tourist foreigners who pay up to 250 yuan (UK £75) a day, and one for the students who pay five yuan for a bed-space. There is one other guesthouse just outside Lhasa, but the distance from town makes it difficult to explore Lhasa properly, and it is therefore best avoided.

The Lhasa Public Security Bureau is said to be very good with permit extensions and some people travelling on their own have reported being able to spend a month and more in Tibet. One American was even taken on by the Lhasa Languages Institute as an English teacher with the knowledge and approval of the regional government, almost certainly the first Westerner to be employed in Tibet since the handful of foreigners working for the Dalai Lama were kicked out in 1951. But after two months, Peking apparently found out and ordered that he be removed.

Until mid-1981, it was possible to travel out of Tibet via Shigatse to Nepal – a three- or four-day trip by bus – but the road was washed out by floods in mid-1981 and, at the time of writing, had still not been re-opened. In 1980, the Chinese authorities were considering starting tours into Tibet from Katmandu, which is far closer to Lhasa than is Peking, and the idea will presumably be revived once the road is re-opened.

XINJIANG (Sinkiang) AUTONOMOUS REGION

The history of the far northwestern 'autonomous region' of modern Xinjiang, or Eastern Turkestan as it was once called, is fascinating, little known and bears re-telling. It has always been one of the crossroads of Asia, and in the past 100 years has seen endless wars, rebellions and intrigue, with the Chinese, the Russians and the local Muslim population all trying to gain the upper hand.

For most of the past 2000 years, the area now known as Xinjiang has been controlled by a succession of kingdoms, sometimes large, sometimes small, but all centred on the string of oases which dot its forbidding deserts. Occasionally, Chinese dynasties have gained control over the area, including that of the Manchus, the last imperial dynasty which established its rule by quelling rebellions of the local Muslims. By the late nineteenth century, however, Chinese rule was slipping as the Manchu dynasty began its slide into oblivion, largely due to the imperialist pressure of the Western powers.

By 1911, when the empire fell and the Republic of China was born, Xinjiang was well out of reach of the government in Peking, and remained so, more or less, until the Communists came to power in 1949. But it was still nominally part of China, and the nationalistic aspirations of the various local peoples, particularly the farming Uighurs and the nomadic Kazakhs, failed to bear fruit. The main reason for this was the warlord Yang Zhengxin, who ruled Xinjiang as his private kingdom from 1911 until his assassination in 1928. While the Soviets were pushing in from the north, many of the local people wanted to try out the new-fangled ideology known as nationalism, but by a clever policy of coming to terms with the Soviets and appeasing the Muslims, Yang kept his hold on the region.

In the early 1920s, the civil war between the Bolsheviks and the White Russians was raging across central Asia just to the north of Xinjiang. Yang shrewdly decided to support the Bolsheviks, and when the war ended with their victory, the Soviet Union signed a special friendship treaty with Yang which resulted in increased trade.

Moscow was clearly trying to shift Xinjiang into its own orbit, and with the Chinese heartland thousands of miles away and in the midst of turmoil, it was not hard to do.

With Yang's death in 1928, he was succeeded by an official named Chin who unfortunately did not continue his relatively enlightened policies. Rampant corruption and oppression caused a number of revolts by the Muslim peoples, one of which forced Chin to flee in 1933. Another Chinese warlord rose to replace him, and this one, Sheng Shih-tsai, remained in power almost to the end of the Second World War. He was, by all accounts, a cruel, brutal despot, and was hated by the Muslim population, but he gained the support of the Soviet Union who sent him advisers and technicians in return for huge influence in the region. The Soviets helped Sheng crush the intermittent Muslim rebellions, and the warlord, in emulation of his Stalinist allies to the north, organised purges of his many opponents. By the late 1930s, the Soviet Union had a virtual monopoly on trade with Xinjiang – contacts with China proper being limited by the poor roads and the weakness of the central government.

The Soviet Union's entry into the Second World War marked the beginning of the end for its client, Sheng. The Soviets no longer had the time or the resources to help him, and he was forced to come to terms with Generalissimo Chiang Kaishek, the Nationalist president of China. But Sheng managed to annoy both the Nationalists and the Soviet Union, and he was finally driven from power in 1944.

The local Muslims now made their most serious attempt yet at gaining independence. A Kazakh leader named Osman arose who, by 1944, controlled most of southwest Xinjiang. He was joined by the Uighurs, the Mongols and others, and an independent Eastern Turkestan Republic was established in January 1945. As it happened, the Soviets were at that point trying to woo the Nationalist Chinese, and succeeded in arranging an agreement between the Chinese and the Muslims under which the new republic was abolished about a year after its formation, in return for a pledge of real autonomy from the Nationalist government. The Nationalists failed to live up to these assurances, but with the civil war against the Communists now raging, they had little opportunity to fully establish their control over the region.

In late 1948, the Nationalists appointed a Muslim named Burhan as the provincial chief, unaware that he was secretly a supporter of the Communist Party. An organisation called the 'Sinkiang League for the Protection of Peace and Democracy' was formed by the Muslim nationalists opposed to Chinese rule, but in August 1949, a number of the most prominent Muslim leaders of the Xinjiang region died in a mysterious plane crash while on their way to Peking for talks with the Communists. The Muslim nationalist movement never recovered from this blow, although the Kazakh leader Osman continued the fight against the Chinese until he was captured and executed in early 1951.

The Chinese began a policy of resettlement of people from the Chinese heartland into Xinjiang, radically changing the racial mixture of the region's population. In 1953, Xinjiang had a population of about 4.9 million of whom 3.6 million were Uighurs, and only a very small number were Han Chinese, but by 1970, the number of Hans was estimated to have grown to about four million. According to the 1982 census, Xinjiang's population is 13 million of whom only six million are Uighurs.

During the 1950s, there were continuing problems with the Muslim people, particularly the nomadic Kazakhs, who were greatly angered by the institution of the communes in 1958. 'Fortunately for the Party,' wrote one historian, 'the Lanzhou-to-Hami railway was completed in 1959 and brought in its wake a large-scale influx of Chinese settlers.' About 60 000 Kazakhs crossed into the Soviet Union in 1962.

Full-scale rebellions and uprisings by the Muslim people of Xinjiang may be a thing of the past, but there is still friction between Han Chinese and locals, and occasional reports of trouble.

Another source of problems for the provincial government in Xinjiang is the huge number of Han Chinese who were settled in the region during the Cultural Revolution of the late 1960s. Most of them were put to work on state farms, and many, particularly those from Shanghai and other urban areas, are very unhappy and would dearly love to return to their homes. There have been reports of demonstrations and strikes by these people, particularly in late 1980 when a large number returned to Shanghai illegally and refused to go back. These two 'contradictions', as the Chinese would put it – friction between the Hans and the Muslims and problems with the educated youth forced to stay in Xinjiang against their will – are not going to be solved quickly.

And what of the future? 'China's future lies in China's northwest,' said the Peking university professor, Chen Changdu. Xinjiang is rich in natural resources, Professor Chen declared, but lacks manpower.

'Population emigration to the northwest from other areas should be actively encouraged.'

Virtually all of Xinjiang is still closed to foreigners, and is likely to remain so for some time to come for several reasons – lack of facilities, poverty and the various problems of social order.

Of the places still not normally 'open', the most interesting is certainly Kashgar, a lively Uighur city with a long, colourful history in the extreme west of Xinjiang, only a few dozen miles from the Soviet border. It is a five-day bus or car ride from Urumqi, but has been visited in the past few years by a handful of foreigners in one capacity or another. One visitor said he was told by the Kashgar police that the city may be 'opened' in 1983.

The climate in most of Xinjiang is diabolically hot in the middle of summer and just as cold in mid-winter. The best times to visit the area are spring and autumn with late September best of all, if for no other reason than because that is the time when the famous grapes and melons are available.

Urumqi

Urumqi is the capital of Xinjiang. In the 1930s, two nuns, Mildred Cable and Francesca French, described it in their book, *The Gobi Desert*: 'The town has no beauty, no style, no dignity and no architectural interest.' It hasn't essentially changed much since then although it has grown from a small settlement to a city of more than 800 000 people.

About three-quarters of the city's population are Han Chinese, and the rest Muslims, but Urumqi has always been a Han town in a sea of Muslims.

There is little to see and very few historical relics. A few old mosques can be found, particularly around the small 'ethnic' section of the city near the SOUTH GATE (Nanmen; take a No. 1 bus to its terminus) but none of them in is in good condition. One of the most impressive buildings in town is the FORMER RUSSIAN CONSULATE, now used by the provincial song-and-dance troupe. There is also a MUSEUM, which basically used to detail the history of the Chinese occupation of Xinjiang. At last report, the displays were being 're-adjusted' to give a greater place to the history and culture of the local Muslim peoples.

How to get there and where to stay
Urumqi is connected to Peking and Lanzhou by regular air services, and there is a railway line all the way from central China. The train journey is very long (three days or more from Peking) but some of the scenery is magnificent – the track passes through long stretches of the Gobi desert.

The usual hotel used by foreigners is the *Eight-Storey Hotel* (Ba Lou Binguan; take a No. 2 bus from the railway station). Dormitory beds are available for five yuan.

It is possible to book train tickets back to Peking or Shanghai at the hotel, but do so a couple of days in advance to be sure of a place.

Tianchi
The main excursion from Urumqi is to Tianchi (heavenly lake), an hour's bus-ride northeast into the mountains. Towering over the pretty lake is a snow-capped mountain known as BOGDA FENG (the peak of God), and the area's alpine look is reminiscent of Switzerland. If you intend to go by local bus, buy your tickets the day before from in front of the People's Park (Renmin Gongyuan). Buy only a one-way ticket if you intend to spend the night at Tianchi, which is highly recommended. The bus leaves from outside the park at 7.00 a.m.

Up at the lake, there are a number of accommodation possibilities. The guesthouse is cheap, clean and comfortable, although there is no running water. There are also tourist versions of the local herdsmens' yurts available at about two yuan a night, and if you hike up into the mountains, you can probably stay with a Kazakh family in a real yurt for just a little more. If you plan to try the last idea, take some nuts, fruit and sweets with you to give to your hosts in return for the goats' cheese and salted tea they will offer you.

Hiking is one of the best things to do at Tianchi, and a good way to start is to hire the guesthouse ferry to take you across the lake. You can also arrange for it to meet you again at sunset. Buses returning to Urumqi leave Tianchi at 4.00 p.m., but get there early to be sure of a seat.

Another excursion from Tianchi is northwest to the town of SHIHEZI (stony creek), which is even less attractive than Urumqi. It is perhaps only interesting as an example of a Han colony: almost all its inhabitants are Han Chinese. It is possible to visit a state farm in the area.

Turfan (Turpan)

Of all the places which foreigners are allowed to visit in Xinjiang, Turfan is undoubtedly the most interesting, and is worth three days on its own. It is the one 'open' city with any real Uighur history, having served for several centuries as the capital of an Uighur kingdom over-run in the thirteenth century by Genghis Khan and his Mongol hordes. Like other oases in the region, Turfan served for hundreds of years as an important staging post on the northern Silk Road. It was originally a centre of Buddhism, but became converted to Islam in about the eighth century.

During the periods when the various Chinese dynasties expanded their control into the region, Turfan was an important garrison town, and the TURFAN CEMETERY, a few miles from the town, contains hundreds of graves of Chinese officials and soldiers who died there, including some from the Jin dynasty (A.D. 265–420) and the Tang dynasty (A.D. 618–907). Some of the tombs are open with the mummified corpses inside on display. Outside town, you will also see some Islamic-style tombs being built in the hills.

Turfan is a good town to walk round because of its authentic Uighur character. The FREE MARKET-CUM-BAZAAR (across the street and down the alley from the bus terminal) has a definite Middle East feel to it. Buy one of the Hami melons or get your own personal chop carved,

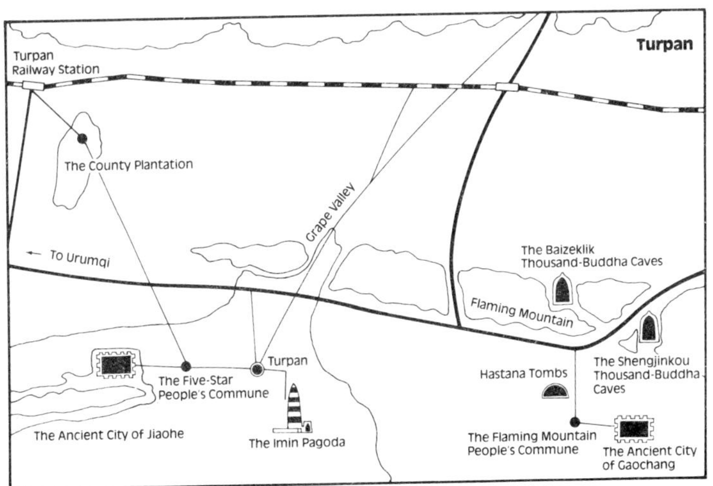

'while-you-wait', in Arabic, Chinese or English for less than three yuan. The night bazaar is good, too. Try some of the food on sale, particularly the mutton kebabs roasting on long, open barbecues, the flat Uighur bread known as *nan*, or *polow*, a mixture of rice, meat and onions known throughout much of the Middle East and India as 'pilau'. The famous Turfan grapes are tasty, but wash them before eating.

As a thriving Muslim town benefiting from the Communist Party's more liberal policy on religion in recent years, Turfan has a number of mosques open to worshippers, and local people are building more themselves. The IMIN PAGODA to the west of the town is a long walk or a short donkey-cart ride. Try to get the old caretaker who lives at the back to let you climb up the minaret/tower to get a good view of the area.

There are a number of excursions to take from Turfan, the best-known of which is the ruined town of JIAOHE (confluence of rivers) about ten miles (16 kilometres) east, which was a Chinese army camp until it was destroyed by Genghis Khan. Many of the mud-brick buildings are still reasonably intact, and visitors can walk around the streets of this long-dead town.

Another town which fell to the Mongols is GAOCHANG, similar to Jiaohe but in better shape. Not too far away from Gaochang are the Buddhist caves at BEZEKLIK, which were defaced by Muslims or robbed of their remaining art treasures by Western adventurers around the turn of the century. Particularly active was Albert von Le Coq, a German who removed whole frescos from the stone walls of the caves and transported them back to Berlin where they were placed in the Berlin Museum and largely destroyed by Allied bombing during the Second World War.

Most foreigners visiting these sites will take a taxi, or join a bus tour organised through the guesthouse. But it is also possible to take a local bus from the bus station (destination: Yalkuntaq) which only goes as far as the junction at which the roads to Gaochang and the Buddhist caves diverge. It is about a three-mile (4.8 kilometre) walk to either site from there (not recommended if it is hot), or else try to hop a ride on a passing donkey cart. An old woman lives at the crossroads who sells tea and meat dumplings (jiao-zi), and you can wait there for the public bus on your way back.

For those of a scientific bent, it is worth investigating Turfan's WATER SYSTEM, which consists of a huge network of underground tunnels stretching out under the desert, draining the water table in what is said to be a unique fashion.

People visiting Turfan during the summer should keep in mind that it is 504 feet (154 metres) below sea level and the hottest place in China. Temperatures in July can reach 116°F (47°C).

How to get there and where to stay

The main railway line through to Urumqi passes to the north of Turfan. The bus from the station to Turfan leaves from a nearby bus depot – walk out of the station, take the first road on the right and the depot is about 100 yards (90 metres) along on the left. There are also local buses to and from Urumqi.

The *Turfan Guesthouse* is on the main road quite a way from the bus terminal: it's a stiff walk or a 10–30 fen ride on a donkey cart (watch your valuables).

Lop Nor

Out in the desert wastes of Xinjiang, 1300 miles (2090 kilometres) due west of Peking, is the depression known as Lop Nor, the lake of Lop, an area of salt flats into which empties the occasional waters of the River Kongqi. Once there was a number of oases and cities in the area which were stops on the great Silk Road into central Asia. But the desert claimed virtually all of them in the end, leaving them buried and forgotten until the European explorers of the late nineteenth century came through the area looking for traces of the past.

After the Communist victory in 1949, Lop Nor took on a new significance: it became China's principal nuclear and missile test site. The story of how China joined the nuclear clan is a fascinating one, and although the Soviets gave the Chinese some assistance before the break in the early 1960s, the tale really revolves around two men, both brilliant Chinese scientists resident in the United States, who decided to return to their homeland and make it a military superpower.

One of the scientists is Zhao Zhongyao, a nuclear physicist, the other Qian Xuesen, an expert on rocketry and missiles. In the early 1950s, when McCarthyism and the Korean War made life a misery for many Asiatic residents of the United States, both men and a few dozen other Chinese scientists decided they would prefer to return to China under Communism than to stay in the West. Their primary motive was, apparently, nationalism.

Professor Zhao left in 1951 because the American authorities could find no excuse for detaining him. But Qian had to wait four more years, having been accused, along with so many others, of being a Communist.

Qian was born in Shanghai in 1912, and went to the United States in 1935. He studied aeronautics at both the Massachusetts and California Institutes of Technology, contributing, among other things, the 'Qian formula' for jet propulsion. During the Second World War, he was director of the Rocket Section of the US National Defence Scientific Advisory Board and, in 1945, headed a team of scientists sent to dismantle the German rocket centre at Peenemunde for shipment back to the United States. In 1949 he became the director of the Guggenheim Jet Propulsion Laboratory, and probably knew as much about rocketry and missiles as anyone else in the world.

In 1950, he decided to return to China, but was prevented by the FBI from leaving the United States. He went to see a friend of his, who was Under Secretary of the Navy, to try to get clearance to leave, but he declined to help.

'I'd rather shoot him than let him leave the country,' the Under Secretary is reported to have said. 'He knows too much that's valuable to us. He's worth five divisions anywhere.'

At a typical McCarthy-era trial, Qian was accused of having been a secret member of the American Communist Party, a charge he denied. His testimony revealed how such a man as Qian could decide to return to help the Communists.

'Do you owe your allegiance to Communist China?' the prosecutor asked him.

'I do not,' Qian replied.

'To whom do you owe allegiance?'

'I owe allegiance to the people of China.'

In 1955, Qian was finally allowed to leave the country. The reason for the timing is unclear. Some say that the US government had decided that what Qian knew was already outdated; others say that he was, in effect, swapped for a number of American pilots released by the Chinese at about the same time.

Qian made his way to China via Hong Kong, and virtually disappeared from sight. He became a Communist Party member in 1958, and survived the Cultural Revolution, when so many other intellectuals were attacked and persecuted, without even being criticised. During those years, it is believed that he was in charge of China's nuclear missile programme, centred at Lop Nor.

In recent years, Qian has been best known for his public statements in support of research into para-psychology, centring around children found in various parts of China who reportedly have strange supernatural powers, including the ability to 'read' or visualise words and characters with their ears. In 1981, a senior Communist Party official denounced the research into the so-called supernatural powers, which he said was just carnival trickery. Qian, however, has conspicuously refused to retract his previous statements.

Lop Nor, a place shrouded in mystery, became even more mysterious in 1979 when another prominent Chinese scientist, Peng Jiamu, disappeared into thin air while on an expedition into the area. Peng, a well-known biochemist, was with a number of other scientists who left him alone with a jeep while they went off into the sand dunes to do some tests. When they returned several hours later, Peng had disappeared. All sorts of rumours grew around this vanishing act. People speculated that he may have been kidnapped and taken over the Soviet border, 500 miles (805 kilometres) away. Another wrote to a Hong Kong newspaper reporting that he had seen Peng alive in a restaurant in Washington with Deng Zhifang, the son of Chinese strongman, Deng Xiaoping, who is studying in the United States. Peking denounced the report as a 'vicious fabrication'.

The search for Peng continued for many months with huge numbers of troops and aircraft mobilised to try and find some trace of him. But no clue was ever found, although the official press, trying to sound convincing, said 'investigations prove the theory that he lost his way while looking for water and that his body was buried by the shifting sands.'

How to get there

Of all the sensitive areas in China closed to foreigners, Lop Nor is probably the most sensitive and the least accessible. It is situated in the eastern part of Xinjiang on the edge of the Taklimakan desert and the nearest substantial town is Turfan, about 150 miles (240 kilometres) to the north. I have to admit that I have included it here simply as an excuse to tell the stories of Qian Xuesen and Peng Jiamu . . .

THE YANGTSE RIVER (Chang Jiang 'long river')

The ferryboat ride from Chongqing down the Yangtse River and through the famous gorges is one of the most interesting journeys available in China. The trip to Wuhan takes just under three days, but unless you have a particular reason for going on to Wuhan or Shanghai, it is better to get off the ferry at Yichang, the town just below the gorges. Once past there, the river widens and the trip becomes rather tedious – the river banks are usually too far away to see clearly.

The Yangtse, 4000 miles (6400 kilometres) long, is one of the world's greatest rivers. It rises on the Qinghai–Tibet plateau to the west and bisects China neatly in half, traditionally, marking the dividing line between the north and south of the country. It flows into the East China Sea just north of Shanghai.

The ferries from Chongqing sailing downstream, mostly named *The East Is Red*, stop at a number of towns along the way. At the end of the first day of the cruise, the boats dock at WANXIAN and spend the night there so that they will arrive at the Yangtse Gorges in daylight. Passengers are allowed to get off the boat and wander round this colourful river town, which also features a lively free market.

The first of the three gorges is the QUTANG GORGE, the shortest but also the most spectacular. At its narrowest point, the sheer precipices rising steeply on either side of the river are less than 100 yards (90 metres) apart. One ancient poet described the sight of the Yangtse forcing its way into the gap as being like 'a thousand seas pouring into one cup'. High up on the cliff face, coffins have been found which were placed there according to the strange funeral rites of some long-vanished tribe.

Next comes the WUXIA GORGE, about 25 miles (40 kilometres) in length, where the cliffs on either side rise to over 3000 feet (914 metres). The most famous of the nearby peaks is the GODDESS MOUNTAIN, named for its female contours, for which a Song dynasty poet wrote:

See the Goddess Peak from afar,
Her form is true loveliness.
Reflected in the water is the long knot of her hair.
Sun-filled clouds caress her flowing robes.

The third and longest of the gorges is the 50-mile (80 kilometre) XILING GORGE, at the end of which a huge hydroelectric dam is under construction to supply electricity to Wuhan. The GEZHOUBA DAM is also expected to make the waters of the Yangtse Gorges safer to navigate.

In the past, every boat making its way up the Yangtse had to be pulled up through the gorges by trackers. Sometimes hundreds of them were needed to pull a single junk up through the rapid currents, but the greater use of steam-driven boats in the past few decades has, thankfully, meant an end to the large-scale use of river trackers. However, people can still occasionally be seen hauling smaller boats up the channel.

How to get there

There is usually only one boat a day from Chongqing heading down the river, so getting a berth can sometimes be difficult. It is best to book in advance through CTS. If you travel to Chongqing from Chengdu, ferry tickets can be booked at the CTS office in the Jinjiang Hotel in Chengdu.

The ferries generally leave Chongqing at 7.00 a.m. and arrive at Wanxian at about 8.00 that evening. They start out again at 4.00 the next morning and dock at Yichang at 6.00 p.m. that night. They arrive at Hankou in Wuhan at about 4.30 p.m. on the third day. The upstream journey from Wuhan to Chongqing takes five days.

From Wohan it is possible to continue down the Yangtse to Nanking (three more days) and Shanghai (four days).

The *East Is Red* ferries have five classes of accommodation. A number of berths and an exclusive lounge are often reserved for foreign tourists, but they can also travel second, third or fourth class. The Chongqing–Hankou (Wuhan) tickets cost 101 yuan for the top class and 29 yuan for fourth class.

The food provided on the ferries is generally considered to be awful, so it is wise to buy some provisions in Chongqing before starting out, although food can also be bought at the numerous stops along the way.

YUNNAN PROVINCE

Yunnan, on China's southwest flank, has been a frontier province for centuries and a place of exile for disgraced officials. Over half of China's minority races are represented in the province, but none of them is as numerous as the large minorities in, say, neighbouring Guangxi – the Zhuang people – or the Uighur people in Xinjiang. The minority people of Yunnan, mostly very poor mountain tribes, add a touch of exotica and colour to the province.

In 1977 and 1978, about 200 000 refugees from Vietnam flooded across the border into Yunnan and Guangxi provinces, placing a huge burden on the local administrations. Most of the refugees were of Chinese origin, and had been forced out by the Vietnamese government apparently as part of a co-ordinated plan to rid the country of its Chinese minority. They have largely been settled on state farms in Yunnan, Guangxi and Guangdong (*see* Hainan Island, p. 117) with some help from the United Nations. China went to war against Vietnam in early 1979, in what was called a 'Self-Defence Counter-Attack', and temporarily seized a strip of Vietnamese territory several miles deep along the border, at a reportedly huge cost in casualties. The border remains tense, and both sides regularly report armed clashes of a minor nature.

Yunnan also shares a frontier with Laos and Burma, and is very close to the famous 'Golden Triangle' region which produces a large proportion of the world's opium supplies. The Communists wiped out virtually all drug addiction and trafficking in China when they came to power, but there has been an upsurge in both during the past few years, although to exactly what extent is not known. All that is certain is that the *Yunnan Daily* occasionally attacks people that it says are engaged in drug-taking and drug-trafficking.

During the civil war in the late 1940s, the Nationalist armies in southeast China proved to be particularly tenacious, and the Communists succeeded only in driving them into the remote mountainous areas of eastern Burma and Thailand, where they survive in a drastically altered form even today. Some of the Nationalist soldiers elected to stay in the jungles rather than accept re-settlement in Taiwan, and have become an important link in the opium trade.

In the Cultural Revolution of the late 1960s, Yunnan became a stronghold of the Maoist radicals, and the provincial leadership allegedly planned an uprising in co-ordination with the radicals in Shanghai after the so-called 'Gang of Four' leaders were seized in Peking. But for reasons never satisfactorily explained, the uprising never took place.

Kunming

Kunming, the capital of Yunnan Province, is known as the 'city of eternal spring' because of its cool, pleasant climate all year round. The large number of pre-1949 buildings makes it a nice city to walk round, particularly the lanes on either side of Dongfeng Dong Lu (Dongfeng Road East) to the west of the Panlong River. Kunming has quite a large community of Muslims, and their MOSQUE is worth visiting (on Zhengyi Lu, just north of the main roundabout on Dongfeng Dong Lu). The city also has many TEAHOUSES along its streets, an old Chinese institution which has been snuffed out in most cities, and a cup of tea in one of them is a 'must'. Some of the better ones offer musical entertainment or story-telling. The KUNMING CULTURAL CENTRE also features snake shows every day with snake charmers doing tricks with deadly cobras, entrance fee 10 fen.

Another point of interest is the DAGUANLOU (tower of great vistas) in the southwest of the city on the shores of the Dianchi Lake, the sixth-largest freshwater lake in China. (Take a No. 4 bus heading west to its terminus.) From the lake take the No. 4 bus to the terminus at the other end of the route to visit the YUANTONG TEMPLE, the largest in Kunming. The local zoo and a good free market are in the same area.

The best excursion close to Kunming is to the WEST HILL (Xishan), a couple of miles to the southwest. There is a path up the forested slopes to the summit which passes by a number of Buddhist temples, some damaged in the Cultural Revolution, but now restored as tourist attractions. To get there, make your way to the No. 6 bus terminus in Kunming. There are two No. 6 bus routes: the first goes to Gaoyao near the foot of the West Hill and the second to NIE ER MU – the grave of Nie Er, a famous composer – about an hour's walk further up. There is also another bus which operates between the two points. From Nie Er's grave, climb up to the DRAGON'S GATE at the summit

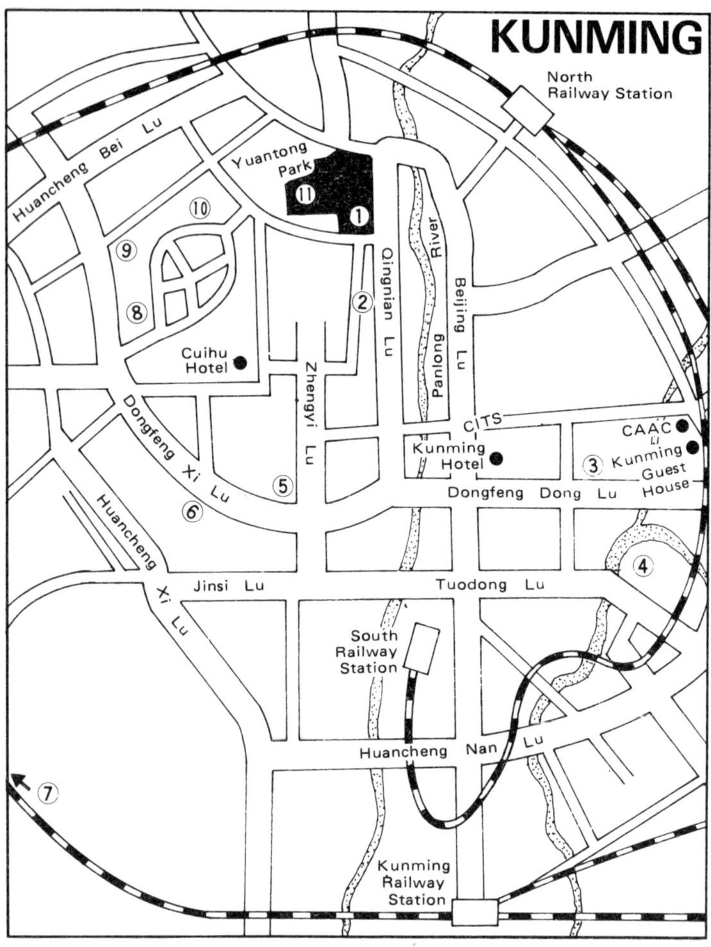

1 Yuantong Temple
2 Kunming Arts and Crafts Factory
3 Yunnan Province Antiques Store
4 Tuodong Stadium
5 Dongfeng Department Store
6 Yunnan Province Museum
7 Grand View Mansion (Daguanlou)
8 Agricultural Exhibition Hall
9 Industry and Communications Exhibition Hall
10 Green Lake (Cui Hu)
11 Kunming Zoo

which was carved out of the rock by a Taoist monk and his assistants over a period of nearly 30 years from the beginning of the nineteenth century. Below, is a Taoist temple called SANQINGGE (Hall of the Three Purities) dating from the Yuan dynasty. Further down are the TAIHUA TEMPLE and the HUATING TEMPLE, both built during the fourteenth century.

Most visitors to Kunming also go to see SHILIN (the stone forest), one of the most extraordinary sights in China – literally a forest of fantastically shaped stones jutting out of the ground. The stone forest is in Lunan County, about 60 miles (96 kilometres) southeast of Kunming. (*Take a No. 2 bus to the terminus in the western part of Kunming from where the No. 17 bus leaves for Shilin. It is best to go to the terminus the day before and buy a ticket (3.50 yuan) to be sure of a seat. The bus leaves at 7.15 a.m. The local CTS office also operates tourist buses to the stone forest and back for ten yuan a head. Bus leaves at 7.00 a.m. and leaves Shilin at 3.00 p.m. Avoid going on Sundays if you want to miss the crowds.*)

It is possible to stay overnight at Shilin. There is a good hotel with rooms renting for 12 to 16 yuan each. In the evening, there are minority dancing displays at the hotel, arranged by CTS for the tourists.

There is also a small village in the 'forest' where the local minority people live, which is well worth visiting.

Yunnan's main specialities in food are Yunnan ham, famed throughout China, Yunnan duck and Guo Qiao Mian ('crossing the bridge noodles'). The *Chuncheng Restaurant* (Dongfeng Xi Lu) is supposed to be good and cheap, and also try the *Beijing Restaurant* (Xin Xiangyun Ji) and the *Shanghai Restaurant* (Dongfeng Xi Lu).

The Kunming Public Security Bureau has the reputation of being very helpful with travel permits and visa extensions.

How to get there and where to stay

Kunming is on the national rail network on the line between Guiyang and Chengdu. There are also flights to and from Canton, Guilin, Nanning and Guiyang, as well as to and from Hong Kong, and Rangoon in Burma.

Most foreigners stay at the *Kunming Hotel* (145 Dongfeng Dong Lu; take a No. 23 bus from the station, get off at the third stop, walk south to main road and then east for 10 minutes or so. Alternatively, take a motorised pedi-cab). The hotel has pleasant double rooms, and dormitory beds too, and is close to the city centre.

Other hotels are the *Kunhu* (44 Beijing Lu; take a pedi-cab or a No. 3 bus from the railway station, get off at the first stop. The dormitory is room 629), and the *Cuihu* (green lake) *Hotel* (6 Cuihu Nan Lu; take a No. 2 bus from the station, and get off at the seventh stop).

Xishuang Banna

This region of Yunnan Province close to Laos and Burma is most famous for the Water-splashing Ceremony which the local Dai people hold as part of their own New Year's celebrations. Visitors stay in JINGHONG, the main town of the district, only 18 miles (30 kilometres) from the Burmese border. It is situated on the Lancang River which further down becomes the Mekong, and the whole area is green, tropical and very beautiful. There are still huge expanses of virgin forests in Xishuang Banna, although indiscriminate deforestation has taken its toll. A number of rare animal and bird species live in the jungle, including helmet-crowned hornbills, black gibbons, wild boar and elephants. The area is also famous for its flowers.

Ten minority races live in the Xishuang Banna area, of whom the most numerous are the Dai, a race related to the Thai people. Another race is distinguished by their long, pendulous earlobes which they cultivate by hanging weighty objects from their ears. Officials will tell you that, under the 'Gang of Four', the minority peoples were maltreated, but that now relations between the Han Chinese and the local tribes are excellent.

The New Year's celebrations of the Dai people usually take place in mid-April although the dates vary slightly each year. Traditionally, the festival should last three days. On the first day, there is a large market, and on the second, dragon-boat races are held on the river. On the third day, everybody throws buckets of water at each other with wild abandon, a tradition said to stem from a battle against a fire demon in the legendary past.

The Dais, who are Buddhists, become totally wrapped-up in the celebrations, which also involve a large amount of eating and drinking. Buffaloes are slaughtered in a highly ritualistic fashion, and there is dancing and singing which gets wilder and fiercer as the celebrations progress. There are Dai villages near Jinghong which can be visited under the eye of an official guide, and also a Tropical Plant Research Unit in the jungle.

Everyone who goes to Xishuang Banna remarks on the beautiful scenery and the relaxed atmosphere.

How to get there and where to stay

Foreigners have to take a plane from Kunming to Simao, about 200 miles (320 kilometres) southwest. There is a local bus which goes from there to Jinghong, a bumpy, scenic drive of about five hours. Simao has a nice hotel if you have to stay the night there.

The hotel in Jinghong is spartan but pleasant, with the cheapest beds costing four yuan a night.

The local Public Security Bureau apparently has a rule that foreigners are allowed to stay in Jinghong for only five days maximum, the only 'open' place in China known to have such a rule.

ZHEJIANG PROVINCE

Wenzhou

This lively port city on the coast of Zhejiang Province south of Shanghai is officially closed to foreigners, although some tourists have been given permission to go there.

Wenzhou has a reputation of being a rather independent-minded place. A large percentage of its residents have relatives living overseas, and these contacts, plus the local fishing fleet, have led to large-scale black-marketeering. Together with Hangzhou, Wenzhou was one of the places most seriously affected by factional disorders during the Cultural Revolution. In the early 1970s, the radicals in the central leadership took over from the local military government ruling groups which had taken power at the end of the Cultural Revolution. The people of Wenzhou, however, seem to have strongly resisted the imposition of their radical policies.

According to local radio broadcasts in 1977, after the so-called 'Gang of Four' radicals had been purged, the communes in Wenzhou at one point in 1975 or 1976 were disbanded and the land distributed to the peasants for individual farming. Underground factories were set up and the black market flourished. One article said that communications with Wenzhou were 'restored' after the fall of the 'Gang', suggesting that the city had cut itself off from the rest of the country for a time.

What exactly happened in Wenzhou in the mid-1970s is not known, but the few hints we have suggest that, whatever it was, it was interesting. The city itself is very isolated, and it would be comparatively easy to cut it off. There are no railways within 100 miles (160 kilometres) and roads in the mountain areas of Zhejiang are very primitive.

Hangzhou (Hangchow)

The first advertising blurb in the history of Chinese tourism was probably the old Chinese saying: 'Above there is Heaven, below there is Suzhou and Hangzhou.' The city itself is nothing special, but the surrounding countryside, and particularly the West Lake beside the town, are very pleasant. The town rose to prominence largely because it marks the southern end of the Grand Canal, the mammoth waterway built largely in the seventh century to supply grain to the north of China. (The northern end of the canal is at Tongxian, east of Peking.)

Hangzhou was the capital of the southern Song dynasty for more than a century from 1138 until the Mongols took the city in 1279. Marco Polo visited the city in the late thirteenth century and described it as 'without doubt the finest and most splendid city in the world'. He waxed lyrical, as usual, about the city's size and the variety and quality of goods for sale in the markets. But he saved a special compliment for the city's courtesans whom he said were so accomplished 'that foreigners who have once enjoyed them remain utterly beside themselves and so captivated by their sweetness and charm that they can never forget them'. The city remained prosperous, and became an important silk centre over the following centuries, but it was almost completely destroyed during the Taiping Rebellion in the middle of the nineteenth century. Since the Communist take-over, the city has grown considerably and now has a large number of factories and a population approaching one million.

In 1976, Hangzhou was the scene of some of the biggest upheavals in the mid-1970s, as radicals and non-radicals fought it out for supremacy. In March 1977, nine people were executed in Hangzhou for 'vilifying Chairman Hua Guofeng' (the leftist successor to Chairman Mao, who was deposed in 1981 by Deng Xiaoping). The deaths were unfortunate, for within four years, Chairman Hua was himself being vilified. In the late 1970s, the two sons of a high Communist Party official in Hangzhou, known as the 'Bear Brothers', shot to brief infamy when they were accused of raping more than 100 girls in their father's house. One of the brothers was executed. However, the Chinese meaning of the word 'rape' is rather different from that in the West. Here, it can simply mean pre-marital sexual intercourse.

The main tourist attraction in Hangzhou is the WEST LAKE, a large freshwater lake surrounded by wooded hills, pagodas, temples and gardens. A number of emperors spent time in Hangzhou and had structures built there, most notably the Manchu emperor Qian Long of the late eighteenth century. Qian Long fancied himself as a poet, and the Hangzhou area is littered with his poems and inscriptions. The SU DONGBUO CAUSEWAY, which runs along the western bank of the

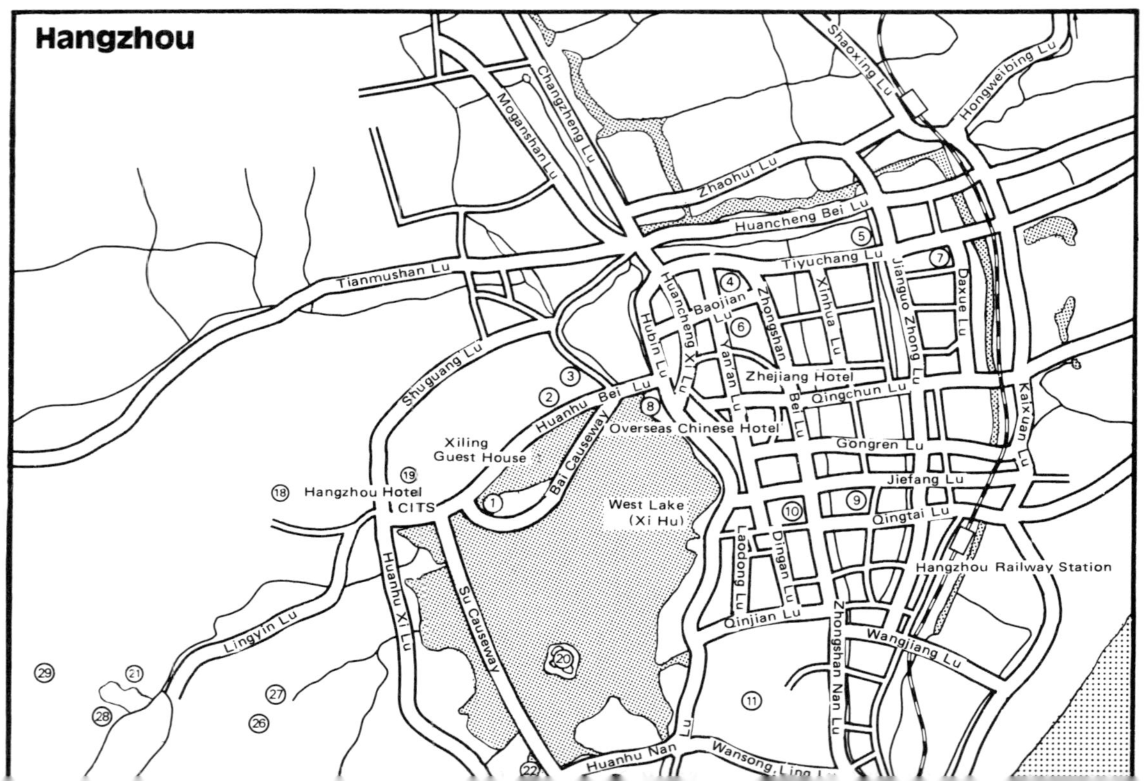
Hangzhou
Shaoxing Lu
Hongweibing Lu
Changzheng Lu
Moganshan Lu
Zhaohui Lu
Huancheng Bei Lu
Tiyuchang Lu
Daxue Lu
Jianguo Zhong Lu
Xinhua Lu
Zhongshan
Baojian Lu
Huancheng Xi Lu
Hubin Lu
Yan'an Lu
Zhejiang Hotel
Qingchun Lu
Bei Lu
Kaixuan Lu
Tianmushan Lu
Shuguang Lu
Huanhu Bei Lu
Overseas Chinese Hotel
Gongren Lu
Jiefang Lu
Qingtai Lu
Xiling
Guest House
Bai Causeway
Hangzhou Hotel
CITS
West Lake
(Xi Hu)
Laodong Lu
Dingan Lu
Hangzhou Railway Station
Qinjian Lu
Zhongshan Nan Lu
Wangjiang Lu
Huanhu Xi Lu
Su Causeway
Lingyin Lu
Huanhu Nan Lu
Wansong Ling
1
2
3
4
5
6
7
8
9
10
11
18
19
20
21
22
26
27
28
29

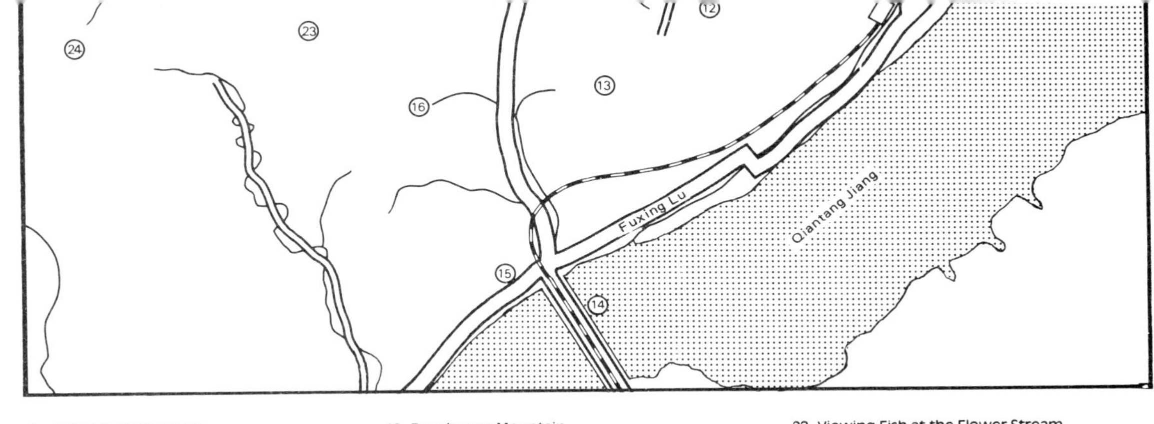

1 Solitary Hill (Gu Shan)
2 Precious Stone Hill (Baoshi Shan)
3 Great Buddha Temple (Dafo Si)
4 Zhejiang Province Exhibition Hall
5 Hangzhou Friendship Store
6 Antiques Store
7 Zhejiang Province Library
8 China Liberation Monument
9 Department Store
10 Branch of Xinhua (New China) Bookstore
11 Wu Mountain
12 Fenghuang Mountain
13 Yuhuang Mountain
14 Qiantang Bridge
15 Six Harmonies Pagoda (Liuhe Ta)
16 Running Tiger Cave (Hupaodong)
17 Nanping Hill
18 Jade Spring (Yuquan)
19 Geling Hill and Tomb of Yue Fei
20 Three Pools Mirroring the Moon (Santanyinyue)
21 Monastery of the Spirits' Retreat (Lingyin Si)
22 Viewing Fish at the Flower Stream (Huagang Guanyu)
23 Dragon Well (Longjing) Temple
24 Tianzhu Mountain
25 Shangtianzhu Mountain
26 Zhongtianzhu Mountain
27 Xiatianzhu Mountain
28 Peak that Flew from Afar (Feilai Feng)
29 Northern High Peak (Beigao Feng)

lake was built in the eleventh century by a poet who was prefect of Hangzhou. SOLITARY HILL ISLAND (take a No. 7 bus from town or walk from the Hangzhou Hotel) near the north shore has a number of interesting buildings, including the remains of an eighteenth-century palace which now houses the PROVINCIAL MUSEUM. The 'THREE POOLS MIRRORING THE MOON' ISLAND, close to the southern shore, is pleasant to wander round. There are ferries from a number of points around the lake shore.

In the hills to the west of the lake is the LINYIN TEMPLE (take a No. 7 bus), one of the oldest Buddhist temples in China, set in a delightful wooded valley. The main temple buildings were destroyed during the Taiping Rebellion and were only re-built in the 1920s. Behind the temple is the FEILAIFENG (literally 'the hill that arrived by air'). There is a cable car to the top or you can walk up.

Close to the Hangzhou Hotel on the northeast shore of the lake is the TEMPLE honouring the memory of Yue Fei, a great general of the twelfth century who fought the Tartar invaders but was betrayed and murdered by the prime minister Qin Gui. Yue Fei's tomb lies behind the temple, and in front of it are four statues representing the evil prime minister, his wife and two other accomplices in the murder. For centuries, it has been a tradition for visitors to spit on the four statues.

In the hills to the south of the Linyin temple (take a No. 27 bus) is DRAGON WELL, home of the most famous type of green tea in China – Dragon Well (Longjing) tea. The well in question can be seen although there is no sign of dragons.

There used to be canals running throughout the central city area of Hangzhou, but most have now been filled in. However, there are still a couple of waterways running north–south through the town, and the terminus of the Grand Canal is to the north of the city.

The main excursion from Hangzhou is to the towns of SHAOXING and NINGBO to the east, linked to Hangzhou by train. Shaoxing is a picturesque little town with canals and old houses, and it is famous for a type of rice wine. It was also the birthplace of the writer Lu Xun. (For details on Ningbo, *see below*.)

How to get there and where to stay

There are flights to Hangzhou from Canton, Peking and Hong Kong, and it is on the main railway line between Shanghai and Canton. Some foreigners have managed to take a ferry along the Grand Canal north to Suzhou, but others have been refused tickets.

The best hotel is the *Hangzhou Hotel* (take a No. 7 bus from the railway station), situated right on the lake shore, away from the centre of town. It has nice standard hotel rooms and also a dormitory. Other hotels include the *Xiling Guesthouse*, east of the Hangzhou Hotel), and the *Overseas Chinese Hotel* in the city, on the east bank of the lake (also take a No. 7 bus from the railway station).

Ningbo

Ningbo was one of the old Treaty Ports opened up to foreign trade by the British in 1842 after the first Opium War, and it contains many buildings from that era, especially down near the harbour. The town was a busy commercial centre long before the foreigners arrived, and only began to decline when its position as the premier port of the region was usurped by Shanghai. The wily Ningbo traders followed the money and founded the basis of the Chinese business community in Shanghai, being particularly strong in the banking sector.

The town is rather dark and dingy with a lot of broken-down old buildings which no one has bothered to repair. The liveliest place is down near the harbour but, generally speaking, there is not much to see. Chinese tourists visit Ningbo on their way to PUTUO ISLAND, the site of one of the largest Buddhist temples in China. According to legend, the Buddha Guan Yin (goddess of mercy) floated to the island on a water lily, and her throne is still there. The catch is that the island is out of bounds to foreigners.

In the hills around Ningbo, there are some interesting Buddhist temples and monasteries, particularly at TIANTAI SHAN, about 50 miles (80 kilometres) south of the town. There are local buses, but it is sometimes difficult to obtain permission to go there.

How to get there and where to stay

Ningbo is linked by rail to Hangzhou, and there are also ferries to and from Shanghai. The town's main hotel is the *Overseas Chinese Hotel* (Huaqiao Fandian), which has double rooms for 12 yuan each. If you're on your own, take a pedi-cab from the railway station, a 15-minute ride.

INDEX

NOTES

Notes

Notes